Church-State
Relationships in
America

Recent Titles in Contributions in Legal Studies
Series Editor: Paul L. Murphy

CHURCH-STATE RELATIONSHIPS IN AMERICA

Gerard V. Bradley

CONTRIBUTIONS IN LEGAL STUDIES, NUMBER 37

Greenwood Press

NEW YORK
WESTPORT, CONNECTICUT
LONDON

Library of Congress Cataloging-in-Publication Data

Bradley, Gerard V., 1954-
    Church-state relationships in America.

    Contributions in legal studies, ISSN 0147-1074;
no. 37)
    Bibliography: p.
    Includes index.
    1. Religious liberty—United States. 2. Church and
state—United States. I. Title. II. Series.
KF4783.B69   1987   342.73′0852   86-27149
                          347.302852
ISBN 0-313-25494-X (lib. bdg. : alk. paper)

Library of Congress Catalog Card Number: 86-27149
ISBN: 0-313-25494-X
ISSN: 0147-1074

First published in 1987

Greenwood Press, Inc.
88 Post Road West, Westport, Connecticut 06881

Printed in the United States of America

The paper used in this book complies with the
Permanent Paper Standard issued by the National
Information Standards Organization (Z39.48-1984).

10 9 8 7 6 5 4 3 2 1

For Pamela,
and for Jennie, Kevin, and Daniel

Contents

Acknowledgments

This is a book about constitutional law. Although its conclusions are based largely on the words and deeds of those Americans who adopted the Bill of Rights in 1791, they are offered as what today's law should be. My chief intellectual debt is thus understandably to my teacher in constitutional law, Henry Monaghan, who is currently at Columbia Law School but who taught at Cornell when I studied law there in the late 1970s. Cornell historian Joel Silbey has been my primary mentor in things historical at both the undergraduate and graduate levels and is the person most responsible for whatever sensitivity to the past is evident in the following pages. Silbey's colleague, and my teacher, R. Laurence Moore, has always been an invaluable guide to religion in the American experience. None of these fine teachers should be understood to vouch for the project, though I hope each takes some pride in a grateful student's endeavor.

The brief discussion of divisiveness rhetoric in chapter 2 appeared previously in 30 *Saint Louis Law Journal* 275 (1986) and is reprinted here with permission. I am especially grateful to Greenwood Press for permission to publish a substantially similar version of chapter 6 (along with some paragraphs from the Introduction) in the summer 1986 issue of *Connecticut Law Review*, as my contribution to a symposium issue on religion and the law.

Able research assistance was provided by several University of Illinois College of Law students, including Charles Stone, Andrew Goldstein, Jeffrey Liskar, and Susan Atwood. Paul Byrne did outstanding work on schooling in early America; William Enos performed superbly in preparing the manuscript for publication. The College of Law also provided me a summer research stipend, which permitted uninterrupted composition. Kay Tresslar tirelessly and efficiently typed more versions of the manuscript than either of us cares to remember. Responsibility for errors is indivisibly my own.

Words miserably fail to describe the debt I owe to my parents, Vincent and Katherine Bradley, and to those to whom this book is dedicated.

Introduction

What persons believe to be ultimately true forms the core of their "religion" and influences, when it does not control, every significant decision they make.[1] Besides directing the purely spiritual life and affecting sundry matters of mere life-style, religious beliefs inform such decisions as choosing a spouse, how many spouses—both concurrently and consecutively—one may choose in a lifetime, how spousal obligations are defined, family size, selection of a profession, and schools for one's children. More important, what people believe to be ultimately true invariably begets some kind of moral code that determines how they treat others. Whether it be the Decalogue, the Golden Rule, or the principled egoism of Ayn Rand, religiously grounded morality supervenes and trumps society's own assignment of duties as contained in the law. The U.S. Supreme Court has made this primacy of conscience the sine qua non of its definition of religion as a "faith, to which all else is subordinate or upon which all else is ultimately dependent."[2] This intimate relation is hardly coincidental. Theologian Langdon Gilkey observes: "if one holds . . . that God is the ever-present ground of all of our existence . . . then necessarily our being and our activity will in every facet disclose a religious dimension."[3]

The political significance of religious belief is not comprised solely of the public repercussions of these individual, more or less private, decisions. Each of the three great Western religions—Judaism, Christianity, Islam—characteristically subsumes all history within it, as does a characteristically American faith, Mormonism. Put differently, the claims of those religions encompass the fates of persons and nations, and if true, are true for believer and nonbeliever alike. Adherents therefore (and again necessarily) perceive their fate, and the

fate of their society, through the interpretive medium of faith.[4] It is important
to recall that each of the three faiths understands itself as explicating the same
God as each of the other two, albeit by different revelations. For instance, Allah
is Islam's name for God; the Jews named the same deity Yahweh. One effect
of this convergence is that each also carries a rather specific account of the
infidels within the three deviating religions.

The gloss of belief thus shines no less intensely on collectives than individuals.
Plenty of contemporary societies, and not just Islamic ones,[5] conspicuously
understand themselves and their relationship to other societies in religious terms.
Even the great twentieth-century movement of atheism confirms the public importance of faith through the continuing efforts of communist states to capture
or annihilate religion, thereby confirming Marx's dictum that the beginning of
all social criticism is criticism of religion.

Historians tell us that collective political activity in the United States has been
an intensely religious enterprise. Americans perennially have joined political
parties and voted for public officers according to church membership and religious
belief,[6] and it is impossible to disentangle great nonpartisan political movements
like abolition,[7] the creation of a free public school system,[8] prohibition,[9] and
the civil rights and antiwar movements of the 1960s not only from their proponents' religious motivation but from their religiously grounded vision of the
United States as well.[10] More recently, the high-visibility participation of clergy
and religiously propelled laypersons in the abortion, sanctuary, and antiapartheid
controversies has caused a serious reexamination not of whether, but how, religious people, institutions, habits, and beliefs should affect public policy. The
declining influence of parties in recent years has accentuated the religious content
of politics. Without the moderating and aggregating influence of parties, single
issue believers invade the public realm unrestrained by entangling political al-
liances so that the religious substance of their political program is closer to the
surface.

It is therefore natural to assume that a people associating politically for their
common good would consider religion a fit subject of public regulation, perhaps
even that religious association would precede and produce political bonds. America's religious and religiously homogeneous founding generation, which commonly interpreted its political experiences, including the Revolution, by the light
of Christian theology, is no obvious exception to this rule. The Supreme Court,
then, unexpectedly observes that the founders self-consciously and deliberately
erected a wall of separation between church and state[11] and that the U.S. Constitution's framers declared religion a private matter entirely distinct from the
public agenda,[12] effectively ordaining that the concerns and competence of religion and of government arrange themselves on opposite ends of some linear
construct and that the Constitution, or at least the Court, intends to keep them
there. At a minimum, the basis for these conclusions is not apparent. Most
important, and just as surprising, is the constitutional law doctrine engendered
by these judicial observations and which actually decides cases: neither the state

nor the federal government may promote, aid, or encourage (or inhibit) religion, even on a basis that does not discriminate among churches, sects, or beliefs. Finally, that the prohibition of religious establishments contained in the First Amendment reflected and promoted these unlikely ambitions is no less obscure.

As perplexing as how such a paradigm of mutual abstention by religion and law might actually govern what appears to be actually inseparable is that proffered justification for it: history. Specifically, the justices (and many commentators) proclaim these curious propositions as the unalloyed command of those who wrote and ratified the Religion Clauses of the First Amendment to the federal Constitution in between 1789 and 1791. The intent of these framers sufficiently warrants the relegation and isolation of religion. That these counterintuitive judicial commandments are also historically counterfactual is demonstrable. Rather, the intuitively plausible conclusion—that government interaction with religion be conditioned on a neutrality among sects—is the historically demonstrable meaning of nonestablishment, and represents the fundamental alternative to what the Court has wrought.

NOTES

1. P. Tillich, *Dynamics of Faith* 1–2 (1957); P. Tillich, *The Courage to Be* (1952). This is effectively the definition of religion adopted by the Supreme Court. See *Torasco v. Watkins*, 367 U.S. 488, 495 (1961) (neither state nor federal government "can aid those religions based on a belief in the existence of God as against those religions founded on different beliefs" (*e.g.*, buddhism, taoism, ethical culture, secular humanism, 367 U.S. at 495 n. 11.)) *See also Welsh v. United States*, 398 U.S. 333 (1970); *United States v. Seeger*, 380 U.S. 163 (1965).

2. *United States v. Seeger*, at 163, 176 (1965).

3. L. Gilkey, *Society and the Sacred* 18 (1981).

4. R. Neuhaus, *The Naked Public Square* 15 (1984).

5. On the public significance of Islam, see D. Pipes, *In the Path of God: Islam and Political Power* (1984).

6. R. Kelley, *The Cultural Pattern in American Politics* (1970); P. Kleppner, *The Third Electoral System 1853–1892* (1979); W. McLoughlin, "The Role of Religion in the Revolution: Liberty of Conscience and Cultural Cohesion in the New Nation," in *Essays on the American Revolution* 197 (S. Kurtz & J. Hutson eds. 1973).

7. C. Griffin, *Their Brothers' Keepers* 152–97 (1960).

8. D. Tyack & E. Hansot, *Managers of Virtue: Public School Leadership in America 1820–1980* (1982); V. Lannie, *Public Money and Parochial Schools* (1968).

9. Kleppner, *Third System*, at 336–49.

10. *See* Generally A. James Reichley, *Religion in American Public Life* (1985).

11. *Everson v. Board of Education*, 330 U.S. 1, 16 (1947). First articulated in letter from Thomas Jefferson to the Danbury Baptist Association (January 1, 1802), the Supreme Court's initial use of the term came in a free exercise case. *Reynolds v. United States*, 98 U.S. 145, 164 (1878), involved a polygamy prosecution of a Mormon living in Utah

territory. *Everson* was the first Establishment Clause case employing the "wall" metaphor and the first since *Reynolds* to use it at all.

12. Justice Frankfurter wrote fourteen years after *Everson* that the Establishment Clause

withdrew from the sphere of legitimate legislative concern and competence a specific, but comprehensive, area of human conduct: man's belief or disbelief in the verity of some transcendental idea and man's expression in action of that belief or disbelief. Congress may not make these matters, as such, the subject of legislation, nor, now, may any legislature in this country. Neither the National Government nor, under the Due Process Clause of the Fourteenth Amendment, a State may, by any device, support belief or the expression of belief for its own sake, whether from conviction of the truth of that belief, or from conviction that by the propagation of that belief the civil welfare of the State is served, or because a majority of its citizens holding that belief, are offended when all do not hold it. (*McGowan v. Maryland*, 366 U.S. 420, 465–66 1961.)

In *Lemon v. Kurtzman*, 403 U.S. 602 (1971), Justice Douglas wrote: "The Constitution decrees that religion must be a private matter for the individual, the family, and the institutions of private choice, and that while some involvement and entanglement may be inevitable, lines must be drawn." 403 U.S., at 625 (Douglas, J., concurring).

Church-State
Relationships in
America

1 ———————————————————

Everson's History: The One (and Only?) Justification of the No-Aid-to-Religion Rule

Arthur Sutherland wrote in 1962 that the Supreme Court's proscription of non-discriminatory support of religion was the "most influential single announcement of the American law of Church and State."[1] Another score or so years has proved this an understatement. The ban on even sect-neutral promotion of religion was proclaimed in the 1947 case of *Everson v. United States*, a case that effectively opened the modern era of church-state jurisprudence. Writing for the Court, Justice Hugo Black determined:

The "establishment of religion" clause of the First Amendment means at least this: Neither a state nor the Federal Government can set up a church. Neither can pass laws which aid one religion, aid all religions, or prefer one religion over another. . . . No tax in any amount, large or small, can be levied to support any religious activities or institutions, whatever they may be called, or whatever form they may adopt to teach or practice religion. . . . In the words of Jefferson, the clause against establishment of religion by law was intended to erect "a wall of separation between church and State."[2]

Since the publication of Sutherland's observation, the no-aid injunction has taken its place as the second of the Court's three-pronged test (first articulated in the case of *Lemon v. Kurtzman*) for sorting out unconstitutional government actions: a statutory program must not have an effect that advances religion (as well as a secular purpose, and it must avoid excessive entanglement with religion).[3] And although one cannot say that no aid or advancement explains all of the Court's Establishment Clause holdings, all of the numerous private school assistance programs invalidated since 1947, as well as the Bible reading and school prayer decisions, have impaled themselves on this prong. Even the occasional reservations expressed by the Court about *Lemon*[4] have never hinted at abandoning the *Everson* no-aid formula. That prohibition has been and is the principle that governs the cases, orders debate, and by which any disorder is measured.

The practical importance of *Everson*'s holding is amplified by the Court's increasing reliance on nonestablishment analysis, instead of free exercise inquiry, in cases where both apply. Each of the four cases decided in 1985,[5] for example, employed the *Lemon* Establishment Clause formula, though each of the challenged state practices was effectively and (with the possible exception of the moment of silence case) purposefully a sect-neutral enhancement of the free exercise of religion with no uninvited intrusion on conscience.[6] In other words, each of the cases would likely have come out differently if the justices had chosen to highlight religious liberty concerns or (more important here) if they had applied a sect equality reading of the Establishment Clause. In 1986 the Court avoided direct constitutional inspection of laws requiring equal access for student religious groups wishing to meet in generally available classrooms but still made clear that the issue was one of religious establishment instead of religious freedom.[7] At the same time, the Court did overrule a state court's exclusion of a blind student from a benefit program for the handicapped simply because he was studying for a lay Christian ministry. (The state judiciary had thought religion was impermissibly advanced by treating this student like all others). The Supreme Court, however, declined an invitation to hold that the Free Exercise Clause required such nondiscriminatory treatment and said that the subsidy might still constitute an establishment of religion, depending on further development of the factual record.[8] Finally, the only unabashedly free exercise case in 1986 resulted in a resounding defeat for individual liberty. In an opinion that was unimpressed with religious freedom concerns, the Court upheld the military's refusal to permit an ordained Jewish rabbi, serving as a U.S. Air Force psychologist, to wear his yarmulke while on duty.[9]

The justification for the imposition of the unlikely no-aid or advancement norm on the fifty-odd sovereignties of the United States is therefore significant. The Court's persistent posture has been, in Mark deWolf Howe's words, that the "command of history, and not the preferences of the Justices" compels it.[10] The commanders are said to be the American people who wrote the Establishment Clause into the Constitution. Indeed, "no other constitutional provision has been so closely tied to the generating history which gave it life" than the Establishment Clause, Justice Rutledge wrote in *Everson*,[11] and the Court's justificatory account begins and largely ends with the historical analyses in that case.

The various opinions in *Everson*, especially that of Justice Wiley Rutledge, are steeped in historical detail, but each traverses the same path, draws the same conclusions, and is easily capsulized. Justice Black pursues the shorter route and begins by recounting the intolerance, persecution, and establishmentarian practices the colonists carried with them from Europe and soon transplanted in America.[12] These practices became "commonplace,"[13] according to Justice Black, so much so that the people finally decided to turn it around. The now "freedom-loving"[14] colonists were shocked into a feeling of "abhorrence"[15] and were especially aroused by tax support of ministers and churches. "It was this feeling which found expression in the First Amendment," Justice Black decided.[16] Then, while conceding that no one group can claim a monopoly on the formation of the First Amendment, Justice Black reduced the religion clauses of the federal constitution to Thomas Jefferson's Bill for Establishing Religious Freedom (appendix I), the denouement of the 1748–1785 Virginia controversy over a bill providing public stipends for Protestant clergymen (appendix 2).[17] The no-aid formula is then assertedly grounded, if not mimicked, in Jefferson's statute.

Justice Rutledge pursued the Virginia analogy with still more vigor and differed from the majority only in assigning Jefferson a supporting role to that of James Madison. Rutledge ostensibly broadened the inquiry to include the proceedings of the First Congress, but the single exchange quoted turns out to devastate his argument.[18] The justice determined that the amendment was the "compact and exact" summation of its author's views,[19] and its "author" was Madison.[20] The opinion traced the general assessment described as not "more or less than a taxing measure for the support of religion"[21] and concluded essentially that Madison's Memorial and Remonstrance (appendix 3) was indistinguishable from the First Amendment. Justice Rutledge even appended to his opinion the complete text of both the proposed general assessment and Madison's "memorial" in opposition.[22]

Stripped to essentials, *Everson* held that the First Amendment's governing principles are those put there by the amendment's "authors," and Jefferson and Madison exhaust the list of authors. The views discussed, however, are not their views of the First Amendment but almost exclusively those expressed in Virginia during 1784–1785. The Court provided no foundation for this historical convergence.

Everson's analysis is pivotal because the justification from original intent is much more than the only one dispensed; it seems to be the only one available. The language of the Establishment Clause is certainly no ally of the justices. If the words "respecting an Establishment of religion" are themselves opaque, the Court has resolutely, even proudly, rejected the most accessible, standard definitions. Modern dictionaries define *establishment* as a state church, such as the Church of England or Church of Scotland.[23] Traditional legal sources are in accord. Blackstone said that "by establishment of religion is meant the setting up or recognition of a state church, or at least the conferring upon one church of special favors and advantages which are denied to others."[24] The *Everson* Court, however, expressly eschewed "narrow interpretations" such as the mere prohibition of a "national church" or "no sect preference." It also rejected the modest option of simply outlawing some cluster of discreet, too cozy, relations between church and state falling short of a "state church," like that now prevailing in England.[25] Instead, the justices found an intention to uproot and extinguish all traces of reli-

4   CHURCH-STATE RELATIONSHIPS

gion in politics, to erect the wall of separation between church and state.[26] Whatever the validity or value of their handiwork, it is at least clear that the plain meaning of nonestablishment has long since ceased to instruct.

Thomas Curry's excellent recent work on the meaning of nonestablishment
in the eighteenth century, as revealed in common usage among religious, political, and educational elites, testifies to the prevalence of this definition.[27] Curry's
monograph, although not an examination of establishment as a legal or constitutional construct, evidences that some people (not many) regarded minor sectarian preferences as consistent with nonestablishment, while others insisted on
complete, even mathematically precise, sect equality. In either event, everyone
agreed that nondiscriminatory treatment of religious groups satisfied the demands
of nonestablishment. Americans, Curry concludes, carried with them from the
colonial period onward a definition of establishment as an exclusive government
preference for one religion.[28]

Despite the Court's sometimes turgid rhetoric to the contrary, neither "our
federalism" nor the structure of the national government is dependent on a choice
between the Court's principles and, for example, a no sect preference interpretation of the Establishment Clause. The *Everson* Court opined that "[T]he structure of our government has for the preservation of civil liberty, rescued the
temporal institutions from religious interference. On the other hand, it has secured
religious liberty from the invasion of the civil authority."[29] This is not a classic
structural argument in the vein expounded by Charles Black,[30] for neither the
relationship among the three branches of the federal government nor that between
the states and the United States is implicated. Although lacking a Blackian
pedigree, this argument from mutual abstention in the interest of civil peace has
nevertheless been a mainstay of Establishment Clause analysis. The entanglement
prong of the *Lemon* formula, for example, serves this master and is designed to
preclude chronic frictional conduct between governmental and religious bodies.
Another intriguing scion of the civil peace argument is the so-called divisiveness
doctrine. Without a complete separation of religion and government, political
factions "were bound to divide along religious lines, one of the principal evils
against which the First Amendment was intended to protect."[31] Therefore courts
enforcing the constitutional command of nonestablishment should combat this
dangerous tendency by, for instance, defusing explosive issues—that is, by
settling them judicially, before sectarian energies ignite. This argument really
just restates the issue: that the constitution built a wall between religion and
politics—church and state—is the proposition being examined. Still, it is difficult
to exaggerate the buoyancy of this ostensible fear of zealotry in the populace,
and academic and judicial writers reiterate divisiveness concerns with regularity.
In addition, curtailing or prohibiting religiously grounded political behaivor
obviously buttresses the *Everson* rule, for no aid stymies religion's enthusiasm
for governmental favor by eliminating the prospect of success. The pyrrhic
benefits of persuading legislators to adopt laws promptly invalidated by the
Supreme Court would not escape even the most excited zealot.

Initially there are three historically grounded critical observations. First, divisiveness as constitutional doctrine has no historical basis. The founders were indeed concerned with specific threats to religious liberty that might be contained in legislation, but they did not anticipate a legislative breakdown due to religiously inspired political activity. In fact, Madison explicitly consigned the insurance of religious liberty to the political process, where the multiplicity of sects would cure the mischief of religious faction.[32] Second, the framers not only contemplated the "evil" of religious intolerance, they devised a solution to it: nonestablishment. The Court's use of divisiveness is almost the antithesis of constitutional interpretation, for the justices merely restate problems already addressed by the framers and proceed to their own preferred solution to them.[33] Third, if the Court could accurately identify "religious" issues (the religious content of them is frequently beneath the surface), it could not "defuse" them. Judicial attempts at stilling religiopolitical agitation have not elsewhere been noticeably successful, as the *Dred Scott*[34] (slavery) and *Roe v. Wade*[35] (abortion) decisions illustrate. Nor have its voluminous Establishment Clause opinions diminished religiopolitical activity, as the recent history of the sanctuary and antiabortion controversies attests.[36]

The general notion of nonestablishment as guarantor of civil peace is fundamentally misconceived in other ways. The Court ignores the basic controversy in the area: has religion divided and endangered political communities, or have political factions used religious symbols, affiliations, and authority to fight their political wars? Although the issue undoubtedly permits no categorical answer, the justices offer no analysis at all. More important, although there is indeed a history to the idea that religious conflict threatens civil tranquility, the Court overstates it and in the process denies the overwhelming preponderance in U.S. history of almost precisely the opposite: Christianity has united, if not defined, the United States, and because political liberty presupposes a religious citizenry, government must aid religion to ensure its own survival. That the generation that enacted the First Amendment held the latter, more favorable, view of religion and the polity is beyond question.[37]

The historical foundations of divisiveness doctrine are shoddy; perhaps consequently, contemporary functional justifications are frequently offered. Put differently, regardless of the framers' intentions, U.S. society is better off—by being more peaceful—with judicial commitment to the doctrine. After all, there is little to recommend sectarian warfare. The question here is, What is the divisiveness rationale for no aid, and is there anything to recommend it?

The "divisiveness" then, is not strictly that putative fourth *Lemon* prong, or second spur—political as opposed to administrative entanglement—of the third *Lemon* inquiry. It is instead more generally half of the answer (oppression being the other half) to these questions: Why is religion a bad influence on political society? Why should it be separate from public activity—something about which government should be neutral and refrain from advancing? As a discreet doctrinal pigeonhole, the checkered career of divisiveness is relatively uninteresting, although Justice Brennan has indicated a willingness to resolve cases on its strength alone.[38] Its vital uses are justificatory and integrative. It warrants and unifies subservient themes, doctrines, and precedent, especially no aid. As such a fundamental rationale, divisiveness has a long and distinguished pedigree. Justice Jackson opined in *Everson* that the First Amendment "above all" was designed to "keep bitter religious controversy out of public life" by denying access to public influence.[39] The end of such strife, Justice Rutledge wrote in the same case, will either be domination by the strongest sect or constant turmoil and dissension engulfing the entire society.[40] Justice Black, author of the majority opinion in *Everson*, wrote in 1968 that the Establishment Clause "was written on the assumption that state aid to religion . . . generates discord, disharmony, hatred, and strife among our people.[41] Justice Rutledge continued in *Everson*: "Public money devoted to payment of religious costs . . . brings the quest for more. It brings too the struggle of sect against sect for the larger share or for any."[42] Even Justice Harlan, normally not easily alarmed, observed in 1970 that "political fragmentation on sectarian lines must be guarded against" and expressly deputized "voluntarism" and "neutrality" as humble servants of this paramount concern.[43] The seminal *Lemon* opinion fully explained:

Ordinarily political debate and division, however vigorous or even partisan, are normal and healthy manifestations of our democratic system of government, but political division along religious lines was one of the principal evils against which the First Amendment was intended to protect . . . The potential divisiveness of such conflict is a threat to the normal political process . . . The history of many countries attests to the hazards of religion's intruding into the legitimate and free exercise of religious belief.[44]

By 1985, a virtual shorthand was sufficient to trigger the now subliminally embedded sanguinary connotations. Religion can serve "powerfully to divide societies,"[45] parochial school aid offers "an all-too-ready opportunity for divisive rifts along religious lines in the body politic."[46] Leonard Levy cites the Clause's pacifying function: it "substantially removes religious issues . . . from politics . . . It thereby helps to defuse a potentially explosive situation."[47] The power of the "divisiveness" image resides solely in the terrors it evokes in the reader's mind, and the mental picture conjured is no less than genuine sectarian warfare. If historical memory falters, contemporary examples abound. And one may fairly claim that the opinion writers want us to think of Northern Ireland and Lebanon, if not the Ayatollah Khomeini himself, when they speak of sectarian divisions in society.

"What is at stake as a matter of policy is preventing that kind and degree of government involvement in religious life that, as history teaches us, is apt to lead to strife and frequently strain a political system to the breaking point."[48] So stated by Justice Harlan, it is easy to see how keeping religion separate from politics follows because if faith is not politically relevant, it cannot lead to political conflict. So stated, however, it is also either terribly odd or terribly reactionary. It is at least peculiar to presume that a judicial decree can handle what a democratic polity cannot. For example, slavery was no less sinful in the eyes of God after *Dred Scott* than before it, nor has the opinion in *Roe v. Wade* shaken pro-lifers' moral condemnation of abortion. The problem is that the obvious cases of sectarian divisiveness involve dividers who regard the entire system, courts included, as illegitimate and oppressive. Deploying constitutional doctrine against actual or threatened extraconstitutional behavior hardly seems a promising modus operandi. The justices most often appear to contemplate a less volatile present but also endeavor to keep the genie in the bottle through a constant vigil for the slightest indication of church-state union or sectarian commotion. In fact, nothing like divisiveness has ever actually happened in a Supreme Court case save for the limp suggestion by the dissenters in *Lynch* that a lawsuit sufficiently proved divisiveness, a proposition that offered a favorable ground of decision for the cost of filing.[49] The Court is clearly engaged in an entirely prophylactic effort, one that has constitutionalized the relationship of church to state without an empirical confirmation of the ''evil'' that assertedly justifies it. Requiring just a ''clear and present danger'' of sectarian strife, for instance, would eliminate the divisiveness rationale from every case that ever employed it. Nevertheless, the Court is prepared to pay for the order of some remote, hypothetical future with the liberty of the present. More obviously repressive regimes at least get an immediate return on their investment.

There is another variant of divisiveness-as-intense-conservatism that is more than the true but trivial observation that the doctrine's raison d'être is preservation of the systemic status quo. Perhaps better labeled divisiveness-as-ideology is that part of the strife-avoidance rhetoric that covers for a highly selective issue agenda, utilized either to accomplish a preferred result on a particular political question or to focus political energy on items the Court deems most pressing. The starting point is Justice O'Connor's suggestion to limit ''divisiveness'' analysis to parochial school aid cases.[50] The apparent logic of the suggestion is straightforward: belief is politically, or peculiarly, salient when religious institutions as such vie for money, thus conforming to the privatist paradigm that irruptions are not pursuits of social turth. But if not, why should believers care more about getting public succor than anybody else? Or if the money is understood to make transmissions of faith from old to young possible or more feasible, why do Roman Catholics run so many of the parochial schools? Do Protestant parents not care about educating their children in the faith? In reality, Catholic schools were, until quite recently, a consequence of the Protestant establishment in the public schools, and state aid has always been an ensuing appeal for a ''rough justice'' in annual educational appropriations. The issue has never implicated religious truths, just public ones like equality and justice. Most importantly, it has never been agitated in a way distinguishable from political conflict generally, and the Court has done nothing except assert, without a scintilla of evidence, the contrary. Now that nonpublic schools, especially inner-city Catholic ones like those affected by the *Aguilar* ruling, are largely, or even predom-

inantly, attended by non-Catholic minorities fleeing public schools, isolation of
this issue is illogical. Quality education, not transmission of the faith, is the
point. Yet the Supreme Court brusquely denied the analytical significance of
those realities, noting in *Aguilar* that it is "simply incredible" to think parochial
schools have abandoned their "religious mission."[51] Even so, the suggestion is
that students now typically attend to acquire not the Catholic faith but the superior
secular education available in Catholic schools. State funding is thus no longer,
if it ever was, an issue portending sectarian strife. Still, the institution remains
subject to the same "divisiveness" scrutiny it earned when parochial school aid
was an issue on which respectable people could express their anti-Catholicism.

The *Walz* opinion of a deeply troubled Justice Harlan suggests another issue
genesis of divisiveness doctrine. The challenged practice in that case—tax exemptions dating from the colonial era—could not have prompted Justice Harlan
to assert (as he did) the primacy of "divisiveness" in church-state law.[52] Edward
Gaffney suggests what did.[53] *Walz* was written in the midst of cleric-led, morally
and religiously inspired, bitterly divisive Vietnam War protests, which followed
on the heels of similar civil rights era demonstrations. Gaffney opines that Harlan
wrote with his eye on those issues,[54] and in fact, Harlan's opinion further refers
to religious agitation on secular issues like birth control and abortion as examples
of public religion "to be guarded against."[55] Whatever Justice Harlan's personal
views on those questions, "divisiveness" is frequently a matter of whose ox is
gored. One classic example is Jerry Falwell's criticism of clerical participation in
civil rights marches as a mischievous mix of religious ministry and politics. A
second example is *Roe v. Wade*'s attempt to defuse the divisive abortion issue,
even while the Court avoided every opportunity to scrutinize constitutionally the
conduct of the Vietnam War. Justice Harlan probably had a truly nonpartisan concern for order. But is it not a sufficient rejoinder, if not enough to quiet his fears,
that, but for public religion, blacks might still be riding the rear of the bus on their
way to fight in Southeast Asia?

A more robust issue agenda underlay the *Lemon* test itself, as the Court's
opinion in that case made explicit:

To have States or communities divide on the issues presented by state aid to parochial
schools would tend to confuse and obscure other issues of great urgency. We have an
expanding array of vexing issues, local and national, domestic and international, to debate
and divide on. It conflicts with our whole history and tradition to permit questions of the
Religion Clauses to assume such importance in our legislatures and in our elections that
they could divert attention from the myriad issues and problems that confront every level
of government.[56]

Here the problem is not whose ox is gored but that anybody's is. Evidently, as
the justices set priorities for the political agenda, any excitement, much less
genuine divisiveness, engendered by state financing is too much. The stakes are
not worth it and not unexpectedly, because the Court's position has always been
that children belong in "common" public schools.

The remarkable claim that the religion clauses authorize the Court to reshuffle the whole political calendar, canceling out what the Court considers unimportant concerns to make room for questions it considers worth dividing on, has not been further explicated by the justices. It nevertheless indicates that tranquility is most definitely not the end of divisiveness concerns. After all, racial justice, including race-conscious politics, is high on the Court's list of approved political activities, even if in the present climate it is undoubtedly more conducive to enduring social hostility than sectarian politics. In fact, roughly the same liberal wing most determined to make race a structural component of the political process is also most determined to remove all traces of religious consciousness from public life. The latter is too divisive, even though the whole of U.S. history witnesses the chronically destabilizing effects of racial politics, which truly dwarf in comparison the disorder traceable to public religion.

None of this implicitly denies either that race-related turmoil has been worth it or that the religious mind has frequently been at or near the surface of political life in the United States. It merely affirms that, evaluated solely according to a volume of discord test, religion warrants no special treatment. Consequently the divisiveness analysis, uniquely applied to the religion clauses primarily by justices who otherwise never hesitate to seek justice at the expense of communal concerns for order, flows from some concern other than harmony, at least understood as the Court describes it as being the absence of palpable, system-stretching conflict. At a minimum, the fears are not fears at all but simple preferences for a regime in which religion is walled off from the public realm and ineligible for governmental assistance. Since the reasons for that naked preference are matters of speculation, critical analysis of the sectarian warfare justification for no aid ends with the observation that whatever value the Court sees in divisiveness concerns, it has nothing to do with avoiding serious conflict.

A third avenue of potential justification for the Court's Establishment Clause principles after the text itself and structural concerns (broadly construed) is one avidly pursued by Justice Frankfurter: the Fourteenth Amendment's guarantee of "liberty." In the context of an aid to parochial school case, he turned to the generation that ratified the Due Process Clause (in 1868) for guidance. (The due process guarantee is the technical medium of decision in most church-state cases; it incorporates the Establishment Clause and applies it to the states.) After a brief recital of historical data in *McCollum v. Board of Education*, Frankfurter concluded "that long before the Fourteenth Amendment subjected the states to new limitations, the prohibition of furtherance by the state of religious instruction became the guiding principle, in law and feeling, of the American people." The Fourteenth Amendment in this regard "merely reflected a principle dominant in American life."[57] We shall see that this was no part of American life when the Bill of Rights was enacted, so the argument thus comprises two separate claims. One identifies what would be a dramatic alteration of practice and belief since the ratification of the First Amendment. The other implies that this state of affairs found its way into the Fourteenth Amendment. Neither assertion has a basis in fact.

Justice Frankfurter's fatal misstep is his equation of nonsectarian with non-religious and it irreparably distorts his reading of the historical record. Horace Mann's mid-nineteenth-century fight to bar sectarian teachings from common schools is consequently an exhortation to separate religion from education.[58] A speech by President Grant as well as the Blaine amendment, both seeking an end to public funding of "sectarian schools,"[59] demonstrate that by 1875 "the separation . . . of the state from the teaching of religion, was firmly established in the consciousness of the nation."[60]

Frankfurter's mistake is that these speakers meant what they said: a separation of sect from education. "Sect" was used solely with respect to Christianity and meant that "spirit of quarrelsomeness and schism, precianism in theology, and refusal to collaborate in common evangelical enterprises"[61] characteristic of American denominationalism. Mann, for instance, believed in "an education which instructed all children in the fundamental ethical norms which were the basis of all religions."[62] In fact, in the words of one historian of American schooling, "no great educational leader before the Civil War . . . would tolerate non-Christian beliefs in the school."[63] What Justice Frankfurter missed most of all was the fact that public schools in 1875 were Protestant.

This explanation of antisectarianism is evident in the language of the Blaine amendment itself.[64] It provided for Bible reading in the schools, and that practice's harmony with nonsectarianism was emphasized by its congressional proponents.[65] The language also belies Frankfurter's assertion that the framers of the Fourteenth Amendment intended a no-aid policy. The framers of the Blaine amendment (many of them were also in the Congress that passed the Fourteenth Amendment, and almost all were politically prominent when that amendment was ratified)[66] evidently contemplated two policies not already binding on the states. That is, they did not believe either that due process liberty contained nonestablishment[67] or that nonestablishment contained a prohibition of nondiscriminatory aid. Most significant, the amendment attempted to add to the non-establishment norm already binding the United States by forbidding aid to sectarian schools, which was at the same time not intended to diminish the religious character of public education.[68]

Everson may have been the Supreme Court's first square confrontation with the Establishment Clause,[69] but it was not the Court's first church-state case. Before 1947, the Court decided three challenges to government payments to religious groups.[70] None supports *Everson*'s interpretation of the Establishment Clause; in each the expenditure was upheld and thus cuts the Court off from a fourth possible support: that of precedent, or stare decisis. The three cases are *Bradfield v. Roberts*,[71] *Quick Bear v. Leupp*,[72] and *Cochran v. Board of Education*.[73] In *Bradfield*, the District of Columbia commissioners, pursuant to congressional enabling legislation, reimbursed the Catholic Sisters of Charity for care administered in their hospital to public charges. *Quick Bear* involved payments by the federal government to Roman Catholic missionaries operating schools on Indian reservations. The state legislature in *Cochran* authorized local school boards to purchase text-books for students in parochial schools. The program was virtually identical to the textbook loan scheme upheld by the Supreme Court in *Board of Education v. Allen*.[74] Although the Court sidestepped the Establishment Clause in each case, the opinions bespeak an indulgent attitude toward state support of religious institutions. The government won in *Bradfield* because the plaintiff could not establish that the hospital was in fact a religious corporation. The documents of incorporation listed the secular names of the individual sisters and did not indicate their clerical affiliation. There was no question on the facts, however, that the Sisters of Charity operated the hospital and that they were a Roman Catholic order. The Court's "four corners" test, however, reflected a remarkable lack of curiosity. That the hospital was controlled by "members of a monastic or sisterhood of the Roman Catholic Church" did not "in the least change the legal character of the hospital, or make a religious corporation out of a purely secular one."[75] The payments in *Quick Bear* were determined to be from a tribal trust fund administered by the federal government. The aid was not therefore out of public monies. The soliciter general argued (citing *Bradfield*) that a "school, like a hospital, is neither an establishment of religion, nor a religious establishment, although along with secular education there might be, as there commonly is, instruction in morality and religion, just as in a hospital there would be religious ministrations,"[76] an argument to which the Court did not respond. Because the Establishment Clause was not yet applicable to the states, the constitutional issue in *Cochran* was whether aid to parochial schools was an appropriation of public money for private purposes. Of the Louisiana legislature in *Chochran*, the Court said, "Its intent is education, broadly; its method comprehensive. Individual interests are aided only as the common interest is safeguarded."[77]

Another prop theoretically available to the Court is again "contemporaneous understanding" but this time those of the justices' contemporaries, not George Washington's. Although the legitimacy of judicial insertion of a perceived societal consensus or community values into the constitution is hotly contested, one need not resolve that dispute to see that the Court draws no comfort here. To sense the Court's isolation, one need only ask whether, at any time since 1947, the Court's wall of separation and complete ban on aid to religion could have mustered constitutional majorities. Is it likely, for example, that the holding of *Engel v. Vitale*,[78] banning nonsectarian voluntary prayer in public schools, would garner a two-thirds vote in Congress and majorities in thirty-eight states? Is it possible that similar majorities would affirm the Court's general proposition that government may not "endorse," "support," or "encourage" religion, even to the extent of prohibiting the display of the Ten Commandments in public schools?[79] To take perhaps the two most visible church-state issues—school prayer and parochial school aid—a late 1984 Gallup poll revealed a majority of Americans in favor of each.[80] Beyond question, then, the justices are way ahead of the American people in this realm. Further, it can be only that it was a politically unthinkable result that saved the most important aid of all—tax exemptions—from the obvious conflict with *Everson*. The same political moderation is probably also at work in the cases saving Sunday blue laws,[81] legislative chaplains, and nativity scenes from invalidation.

Given the critical role of church-state issues in U.S. political life, the centrality of the constitutional requirement of no aid to that life, and the absence of alternative props for the *Everson* rule, it is tragic that a more unfortunate historical analysis than *Everson*'s would be hard to find. The problem is not only that the justices there recover inaccurate historical answers (although they do much of that) but that they ask the wrong questions. Their categories of inquiry into original intent negate every conceivable canon of sound construction. Ratification, not either congressional proposal or authorship, is the operative fact, and thus the meaning apprehended by the ratifiers—the state legislators—is what matters. Not a word of the state-by-state process of ratification is spoken in *Everson*. In fact, one would think from the opinions that the First Amendment was rendered operative by House approval, if not by the simple act of Madison's penmanship. One would further think that another major source of contemporary understanding—newspapers—was nonexistent. They existed, and survive, but the Court makes no use of them. Just as serious, the majority says absolutely nothing of the congressional debate that is readily accessible and sometimes a good (sometimes the only) substitute for the meaning apprehended by the ratifiers. Justice Rutledge footnotes but a single congressional episode because the debates were "sparse," reflecting the fact that [in his opinion] essential issues had been "settled."[82] The justices do not attend their connection between Madison's "memorial" and the First Amendment by, for instance, indicating that Madison told others that at least he thought they were fungible. (In fact, Madison never equated the two.) The Court makes no mention of the state conventions that ratified the 1787 Constitution, recommended amendments, and along the way clearly identified the "evils" the First Amendment protected against.

The simple equation of the First Amendment with the Virginia controversy is just as troubling as the idea that Jefferson plus Madison equals the relevant portion of the founding generation. Equating, without specific supporting evidence, an intrastate contest—any state, any contest—with federally imposed norms is fundamentally ill conceived. Most especially in the founding era, there should be no presumption that what the people thought an appropriate method of governing federal affairs corresponded to their notion of good state government—and viceversa. Justice Black concedes that for a half-century after the First Amendment's ratification, some states continued their establishments.[83] If state norms reveal federal norms willy-nilly, how could so-called establishment states like New Hampshire, Vermont, and Maryland have ratified the nonestablishment clause?

Another difficulty with the general assessment equation is apparent from a careful reading of it[84] and is heightened by the drift of the Court in cases like *Lynch v. Donnelly* into a search for ancient analogues, asking whether the framers countenanced a practice similar to that now challenged and, if so, rebuffing the challenge. The general assessment has no modern analogue and thus cannot guide such a search for original intent. It was a separate, distinct tax, imposed and collected for the twin purposes of paying clergymen and for building and maintaining churches. The effect would have been to place a clergyman on the government payroll in his sacerdotal and ecclesiastical capacities and to fund the system by direct coercion of individuals. It is nothing like any of the modern private school aid programs, which are conceptually closest to the general assessment but which operate much more indirectly to underwrite "secular" educational functions in religious schools. As Morgan rightly points out, given the amounts involved these days for particular taxpayers, "only a conscience of prodigious preciosity could be seriously offended."[85]

Another flaw is the Court's use of the general assessment as a surrogate for no aid, as if one could not oppose the general assessment without being opposed to all support of religion. While Jefferson's and Madison's opposition may have stemmed from such sweeping principles (and it probably did not), no one else's did. Worse, *Everson*'s excessive focus on an outmoded species of financial support is conducive to a definition of establishment that is at once too narrow and too broad—too narrow in that even careful scholars like Leo Pfeffer and Leonard Levy have succumbed to the temptation of making it a necessary condition of an establishment. Where there was a general assessment, Levy and Pfeffer conclude, there was an establishment,[86] ignoring that there are many other material and nonmaterial ways to support religion besides imposing a general assessment. Levy, for instance, labeled New Hampshire, Massachusetts, Connecticut, Georgia, Maryland, and South Carolina as establishment states simply because their laws authorized the kind of support eschewed in Virginia.[87] Yet each of the thirteen original states generously aided and promoted religion and should therefore, according to Levy's methodology, be called establishment regimes. Further, this narrow focus ignores that even a state hostile to general assessments, like Virginia, was establishmentarian in that it found alternative ways to prefer a single sect—Anglicanism—to all others.

Levy succumbs to the broadening temptation of *Everson* as well. Committed to *Everson*'s view that an assessment denotes an establishment, even if generally available and thus sect impartial, he is obliged to invent the term *multiple establishment* to describe the post-Revolutionary era of nondiscriminatory assistance to all Protestant sects.[88] The term *multiple establishment* does not occur at all in the historical materials, and it could not. Since *establishment* meant sect preference, eliminating the preference eliminated, not multiplied, the establishment. *Multiple establishment* is historically an oxymoron; its modern equivalent is *nondiscriminatory preference*. This derailment, then, represents the elevation of *general assessment* into both a necessary and a sufficient condition of an establishment. Whatever the emotive appeal such an elevation possesses for modern political warriors, it is thoroughly ahistorical, a simple projection of the present onto the past.

NOTES

1. A. Sutherland, "Establishment According to Engel," 76 *Harv. L. Rev.* 25, 31 (1962).

2. *Everson V. Board of Education*, 330 U.S. 1, 15 (1947).

3. *Lemon v. Kurtzman*, 403, U.S. 602, 612–613 (1971). As expressed by the Court, the constitutionality of any statute challenged under the religion clause is controlled by three tests: "first, the statue must have a secular legislative purpose; second, its principal or primary effect must be one that neither advances nor inhibits religion; finally, the statue must not foster 'an excessive government entanglement with religion.' " Id., at 612–13 (citations omitted).

4. In Larson v. Valente, 456 U.S. 228 (1982), the Court for the first time ignored *Lemon*; nevertheless, the result in *Larkin v. Grendel's Den*, 459 U.S. 116 (1982), during the same term rested firmly on the *Lemon* test. There the chief justice wrote for the majority: "This Court has consistently held that a statute must satisfy [the] three [*Lemon*] criteria to pass muster under the Establishment Clause. In *Marsh v. Chambers*, 463 U.S. 783, 103 S. Ct 3330 (1983), the Legislative chaplain case, the majority for the second time eschewed the *Lemon* formula. During the same term, in *Mueller v. Allen*, 463 U.S. 388, 103 S. Ct. 3062 (1983), the Court ostensibly applied the test, while it approved a tuition tax credit scheme indistinguishable from that struck down a decade earlier in *Comittee for Public Education and Religious Liberty v. Nyquist*, 413 U.S. 756 (1973), on the strength of *Lemon*. Finally, the majority in the 1984 Rhode Island nativity scene case was unwilling to be confined by any particular analysis, remarking that past cases revealed only that it was "often" "useful to inquire" into secular purpose, primary effect, and entanglement. *Lynch v. Donnelly*, 465 U.S. 660, (1984). The "wall of separation" was now "a useful figure of speech probably deriving from the view of Thomas Jefferson." Id., at 1359. Each of the cases decided between 1984 and 1986, however, unequivocally reaffirmed the governance of the *Lemon* criteria.

5. Those cases are *Aguilar v. Felton*, 105 S. Ct. 3232 (1985); *Grand Rapids School Dist. v. Ball*, 105 S. Ct. 3216 (1985); *Thornton v. Caldor, Inc.*, 105 S. Ct. 2914 (1985); and *Wallace v. Jaffree*, 472 105 U.S. S. Ct. 38 2479 (1985). *Aguilar* and *Grand Rapids* were companion taxpayer challenges to what was originally Title I of the Elementary and Secondary Education Act of 1965, 20 U.S.C. §§ 2701–3386 (1976), which was superseded in 1982 by Chapter 1 of the Education Consolidation and Improvement Act of 1981, 20 U.S.C. §§ 3301–3876 (1982). For convenience, the Court called the questioned provisions Title I. State and local education agencies were authorized to receive federal funds "to meet the special educational needs of educationally deprived children," and the statutory coverage was confined to areas with a high concentration of low-income families. Id., at § 3801. Most importantly, the administering school districts were obligated to meet the special educational needs of all eligible children, whether or not they attended public schools. Id, at § 3806. The Grand Rapids School District implemented this congressional command through the Community Education and Shared Time program, in which public school personnel taught courses in parochial schools during regular school hours to parochial school students. Additionally adult education courses, taught by parochial school teachers working part time for the district were offered after school in the parochial school buildings. The Shared Time courses were remedial or enrichment courses generally unavailable in the private schools. The adult courses duplicated ones available in the local public schools. The Court determined that the program "impermissibly advanced religion" in three ways.

First, the teachers participating in the programs may become involved in intentionally or inadvertently inculcating particular religious tenets or beliefs. Second, the programs may provide a crucial symbolic link between government and religion, thereby enlisting—at least in the eyes of impressionable youngsters—the powers of government to the support of the religious denomination operating the school. Third, the programs may have the effect of directly promoting religion by impermissibly providing a subsidy to the primary religious mission of the institutions affected. (*Grand Rapids, 105 School Dist.* at 3223–24.)

New York City encountered a catch–22 backlash in its implementation of Title I. Only public school teachers, monitored by public school supervisors, provided the remedial and guidance services offered in the largely Catholic private schools. This practice effectively ensured against improper religious advancement but just as effectively ensured an impermissible church-state entanglement. That is, the "pervasive monitoring," as the Court saw it, necessary to survive the second inquiry established in *Lemon* necessarily resulted in a violation of the third *Lemon* inquiry. *Aguilar*, at 3237.

In *Thornton v. Caldor, Inc.*, the following statute was invalidated by the Supreme Court:

No person who states that a particular day of the week is observed as his Sabbath may be required by his employer to work on such day. An employee's refusal to work on his Sabbath shall not constitute grounds for his dismissal. Conn. Gen. Stat. Ann. §§ 53–303 (West 1985).

The petitioner's decedent was discharged from a managerial position in one of the respondent's stores for refusing to work on his Sabbath, Sunday. The Supreme Court concluded that the statute had "a primary effect that impermissibly advances a particular religious practice"—Sabbath observance—in violation of the second *Lemon* test. *Thornton* at 2918.

Parents of children attending Mobile, Alabama, public schools challenged classroom religious observances in *Wallace v. Jaffree*. At issue before the supreme Court was a statute authorizing a period of silence for "meditation or voluntary prayer." Ala. Code § 16–1–20.1 (1984). The convoluted pedigree of the statute persuaded the Court that the addition of "or voluntary prayer" to an existing moment-of-silence statute was the operative event. That the addition was "an effort to return voluntary prayer" to public schools meant it had "no secular purpose" and conveyed a message of "endorsement" (that is, it advanced) of religion as well. *Wallace* at 2491.

6. The Court's argument to the contrary in Wallace was quite unpersuasive. See *Wallace* at 2490–91.

7. *Bender v. Williamsport*, 106 S. Ct. 1326 (1986).

8. *Witters v. Washington*, 106 S. Ct. 748, 253 n. 5 (1986).

9. *Goldman v. Weinberger*, 106 S. Ct. 1310. (1986).

10. M. Howe, *The Garden and the Wilderness* 4 (1965).

11. *Everson* at 38.

12. Ibid. at 8–10.

13. Ibid. at 11.

14. Ibid.

15. Ibid.

16. Ibid.

17. Ibid. at 11–13.

18. Rutledge (at 42–43 n. 34) related: At one point the wording was proposed: "No religion shall be established by law, nor shall the equal rights of conscience be infringed." 1 *Annals of Congress* 729. Congressman Huntington of Connecticut feared this might be construed to prevent judicial enforcement of private pledges. He stated "that he feared . . . that the words might

be taken in such latitude as to be extremely hurtful to the cause of religion. He understood the amendment to mean what had been expressed by the gentleman from Virginia, but others might find it convenient to put another construction upon it. The ministers of their congregations to the Eastward were maintained by the contributions of those who belonged to their society; the expense of building meeting-houses was contributed in the same manner. These things were regulated by by-laws. If an action was brought before a Federal Court on any of these cases, the person who had neglected to perform his engagements could not be compelled to do it; for a support of ministers or building of places of worship might be construed into a religious establishment." 1 *Annals of Congress* 730.

To avoid any such possibility, Madison suggested inserting the word *national* before *religion*, thereby not only again disclaiming intent to bring about the result Huntington feared but also showing unmistakably that *establishment* meant public support of religion in the financial sense. 1 *Annals of Congress* 731. See also IX Madison, 484–87.

19. *Everson* at 31 (1947).

20. Ibid. at 37.

21. Ibid. at 36–41.

22. Ibid. at 63–74.

23. 1 *Compact Edition of the Oxford English Dictionary* 897 (1971); *Webster's New International Dictionary of the English Language* 874 (2d ed. unabridged 1939).

24. *Blackstone's Commentaries* 296 (Tucker ed.).

25. *Everson* at 31 (Rutledge, J., dissenting).

26. Ibid.

27. T. Curry, The First Freedoms: Church and State in America to the Passage of the First Amendment (1986).

28. Ibid. at 210.

29. *Watson v. Jones*, 13 Wall. 679, 690 (1872), quoted approvingly in *Everson* at 15.

30. C. Black, Structure and Relationship in Constitutional Law (1969).

31. *Lemon* at 62–63. Divisiveness doctrine may be traced to one sentence in P. Freund, "Public Aid to Parochial Schools," 82 *Harv. L. Rev.* 1680, 1692 (1969): "While political debate and division is normally a wholesome process for reaching viable accommodations, political division on religious lines is one of the principal evils that first amendment sought to forestall." See also P. Weber, "Building on Sand: Supreme Court Construction and Educational Tax Credits," 12 *Creighton L.* Rev. 531, 553 (1979).

32. Federalist No. 51. in *The Federalist Papers*, 324 (Mentor ed., 1961).

33. This is more generally true of the Court's church-state efforts, which seem to treat the Religion Clauses as no more than an invitation to fashion a general common law of religion and government according to the justices' account of the good society.

34. *Dred Scott v. Sanford*, 60 U.S. (19 How.) 393 (1857).

35. *Roe v. Wade*, 410 U.S. 113 (1973).

36. The necessary implication of the divisiveness doctrine is that to the extent a religously motivated person cares deeply about a public issue, he or she is more likely to be unable to affect the outcome of public debate, since to the same extent the Court is likely to defuse the issue by rescuing it from the arena of political decision making.

37. M. Malbin, *Religion and Politics: The Intentions of the Authors of the First Amendment* 16 (1978). See E. Gaffney, "Political Divisiveness along Religious Lines: The Entanglement of the Court in Sloppy History and Bad Public Policy," 24 *St. Louis U.L.J.* 205, 220–21 (1980) (divisiveness doctrine denies central Madisonian insight into requisites of political stability.)

38. See *Meek* at 385 (Brennan, J., concurring in part and dissenting in part).

39. 330 U.S. at 27 (Jackson, J., dissenting).

40. Ibid. at 53–55 (Rutledge, J., dissenting).

41. *Board of Educ. v. Allen*, 392 U.S. 236, 254 (1968) (Black, J., dissenting).

42. *Everson* at 53.

43. *Waltz*, 397 U.S. at 695 (opinion of Harlan, J.).

44. *Lemon* at 62–63 (citations omitted).

45. *Grand Rapids* at 3222.

46. Ibid. at 3222–23.

47. L. Levy, *The Establishment Clause: Religion and the First Amendment*, ix (1986).

48. *Waltz* at 694 (opinion of Harlan, J.).

49. *Lynch* at 702–3 (Brennan, J., dissenting).

50. Ibid. at 689. So starkly stated, this obviously is a logical possibility only for a distant doctrinal inquiry; divisiveness will always be present as normative alpha and omega. Yet Justice O'Connor's point, and those following, inform subsequent discussion of the precise nature of the divisiveness identified by the Court.

51. 105 S. Ct. at 3238 n. 8.

52. *Waltz* at 694 (opinion of Harlan, J.).

53. See Gaffney, "Political Divisiveness," at 205.

54. Ibid. at 210 n. 29.

55. *Waltz* at 695 (opinion of Harlan, J.).

56. 403 U.S. 622–23.

57. *McCollum v. Board of Education*, 333 U.S. 203, 215 (1948) (opinion of Frankfurter, J.) (emphasis added) (footnote omitted).

58. Ibid. at 215.

59. Ibid. at 218.

60. Ibid. at 217.

61. E. Smith, *Religious Liberty in the United States* 108 (1972).

62. V. Lannie, *Public Money and Parochial Schools* 80 (1968).

63. M. Curti, *The Social Ideas of American Educators* 20 (1959).

64. The version passed by the House of Representatives read:

No state shall make any law, respecting an establishment of religion, or prohibiting the free exercise thereof; and no religious test shall ever be required as a qualification to any office or public trust under any state. No public property, and no public revenue of, nor any loan or credit by or under the authority of, the United States, of any State, Territory, District, or municipal corporation, shall be appropriated to, or made or used for, the support of any school, educational or other institution, under the control of any religious or anti-religious sect, organization, or denomination, or wherein the particular creed or tenets of any religious or anti-religious sect, organization, or denomination shall be taught. And no such particular creed or tenet shall be read or taught in any school or institution supported in whole or in part by such revenue or loan of credit; and no such appropriation or loan of credit shall be made to any religous or anti-religous sect, organization, or denomination, or to promote its interests or tenets. *This article shall not be construed to prohibit the reading of the bible in any school or institution*; and it shall not have the effect to impair rights of property already vested. (Emphasis added)

Anti-Catholicism was the primary impetus for the Blaine amendment. "During the closing days of the Congressional session, Republicans in both houses, hoping to capitalize on anti-Catholic sentiment, pushed unsuccessfully for a constitutional amendment to prohibit

18 CHURCH-STATE RELATIONSHIPS

the use of public funds for parochial schools." K. Polakoff, *The Politics of Inertia* 115 (1973). Polakoff's observation is typical of the historiography of the Blaine amendment.

65. Remarks of Senator Frelinghuysen during Blaine amendment debate:

Institutions supported by the money of all persuasions, even though they be prisons are not to be made schools for teaching presbyterianism, or catholicism, unitarianism, or methodism, or infidelity, or atheism, and this article says so. But this article goes no further. There is nothing in it that prohibitis religion as distinguished from the particular creed or tenets of religious and anti-religious sects and denominations being taught anywhere. *Cong. Rec.*, 44th Cong., 1st sess., vol. 4, pt. 6, p. 5562.

66. F. O'Brien, "The Blaine Amendment 1875–76," 41 *Det. L. Rev.* 137 (1951).

67. O'Brien concludes (correctly) from an analysis of the debates that the Blaine amendment contained a new regulation of the states.

68. For a general treatment of the Blaine amendment, refer to A. Meyer, "The Blaine Amendment and the Bill of Rights," 64 *Harv. L. Rev.* 939 (1951); M. Klinkhammer, "The Blaine Amendment of 1876: Private Motives for Political Action," 42 *Cath. Hist. Rev.* 15 (1956). The Blaine amendment was introduced some twenty times in Congress down to 1929. E. Corwin, "The Supreme Court as National School Board," 14 *J. Law and Contemp. Problems* 3, 12 (1949). The near miss of 1876 (it passed the House 180–7, lost in the Senate 28–16, with 27 abstentions) was the closest it ever came to passing the Congress.

69. *Everson* at 29 (Rutledge dissenting).

70. F. Sorauf, *Wall of Separation*, 18–19 (1976).

71. *Barfield v. Roberts*, 175 U.S. 291 (1899).

72. *Quick Bear v. Leupp*, 210 U.S. 50 (1908).

73. *Cochran v. Board of Education*, 281 U.S. 370 (1930).

74. *Board of Education v. Allen*, 392 U.S. 236 (1968).

75. *Bradfield* at 291.

76. *Quick Bear* at 50, 74.

77. *Cochran* at 375.

78. *Engel v. Vitale*, 370 U.S. 421 (1962).

79. *See Stone v. Graham*, 449 U.S. 39 (1980).

80. *Champaign-Urbana News Gazette*, November 18, 1984, p. 7, col. 1.

81. *McGowan v. Maryland*, 366 U.S. 420 (1961).

82. *Everson* at 42.

83. Ibid. at 14.

84. See Appendix 2.

85. Richard Morgan, "The Establishment Clause and Sectarian Schools: A Final Installment?" in P. Kurkland, ed., *Church and State: The Supreme Court and the First Amendment* 270 n. 134 (1975).

86. L. Pfeffer, *Church, State and Freedom* 141 (1953); Leonard Levy, "No Establishment of Religion: The Original Understanding," in L. Levy, *Judgments: Essays on American Constitutional History* 169–224 (1972).

87. Ibid. at 194–97.

88. See Levy, passim.

2

The Sacred Canopy: Law and Lexicon of Church-State in the Founding Era

Justice Rutledge's "sparse Congressional discussion"— because the essential issues had been settled"[1]—unwittingly, and perversely, contains the key to understanding the Establishment Clause. His statement is only almost literally true. Sparseness is relative, and compared to the discussion of other Bill of Rights provisions, the Establishment Clause was much debated, although it received in absolute terms only a little careful attention. The justice is "perversely" correct because the implication of his comments is subtly misleading. He suggests that the nagging church-state issue was finally settled by the Establishment Clause when only the meaning of *nonestablishment* as sect equality was. The more general issue continues to nag American society, especially the Supreme Court, to this day. But Rutledge could not have more accurately, however unwittingly, explained the relatively little commotion greeting disestablishment in Congress: everyone knew it meant no sect preference and agreed that it was an appropriate federal norm. This consensus or convergence quality of the Establishment Clause—that the meaning of it (like most of the rest of the Bill of Rights) was not novel and represented conventional thought—is apparent throughout this book and impels the discussion first to that terrain in which both prevailing norms of church and state and the legal language transporting those norms were clearly marked. The Constitution and laws of the states, as well as the experiences captured within them, are the indispensable referents, and for three reasons. Before the revolution, there was no nation from which to derive a national norm. Even during the brief Articles of Confederation period, union was so attenuated and the national government so weak that it serves poorly as a prism for focusing the genuine sentiments of the people. The second reason is related but separate. As Walter McElreath wrote more than a half-century ago, "The proper place to begin a study of the origin and development of the new idea of government is in the constitutions of the original states, which deal with the social relations of men with their fellowmen, and with the relation of the individual to the body politic."[2] State practices are thus more likely to reveal deeply held sociopolitical convictions than the bundle of compromises constituting national political behavior.[3] Finally, the relevant inquiry for today's public policy on church-state as contained in the Constitution is the history not of the idea but of the legal term *establishment*. An intellectual history will inform the constitutional lawyer's search for historically grounded meaning, but the tradition culminating in the religion clauses was legal and political, not speculative. Therefore the prevailing meaning of nonestablishment as a term in the constitutional law of the states is the essential background of the First Amendment.

NEW ENGLAND COVENANT POLITICS: MASSACHUSETTS, NEW HAMPSHIRE, CONNECTICUT, AND VERMONT

When twentieth-century commentators and justices look for religious establishment at the time the Bill of Rights was enacted, they are not sure how many there were in America, but they are sure there were some in New England. Supreme Court litigator Leo Pfeffer, in his influential *Church, State and Freedom*, discovered four states retaining a "substantial Establishment:" Massachusetts, Connecticut, New Hampshire, and Maryland.[4] Justice Black relied on the older, 1902 work of Sanford Cobb, a reluctant categorizer whose only certain establishments were Connecticut and Massachusetts.[5] Law professor Morris Forkosch reports six establishments extant in 1789[6] and although he does not list them, he must include New Hampshire, Massachusetts, and Connecticut to get such a high figure. William Van Alstyne, relying on the work of Pfeffer and others, reports five establishments.[7] Recently Justice Rehnquist counted New Hampshire and Massachusetts among the four state establishments extant (the others were Maryland and Rhode Island).[8] Leonard Levy's inspection of the early national era persuaded him that Connecticut, New Hampshire, and Massachusetts were among six states that established religion.[9] All these observers have overlooked Vermont, which proclaimed its independence in 1776 but whose status was uncertain throughout the 1780s. The settlers in what became by 1791 the state of Vermont, however, wrote a constitution in 1777 and enacted laws throughout the Confederation era. The content of Vermont's laws is important because Vermont's ratification of the Bill of Rights was one of those necessary to render it legally operative.[10] Vermonters, like Virginians and New Yorkers, were ratifiers and thus important. If modern observers had looked, they probably would have counted Vermont an establishment state too.

There is certainly some basis for assigning the New England states a place apart from their southern neighbors. This was the land founded upon Calvinist theology, where social organization was rooted in a covenant theory that taught that the people's unity was religious before it was political.[11] The Puritan settlers modeled their government on the Israelite theocracy of the Old Testament, including the views that civilian officials should enforce religious conformity and that the Ten Commandments were a starting point for political order.[12] During the seventeenth century, the laws of Massachusetts and New Haven, for instance, even specified that the word of God governed in cases not comprehended by colonial statutes.[13] More generally, during the colonial era, distinctions among civil and spiritual, political and religious were, at best, embryonic in New Englanders' thought.

The historical inseparability of church and state is evident in the constitutions and laws enacted by the states soon after the Declaration of Independence from Britain obliged them to fashion new legal orders. The Vermont Constitution of 1777 illustrated the pattern by describing the disputed territorial claims of New York and New Hampshire to it as a "violation of the tenth command,"[14] a matter of envying thy neighbor's goods. The people of Massachusetts "covenanted" with each other in their 1780 constitution and acknowledged the goodness and providence of the "great Legislator of the Universe."[15] The preamble to the Connecticut Constitution of 1776 (which did little more than affirm the 1662 charter) looked forward to the "Tranquility and Stability of Churches and Commonwealths."[16]

These pious generalities had practical bite. The constitution of each state required individual public worship,[17] and irregular church attendance cost 3 shillings in Connecticut[18] and 10 shillings in Massachusetts.[19] Each also specified a duty to support and maintain religious teachers and institutions, if only of the Protestant variety.[20] New Hampshire limited elected office to Protestants;[21] Vermont required of its public officials a declaration of Protestant belief, as well as a renunciation of all allegiance, "civil or ecclesiastical," to all foreign princes and prelates.[22] Besides thereby disqualifying Catholics from public office, Vermont guaranteed religious liberty to Protestants only,[23] New Hampshire and Massachusetts extended religious freedom to all "Christians," and Connecticut granted ecclesiastical corporate privileges only to Protestant sects.[24]

More remarkably puritanical in social theory than these constitutional provisions were the statutes that fleshed them out. Publicly maintained, supported, sponsored, and encouraged religious orthodoxy was the legal rule. Provisions governing the Lord's day involved much more than obligatory church attendance and fully warrant Mencken's definition of a Puritan as one whose sneaking suspicion is that somewhere, somebody is having a good time. No one enjoyed themselves on Sunday in New England. Beside the expected prohibition of all servile work, amusements, and gaiety, Massachusetts forbade "unnecessary walking" and empowered wardens "forcibly to stop and detain any person . . . he shall suspect of unnecessarily travelling . . . [and] take into custody . . . those who do not give satisfactory answers." Refusing to give "direct answers" to the warden cost the taciturn traveler a 5 pound fine.[25] Connecticut's Sabbath police—grand jury men, constables, and tithing men—were enjoined to "carefully inspect the behavior of all Persons on the Sabbath or Lord's day; and especially between the Meetings for divine worship on said Day".[26] The regulators were specifically authorized to make warrantless arrests of Sabbath breakers, and anyone "neglecting to afford his utmost Assistance to apprehend and secure" such offenders suffered the same penalty as for failure to assist the sheriff in his other law enforcement duties.[27]

Criminal prohibitions of blasphemy were just as pervasive, even more colorful, and amounted to nothing less than an official declaration of the truth of Christianity. In Connecticut "whipping on the naked body" (as many as forty stripes) along with an hour in the pillory attended "cursing or reproaching the true God or his government of the World."[28] A separate provision disqualified from office anyone educated in the Christian religion who shall "deny the Being of a God; or shall assert and maintain that there are more Gods than One; or [deny] the Old and New Testament to be of Divine Authority."[29] Massachusetts added rejection of the Last Judgment or exposing any of the books of the Bible to "contempt or ridicule" to its definition of blasphemy and authorized a maximum of sixteen months in jail, whipping, fitting in the pillory, or the gallows as penalties.[30] Blasphemy was distinct from the offenses of "cursing" and "profane swearing," but all tended, among other things, to "loosen the bonds of civil society."[31] The New Hampshire legislative session of 1791 revealed the temper of the times. A special committee recommended continuation of the extant blasphemy law, but one delegate moved for an amendment that any person speaking disrespectively of the Bible should have his "tongue bored through with a hot iron." This coddling was rejected by another member, John Sherbourne, who thought death the appropriate punishment. Cooler heads prevailed, however, and existing penalties were ratified.[32]

Further promotion of religion, piety, and morality took a variety of forms, and Connecticut was especially notable for its efforts here. It required every household to keep a Bible[33] and denied copyright protection to anything injurious to religion and morals.[34] "Mountebanks" and medicine shows were suppressed because they too were a "detriment of good Order and Religion."[35] Connecticut, as did the other New England states, exempted church property from taxation.[36] Each taxed its inhabitants specifically for the mantainance of Protestant ministers and houses of worship.

The systems of taxation for religion rested on the basic New England theme of local town autonomy. Article III of the Massachusetts Declaration of Rights[37] was produced by a committee that included future President John Adams and Caleb Strong, a member of the First U.S. Senate, which passed the Establishment Clause.[38] Article III, apparently drafted by revolutionary firebrand Sam Adams on behalf of the committee[39] authorized the legislature to require towns and parishes (parishes were geographical units) to provide at community expense for "public worship" and for the "support and maintenance of public Protestant teachers of piety, religion and morality," where such provision was not made "voluntarily."[40] ("Voluntarily" referred to Boston where a non-coercive system of support for religion prevailed throughout the colonial era.)[41] The New Hampshire Constitution of 1784 empowered the legislature to "authorize" the same undertaking,[42] which meant that towns could not be forced to settle and maintain ministers. Vermont's 1777 constitution did not specifically authorize the legislature to implement its declaration in favor of public worship, but in 1783 the legislature adopted essentially the prevailing town system.[43] There was no effective change since prior to that Vermont towns had been governed by New Hampshire church laws. In Connecticut "ecclesiastical societies" were geographically defined and empowered to settle and maintain ministers.[44] The societies were Congregational, but by 1784 all other Protestant sects were extended the same powers and privileges for maintenance of public worship.[45]

New Hampshire's Senator Paine Wingate explained and faithfully subscribed to the prevailing logic of public taxation for religion:

By this paragraph in the Constitution it is admitted that it is for the public civil welfare and prosperity to support the Protestant teachers of religion, and that every member of society is bound to contribute his proportion for the general good of the whole; for the same reasons that schools, and other means of useful instruction are supported at the public expense, and for the general benefit although each individual may not immediately receive the same degree of advantage.[46]

The mechanics of these systems developed over time in varying bits of legislation and differed some from state to state, but a composite profile of them is available.[47] First, a majority of those legally qualified to vote in a geographically defined town, parish, or society decided which Protestant ministry to settle in the town and voted a tax on all inhabitants to raise funds for church construction and a ministerial stipend. The sect most often selected was Congregational, but (especially in New Hampshire) other sects could and did achieve local hegemony. In Holderness, for example, Samuel Livermore, an active participant in the House of Representatives debate over the Establishment Clause, was a pillar of the settled Episcopal church.[48] Throughout New England, the tax was assessed solely and specifically for these purposes, was locally collected and administered, and the entire process was codified in local rules, or bylaws.

Perhaps the most notable feature of the system was its treatment of those Protestants outside the publicly maintained denomination, known as dissenters. (In New England as elsewhere, non-Protestants occupied an unfortunate category of their own and were not dissenters as contemporaries used that term.) As early as 1693 in New Hampshire,[49] and by the 1780s in Massachusetts,[50] Connecticut,[51] and Vermont,[52] no one was required to support the minister of a sect other than one's own. The aspiring dissenter secured a certificate from his congregation, stating that he was a regular attendee and supporter of it. When lodged with the clerk of the publicly maintained society, the certificate exempted the holder from the general assessment. To qualify for this relief, one had to subscribe to some Protestant church, and each of those churches was required by law to maintain itself through public levy. One result was that a single town might have two or more congregations publicly supported; certainly more than one denomination was so maintained somewhere in each state. These public props persisted into the nineteenth century. Vermont was the first to abandon them in 1807,[53] Massachusetts the last in 1833.[54]

It is now easy to see the possible bases for the establishment conclusions of Pfeffer, Cobb, Forkosch, and the others. Indeed, it is much harder to find Justice Black's "freedom loving" colonists, or to see how Justice Rutledge could conclude (as he did in *Everson*) that no state establishments existed by 1789.[55] Given Rutledge's conclusion that nonestablishment meant at least no aid to religion at all, these were four establishments with a vengeance.

That the Supreme Court's definition of establishment is askew is more apparent from a closer look at the constitutions of these states, which not only enshrined conscience as an inviolable, unalienable right but also forbade religious establishments. Massachusetts and New Hampshire expressed nonestablishment in precisely the same terms: "no subordination of any one sect or denomination to another shall ever be established by law."[56] No other reference to the subject of establishments appears in either constitution. Vermont's constitutions of 1777 and 1786 track the New Hampshire and Massachusetts provisions, forswearing "partiality for, or prejudice against, any particular class, sect, or denomination of men whatever."[57] The preamble to the Connecticut *organic act* of 1784 read: "so . . . that Christians of every denomination, demeaning themselves peaceably, and as good Subjects of the State, may be equally under the Protection of the Laws."[58] Each state guaranteed freedom of conscience to "all men" in Vermont,[59] to every individual in New Hampshire,[60] to all "subjects" in Massachusetts[61] and Connecticut.[62] The men who wrote these provisions fully intended to disestablish religion and understood nonestablishment to be the effect of their work. Providing public support of religious institutions was seen by them as Paine Wingate saw it: "A way to promote political stability and social cohesion by guaranteeing that individuals would receive instruction in moral principles, rooted with common religious sensibilities of the people, which would make them good citizens."[63]

The point is not everybody in New England agreed with the full range of church-state regulations, although the regimes noted undoubtedly received the enthusiastic support of an overwhelming majority. It is that nonestablishment indisputably meant no sect preference and that no sect preference was obviously consistent in the minds of these founders with aid and encouragement of religion. It is more than that, for even the attacks of critics like Isaac Backus and William Plume reveal agreement on the definition of establishment as legally enforced sectarian superiority. Their disagreement was primarily over whether the regimes actually comported with the standard definition. The attack on the systems of public worship and tax support along establishment lines was little more than a claim that Congregationalism was still legally favored and that dissenting sects were still subordinated. One claim of the dissenting (that is, non-Congregational) sects was that the certificate system implied sect subordination by requiring dissenters to secure credentials satisfactory to the majority church before they were permitted to withdraw from its support.[64] The challenge was quite accurate; dissenters had to go to a lot of trouble to achieve what Congregationalists enjoyed simply by being in the majority. This problem was largely de facto and not de jure, however, for only Connecticut deviated from facially sect-neutral laws and then only by recognizing the sociological reality of Congregational hegemony.[65]

A second claim of subordination stemmed from this practicality of numbers. To qualify for relief, dissenters had to show attendance and support of another church. Where the dissenters were separate handfuls of Baptists, Quakers, and Universalists, however, each might be unable to erect and support a ministry of its own.[66] A variety of practices grew up to sustain dissenters in this situation. In Connecticut, Baptists frequently crossed the border to worship in Rhode Island, and Connecticut recognized certification by Rhode Island congregations.[67] More commonly dissenters joined a magnet congregation whose sole purpose was to provide certificates, while the separate parcels of dissenters actually worshipped apart.

A third establishment tendency resided in the laws themselves and constituted a kind of residual preference. For the taxes of newcomers, those who failed to designate a recipient, and dissenters who could not secure certificates from an operating congregation, usually the money went to the majority congregation, usually the Congregationalists.[68]

Fourth, this elaborate minuet had to be administered, and was frequently litigated, in what was for dissenters hostile territory. Litigation meant judges and juries composed primarily of hostile Congregationalists,[69] and contested issues included whether a minister who preached universal salvation was a "Protestant teacher of religion, piety, and morality"[70] and whether a Presbyterian could be compelled to support a Congregational minister because they were really the same sect."[71]

A final preference arose from the Baptist disavowal of professional clergy. Instead they chose ministers from their own congregation to serve without compensation. Baptists therefore did not need the system at all, and its burdens fell on them with no immediate tangible benefit. Baptist leader Isaac Backus claimed that his sect's ministers could not in good conscience accept money involuntarily acquired, so Baptists' taxes usually went to the town's ministers.[72] For these reasons, Backus complained to the Massachusetts delegation of the 1776 Continental Congress about the discrimination suffered by dissenters. The delegates replied that the certificate provisions granted sufficient liberty, and John Adams added that he doubted they could be called an "Establishment" at all.[73]

These arguments from sect discrimination exhausted the establishment critique on the compulsory finance provisions during the pre–First Amendment period. Literally no one suggested an establishment existed simply because religion was aided. As Baptist minister Samuel Stillman remarked in 1779, "There are many ways that the magistrate can encourage religion" while respecting rights of conscience in a nonestablishment regime, which, Stillman noted, Massachusetts was.[74] Indeed the criticisms noted were not of the system as a whole but of discreet features of it. The frontal attack on the idea of compulsory worship and taxation came much later (in the nineteenth century) and was primarily rooted in an elaborate argument derived from freedom of conscience. What the New England dissenters highlighted instead was a potential, if not actual, establishment tendency in systems of compulsory support of the clergy, a flaw detected almost wherever such systems were proposed or enacted. But that flaw was one of preference among sects and simply confirmed that nondiscriminatory aid to religion complied with the nonestablishment norm.

It is perhaps inevitable that historians should focus on the critics who ultimately dismantled the New England church-state regime and who in the process made arguments about religious liberty pleasing to modern ears. It is not inevitable that we forget—and we should not forget—that during the 1780s theirs was not the popular view. The essentials of the New England church-state arrangement were before the people and their representatives repeatedly during the last part of the eighteenth century and every time received their hearty approval. The citizens of Massachusetts, for instance, rejected a proposed state constitution in 1778 because it lacked a bill of rights.[75] Article III of Massachusetts's 1780 constitution's Bill of Rights containing the conscience, establishment, and compulsory public worship and support provisions was "closely scrutinized" and then approved by almost three-quarters of the electorate.[76] The state legislature reinforced the Constitution's religious provisions by an act passed in 1786.[77] New Hampshire residents rejected a constitution in 1779; the one ordained in 1784 and that contained the provisions discussed in this part began a laborious birth in a 1781 convention. The people, from their town meetings, submitted voluminous amendments, which were digested by the convention, and the constitution was finally ratified in 1784.[78] Another constitution (containing substantially identical religious provisions) was ratified by the people in 1791. Article VI of the 1791 Declaration of Rights—the no establishment and pro–public support provisions—was retained in the convention by a vote of 89 to 15.[79] Included was the affirmative vote of Abiel Foster, a Congregational minister and a member of the first House of Representatives, which passed the Bill of Rights.[80] In addition, the New Hampshire legislature enacted additional laws empowering towns to tax for ministerial support in 1791, 1793, and 1794.[81] The people even rejected an amendment to the 1791 constitution, which was no more than a liberalization of the certificate provisions, by a vote of 3993 to 994.[82] The Vermont constitutions of 1777, 1786, and 1793 were not popularly ratified but approved by a popularly elected legislature[83] and reflected no significant change in the church-state regime initially received from New Hampshire. Connecticut offered no constitution for ratification, but all the laws described in this part were part of a comprehensive revision by influential Congressman Roger Sherman and Richard Law that was adopted by the legislature in 1784.[84]

The dissenting sects ensured that the attention of state legislators was continuously focused on church-state issues, especially the funding systems. But chronic legislative tinkering with those systems throughout the final two decades of the eighteenth century yielded only a smoother avenue of relief for dissenters. The systems themselves entered the nineteenth century unsullied. There is, then, no reason to doubt the observation of William Plumer, the foremost adversary of the standing order in New Hampshire, that overwhelming community sentiment was the obstacle to what he defined as progress.[85]

There are two inescapable conclusions to the New England story. First, New Englanders lived in a regime that aided religion, entangled church and state, and hemmed conscience in with overarching social and religious duties simply because they wanted to. Second, even the dissenters from that regime did not dispute the definition of establishment embodied in the constitutions and laws the people and their representatives enacted. That definition was no sect preference.

RHODE ISLAND: "GOD'S COUNTRY"

Those wearied and dismayed by the rigid orthodoxy of New England may find respite in Rhode Island. Roger Williams did. Banished from Massachusetts Bay in 1635 as a religious heretic and thus a political subversive, Williams and a small group of followers settled at the head of Narragansett Bay on land purchased from the Indians.[86] There they endeavored to establish, in the words of Rhode Island's foremost historian, "a pure democracy, which for the first time guarded jealously the right of conscience by ignoring any power in the body politic to interfere with those matters that alone concern man and his Maker."[87] With a mild caveat springing from the autocratic side of Williams's political personality,[88] they did.

From its beginning, the "lively experiment" was governed by assumptions radically different from those of its northern neighbors. In the first articles of incorporation, drafted in 1637 (apparently) by Williams, common political authority extended "only in civil things."[89] The 1663 colonial charter guaranteed full religious liberty to all persons,[90] and a comprehensive 1716 act restated these fundamentals.[91] The same act, in stark contrast to neighboring colonies, ordained that ministerial salaries be "raised by a free contribution and no other way."[92] A 1798 statutory revision put it this way: "no man shall be compelled to frequent or support any religious worship, place or ministry whatsoever."[93] (There had in fact never been compulsory public worship.) Obviously absent from Rhode Island was that comprehensive mingling of civil and religious power over church funds exercised by the New England town governors.

However edifying to modern minds, Rhode Island's separation of church and state was certainly not a product of the Enlightenment political theory that may have prompted similar thoughts in the mind of the revered Jefferson. Indeed it misleads to analyze the lively experiment in political terms at all, for the Providence regime was just as surely and firmly rooted in Protestant theology as was the Puritans' city on a hill. And it is the content of Williams's theology that need be inspected, for only by comprehending the intellectual foundation of Rhode Island "separationism" can we understand the nature of the Baptist assaults on both New England Congregationalism and the Revolutionary-era southern Anglican establishments, as well as the pivotal role of the Baptists in the now-famous Virginia general assessment struggle of 1785.

The Puritans banished Williams chiefly because he rejected the cornerstone of the Massachusetts regime: convenant theology.[94] But it was Jesus Christ, not John Locke, who induced the eviction, for Williams's disagreement arose out of a biblical, not a political, analysis that squarely repudiated the Puritans' intellectual reliance on the ancient Israelites. Quite contrary to Puritan doctrine, Williams admitted no independent significance of the Old Testament, insisting that Jesus had entirely "abrogated" the "Hebraic" system. Christ stripped civil magistrates of all authority and power over religious belief, which was to Williams a matter of "soul liberty."[95] In other words, the magistrate could not coerce belief because God did not.

This encompassing definition of liberty of conscience was the organizing principle of Williams's society, and it produced a kind of separation of church and state. It is thus important to keep in mind that the cleavage was meant to protect the church and the soul from the corrupting influence of the magistrate, to preserve the garden of church from corruption in the wilderness of the world. The quest for spiritual purity quite literally led Williams into the political realm, where he was basically traditional, if not authoritarian.[96] This priority of the spiritual is clearly evident in the legislative explanation for the revised 1798 Act Relative to Religious Freedom, and the Maintenance of Ministers:

WHEREAS Almighty God hath created the mind free; that all attempts to influence it by temporal punishments or burthens, or by civil incapacitations, tend only to beget habits of hypocrisy and meanness, and are a departure from the plan of the Holy Author of our religion, who being Lord both of body and mind, yet chose not to propagate it by coercions on either, as was in his almighty power to do that to compel a man to furnish contributions of money for the propagation of opinions which he disbelieves, is sinful and tyrannical; that even the forcing him to support this or that teacher of his own religious persuasion, is depriving him of the comfortable liberty of giving his contributions to the particular pastor whose morals he would make his pattern, and whose powers he feels most per-suasive to righteousness, and is withdrawing from the ministry these temporary rewards, which, proceeding from an appropriation of their personal conduct, are an additional incitement to earnest and unremitting labours for the instruction of mankind.[97]

Public support of Rhode Island's ministry was unnecessary since Baptists there, as elsewhere, preferred an unsalaried, nonprofessional clergy, frequently designating members of their own congregations as preachers. More notable is the absence of any establishment line of attack or a proffered definition of establishment in Rhode Island's legal corpus. Spiritual liberty, not nonestablish-ment, justified the negation of compulsory tax support.

Since that which justifies also limits, one may see why Rhode Island exempted all church property from taxation. While certainly an aid and benefit to religion, it portended no corruption or stain from the heavy hand of government. One can also understand how Rhode Island, like its orthodox neighbors, prohibited blasphemy,[98] profane swearing,[99] and the sale of liquor to those "known to possess the odious and destructive vice of drunkenness"[100] and enforced various Sabbatarian restrictions (but not compulsory worship).[101] The radical emphasis on spiritual liberty indicated a deep gulf between spirit and the (inherently evil) flesh, which at the behavioral level required taming to prevent individual and societal anarchy. What constituted civily enforceable public decorum was, to Baptist and Puritan alike, largely a function of Christian belief, as each stemmed from a Calvinist root stressing behavioral conformity. If the state thereby sponsored, encouraged, or supported Christianity, the staying hand of spiritual freedom was not implicated. One may also understand, with Elwyn Smith's help, Rhode Island's exclusion of Roman Catholics[102] and Jews[103] from citizenship. Smith notes that Baptists shared with other Protestants a general aversion to the works righteousness of papists.[104] He might have added that the hierarchical order and (perceived) negation of individual autonomy in the Catholic church would aggravate Baptists more than other Protestants. The principled rejection of the Old Testament was also conducive to anti-Semitism.[105] Isaac Backus, for example, castigated the Massachusettts theocrats for drawing their arguments from the old Jewish constitution and ordinances: "As the Jews were required to inflict corporal punishments, even unto death upon non-conformers to their worship, this commonwealth did the like to such as preferred to conform to their way."[106] In Rhode Island, the sizable Jewish congregation at Newport was free to worship as it pleased, but Jews nevertheless remained second-class citizens in the state.[107]

If one accepts the Supreme Court's definition of establishment, then Rhode Island, that polar star of religious liberty, maintained an establishment at the time it ratified the First Amendment in 1790. Clearly separation of church and state, such as it was in Rhode Island, was never rooted in or animated by a no-aid-to-religion stricture. That naked concept simply did not resonate with the colony's theological grounding. The fire of spiritual liberty certainly extinguished forms of aid elsewhere welcomed; indeed those forms of aid were detriments or corruptions of religion in Providence. But Rhode Islanders did not live by the *Everson* ban on nondiscriminatory support and promotion of religion, much less did they ever argue that nonestablishment denoted such a rule.

In the broad spectrum of state practice during the colonial and early national periods, even this definition of religious liberty was iconoclastic, an identifiably Baptist island in the stream of publicly supported and enforced religious orthodoxy. And that is its only influence; it impinged on public events only where Baptists did. Rhode Island's direct influence in national development was virtually nil. Its population minute, Rhode Island ratified the federal Bill of Rights, but it did not participate in the general debate succeeding the Constitutional Convention of 1787 and did not convene a ratifying convention in time to forward, as other states did, suggested amendments to the Constitution. Since it was not represented in the First Congress, no Rhode Island representative affected the debate over the language of the Establishment Clause.

Nor was Rhode Island's experiment one that other states were likely to follow. Historian Perry Miller rightly observes that Roger Williams "exerted little or no direct influence on theorists of the Revolution and the Constitution, who drew upon quite different intellectual sources."[108] Indeed, given his radical departure from Puritan political theory, there is no sense in which Williams and Rhode Island were further along a maturation process that the rest of New England was bound to follow. There is just as much, although different, reason to conclude that Rhode Island was not elsewhere a model for non-Baptists. First, nothing was more common in the political discourse among politicians of late eighteenth-century America than denunciations of Rhode Island's political fortunes. Among the major causes were its erratic participation in national councils during the Confederation and what was widely considered a ruinous emission of paper money in 1785. The result was a string of caustic epithets usually reserved for Tories and Jesuits, and they fell from every patriot's lips. That "unhappy, fallen, lost sister" whose conduct was "unexampled in the history of the world,"[109] Rhode Island was, in the opinion of Theodore Sedgewick, a first congressman from Massachusetts, "a little trollop."[110]

Perhaps the paramount cause of Rhode Island's notoriety was that it was where Baptists lived. Rhys Isaac's pathbreaking article[111] on the nature of the Baptist challenge to the ruling class in revolutionary Virginia reveals a penetrating hostility to Baptists as such, especially to their enthusiastic religious style. The emotional, extremely pious, and in many ways intolerant spirituality of the faithful and the perceived (and, relatively at least, actual) ignorance of their clergy rankled the reserved, ritualistic Anglican gentry.[112] Baptists (not just Rhode Islanders) were widely considered enemies of good government[113] and were ridiculed at a time when religion was not joked about. Thus one unexpectedly encounters the sarcasm of a Confederation congressmen who, embarking for Rhode Island, reported sarcastically to colleagues that he was about to visit "God's country."

THE NATIONAL CHURCH OF THE SOUTH

The best-known historian of the Church of England in the United States described the Anglican church as the national church of the American South.[114] Since James Madison contended that the Establishment Clause was neither more nor less than the prohibition of a "national church," even *Everson* enthusiasts ought to find the contours of the southern Episcopal regimes deeply instructive. More important, with the exception of four counties in and around New York City, the southern colonies—Maryland, Virginia, North Carolina, South Carolina, Georgia—provide the only instances of unequivocal disestablishment in the experience of the ratifying generation. That disestablishment was accomplished there explicitly, deliberately, self-consciously, and so near to the adoption of the First Amendment (1776 for Maryland and North Carolina, 1777 for Georgia, 1778 for South Carolina, and 1786 for Virginia) invites detailed scrutiny. Because legal conditions and popular thoughts in the establishment period, during the disestablishment controversy, and through the era of nonestablishment are all recoverable, one can clearly see just what Americans thought prohibiting an established church meant. The southern experience shows that Anglicanism was established because it enjoyed legal and political privileges other subordinate Protestant sects did not. The proponents of disestablishment sought equality of Protestant sects, and when that was accomplished, nonestablishment conditions prevailed.

Anglican Establishments Defined

James Madison wrote a friend in 1774: "That diabolical, hell-conceived principle of persecution rages among some. . . . There are at this time in the adjacent county not less than five or six well-meaning men in close jail for publishing their religious sentiments, which in the main are very orthodox. . . . So I must beg you to . . . pray for liberty of conscience to all."[115] The preachers bewailed by Madison were no doubt more humanely treated than the Baptist preacher— "Brother Waller"—whose Tidewater meeting was interrupted in the following manner by the local Anglican minister and some of his retainers:

Brother Waller informed us . . . [that] about two weeks ago on the Sabbath Day down in Caroline county he introduced the worship of God by singing. . . . The Parson of the Parish [who had ridden up with his clerk, the sheriff, and some others] would keep running the end of his horsewhip in [Waller's] mouth, laying his whip across the hymn book, etc. When done singing [Waller] proceeded to prayer. In it he was violently jerked off the stage; they caught him by the back part of his neck, beat his head against the ground, sometimes up, sometmes down, they carried him through a gate that stood some considerable distance, where a gentleman [the sheriff] gave him . . . twenty lashes with his horsewhip.
    . . . Then Bro. Waller was released, went back singing praise to God, mounted the stage and preached with a great deal of liberty.[116]

These expressions of Anglican supremacy were perhaps peculiar to Virginia's relatively illiberal establishment, which caused (in part) moderation in establishments farther south by inducing large numbers of dissenters to migrate from Virginia to the inland areas of North and South Carolina.[117] But these incidents were only the cruel visage of a body firmly planted throughout the South, a regime sustained by a far-reaching system of legal and political Anglican dominance over the other Protestant sects, and the episodes well illustrate the principle that made establishments sufficiently unpopular to be overturned in the Revolutionary era.

The reality of Anglican hegemony touched everyone living in the southern states and at various points in life. It started in the structure of local government. In Georgia, South Carolina, and Maryland, the essential unit of local government was the parish, a geographically defined item whose center was the local Anglican church.[118] More significant, and the case in all five states, the vestrymen, or lay governors, of the local Anglican church were both civil and religious officers.[119] They exercised power over the political affairs of all, as well as the religious lives of Anglican communicants. In Georgia, for instance, they were effectively the only locally elected officials.[120] Elsewhere they were supplemented by other petty officials, such as justices of the peace. Among the civil duties of the vestry in all the colonies was to provide for the orphans and poor of the locale.[121] In various states they were also charged with enforcement of morals legislation, administration of political elections [122] and of the wild animal bounty,[123] supervision of fire protection, sanitation, and the cemetery,[124] and regulation of tobacco production.[125] More to the heart of the discrimination so keenly felt, all inhabitants of the parish or county were taxed to support the established church and its minister.[126] (The vestry assessed and collected these tithes as well.)[127] Moreover, the rule rather than the exception in the colonial South was that non-Anglicans could neither vote for nor serve as vestrymen.[128] Ordinarily, then, dissenters were effectively precluded from participation in important aspects of local government, were obliged to pay for Anglican worship, and in addition were left with the burden of underwriting their own churches as well.

The legal dominance of the Anglican vestry was accentuated throughout the South, and especially in Maryland, South Carolina, and Virginia, by the tight fit between vestry service and political officeholding.[129] The Virginia House of Burgesses, for instance, has been described as practically a convention of vestrymen[130] and Virginia's Episcopal church pictured as the religious arm of the tidewater gentry.[131] The South Carolina Constitution of 1776 was written exclusively by churchmen,[132] and the ascendancy of the Charleston aristocracy in South Carolina affairs was largely the ascendancy of Anglican vestrymen.

The fit between a gentry ruling class and the Anglican vestry was perhaps tightest in Maryland. The pre-Revolutionary Maryland legislature governed the temporal affairs of the Anglican church, expressly and separately authorizing tax assessments for the construction of each Anglican church.[133] Although North Carolina's establishment rested on no similar social and cultural foundation,[134] it was equally immoderate. There, the legislature chartered only Anglican schools[135] and permitted only Anglican clergymen to perform marriages (for which they were authorized to charge a fee).[136] An act of 1767 gave Presbyterians the right to be married by their own clergy, but the whole fee had to be given over to an Anglican minister whenever one demanded it.[137] The scarcity of Anglican clergymen in Georgia made exclusivity impossible, but Anglican ministers there still enjoyed monopoly-like privileges over weddings and burials.[138] In South Carolina, only establishment clergy could perform marriages,[139] and although Anglican churches could hold estates and sue at common law, no dissenting church could.[140] In Maryland, publicly supported education was limited by an act of assembly to institutions in which schoolmasters were members of the church.[141] And the travails of the Virginia Baptist preachers owed to the legislative requirement that non-Anglicans procure a license to preach in the Old Dominion.[142]

This system of massive aid, encouragement, sponsorship, and support of religion would certainly have upset disestablishmentarians clinging to a no-aid principle. But there was also much here to disturb even those who defined establishment much less ambitiously as, for example, the privileged inequality of Anglicanism. Fortunately we need not guess which aspect of the regime its adversaries identified as establishmentarian and which features they essayed to remove by disestablishing the Episcopal church. Both the struggle and consummation of disestablishment unequivocally show that sect inequality was an establishment of religion.

Disestablishment Defined

The War for Independence was the occasion, if not the cause, of disestablishment in the southern colonies (now states), and it is one of the intriguing questions of the era whether the causal relationship is more appropriately reversed—that is, to what extent the conflict was one between American dissenters and Anglican establishmentarians on either side of the Atlantic. There is much historical evidence that by disestablishment in the South, the patriot leadership hoped to enlist dissenters in the war effort. The dissenters, in turn, recognized wartime as a perfect opportunity to wrest equality from the tidewater gentries.[143] Disestablishment was, in any event, a multifaceted reality, but not among its realities was hostility to state support of religion.

Disestablishment came to North Carolina in 1776, and historians agree that it was a movement spearheaded by dissenting Protestants.[144] The most careful student of the process identifies the injury as the "oppressive nature of favoritism to church and clergy"[145]—in short, the English establishment. The salient appeal for relief was contained in a pair of instructions to the representatives of Mecklenburg and Orange counties to the state constitutional convention of 1776. The residents advised oppostion "to the utmost any particular church or set of Clergymen being invested with power to decree rites and Ceremonies," the establishment of any mode of worship opposed to the rights of conscience, and compulsory support of any denomination other than one's own. Upon adoption of the constitution, the delegates were instructed to secure repeal of the marriage and vestry laws, the major symbols of Anglican superiority.[146] The 1776 constitution embodied these instructions[147] and recognized the "inalienable right to worship Almighty God, according to the dictates" of conscience.[148] The document went on to "explicitly disestablish" Anglicanism by proclaiming "that there shall be no Establishment of any relgious Church or Denomination in this State in Preference to any other."[149]

The undisputed leader of disestablishment in South Carolina was William

Tennant, a transplanted (from New Jersey) Presbyterian minister. He circulated a petition among backcountry dissenters prior to the legislative session of 1777, and the petition, with "many thousand signatures," prayed that "there shall never be the establishment of any one Denomination or sect of Protestants by way of preference to another in this State," that no Protestant be compelled to support a religious worship that he does not freely join, and that "all Protestants demeaning themselves peaceably under the government established under the [1776 state] Constitution shall enjoy free and equal privileges, both religious and civil."[150] Tenant followed his presentation of the petition with an impassioned plea to the assembly for disestablishment.[151] His theme there was that South Carolina acknowledged one society as a Christian church and "knows the other not at all" and continued to cite Anglican privileges.[152]

The general assembly endorsed Tennant's position in its entirety and incorporated that sentiment in the South Carolina Constitution of 1778, which put all Protestant sects on an equal footing. This document has been almost universally read by contemporaries and historians as effecting disestablishment.[153] Even Leo Pfeffer does not include South Carolina as retaining any substanial establishment in its basic laws.[154] In fact, the constitution of South Carolina, in ordaining a regime of Protestant equality with effective exclusion of non-Protestants from public office, did precisely what all of the other states did. What is puzzling, and unique, is that South Carolina chose to describe Protestant hegemony as an establishment—that is, the "Christian Protestant religion" was the "established" religion of the state. Levy admits that "[N]ever before had an estblishment been known that did not exact religious [tax] assessments." In other words, South Carolina's experience contradicts Levy's definition of establishment, but not ours.[155] Although from our perspective this is perhaps a technically accurate use of the term—its only practical effect was to subordinate Roman Catholics and Jews—the self-consciousness exhibited is unique among U.S. state papers of the time. It is also otherwise inconsequential. That this unparalleled development failed to affect establishment concepts has been recognized by Thomas Curry, who wrote that South Carolina's "establishment . . . corresponded to no previous definition of the term, caused no controversy in the state, and disappeared without comment."[156]

Like most other episodes in Georgia's Revolutionary-era political history, the process by which Anglicanism was disestablished in 1777 remains obscure. What is known reveals that the establishment had been practically ineffective due to the religious heterogeneity and geographic spread of the population, which, combined with frontier conditions, made any social control difficult. Most consequential was the lack of Anglican ministers; the number of clergy never exceeded a handful at any time prior to the close of the Revolution.[157] The constitutional provision effecting disestablishment was understandably simple: "All persons whatever shall have the free exercise of their religion; . . . and shall not, unless by consent, support any teacher or teachers except those of their own profession."[158] That this meant the dawn of nonestablishment in Georgia was the universal understanding at the time.

Disestablishment in Maryland came with the constitution of 1776.[159] It guaranteed that "all persons professing the Christian religion, are equally entitled to protection in their religious liberty"; neither should "any person be compelled to frequent or maintain, or contribute, unless on contact, to maintain any particular place of worship, or any particular ministry." Lest these provisions be thought to forbid all compulsory support of religion, the same article authorized the legislature to lay a "general and equal tax, for the support of the Christian religion."[160]

The drafters and their contemporaries agreed that the Virginia constitution of 1776 was a decisive victory for disestablishmentarians and that it clearly preserved the Anglican establishment.[161] Modern historians concur. The only religious provision of consequence—section 16 of the Declaration of Rights—in the constitution provided

that religion or the duty which we owe to our Creator, and the manner of discharging it, can be directed only by reason and conviction, not by force or violence; and therefore all men are equally entitled to the free exercise of religion, according to the dictates of conscience; and that it is the mutual duty of all to practice Christian forbearance, love, and charity towards each other.[162]

Although Patrick Henry, later a vigorous advocate of a general assessment, proposed this language to the convention, its authors were George Mason and James Madison.[163] This section was intended to guarantee full measure of liberty of conscience, as is apparent from the wording, which was Madison's and an improvement on Mason's original draft.[164] (The original had stated that "all men should enjoy the fullest toleration in the exercise of religion.")[165] And the Virginia legislature, in the light of section 16, promptly repealed laws mandating church attendance and dissenters' support of the Anglican church and modified the legal definition of heresy.[166]

Even more significant are the words left out of the section and what the legislature did not do. Nowhere in the 1776 constitution is found the blanket declaration of sect equality common to other state constitutions of the era, including those in New England. Expressly defeated on the floor of the convention was Madison's direct play for disestablishment. Madison would have added after the free exercise sentence: "and therefore that no man or class of men ought on account of religion to be invested with peculiar emoluments or privileges, nor subjected to any penalties or disability."[167] Henry, sponsoring this language as well as the enacted provision, denied on the floor that even this language portended disestablishment, although Madison so intended it and Henry favored it.[168] The proposal was nevertheless defeated. Stalled in committee was a more subtle inroad into Anglican preeminence. Where the committee- and convention-approved version proscribed "force and violence" in the area of conscience, Madison proposed to substitute the more expansive term *compulsion* for *force*. This fine distinction was also defeated.[169]

Thomas Jefferson, whose skepticism of organized religion was already well developed and well known, was a loser too. Although his work in the Philadelphia Continental Congress precluded his actual presence at the Virginia convention, he participated in it by drafting at least three complete constitutions. Portions were incorporated in the enacted constitution, but left out were all his suggestions pertaining to religion.[170] Jefferson proposed that no one should "be compelled to frequent or maintain *any* religious institutions" [emphasis added].[171] The enactment of section 16 instead prompted Jefferson, according to Edmund Randolph's biographer, to pen his famous Bill for Establishing Religious Liberty, which called for no compelled support "whatever," thereby making clear that in Jefferson's mind, section 16 did not forbid compulsory support of religion.[172]

Section 16 was hailed by dissenters as a great victory, freeing them from a "long night of ecclesiastical bondage."[173] It also served as a launching pad for assaulting the Anglican establishment. Subordinate sects, chiefly the Baptists and Presbyterians, argued in the press and in legislative petitions that genuine freedom of conscience was inconsistent with both an establishment of religion and taxation to pay ministerial stipends,[174] and the battle continued for almost twenty years. Even while significantly abated by the legislative embroglio of 1784–1785, agitation over the Anglican establishment did not completely end until early in the nineteenth century. As closer inspection of the 1785 general assessment proposal will make clearer, the establishment's adversaries, even as they dismantled it, made its definition evident. They made clear that the establishment that they combatted consisted of Anglican hegemony over other sects. Taxation for religous purposes, like the general assessment proposal, constituted a separate evil. Each was assertedly violative of the right of conscience but not necessarily of that defined in section 16. Critically there is no evidence in Virginia, or anywhere else, that disestablishmentarian sentiment was rooted in hostility to all aid or encouragement of religion or that disestablishment in any way encompassed such a notion.

However potent, if not self-evident, the dissenters' calculation of conscience may seem to modern readers, the Virginia legislature of 1776 unequivocally rejected it and reinforced the Anglican establishment. (Even the Constitutional Convention did as much, for one of its last acts was to decree a series of changes in the Anglican liturgy.)[175] Retained, for instance, were the Episcopical monopoly over marriage ceremonies, the vestry's exclusive power to tax for the benefit of the poor, and the vestry's administration of that fund. Tax-exempt glebe lands continued to be held only by the Episcopal church. Indeed despite numerous loosenings of the establishment's grip between 1776 and 1784, none of the changes (as Elwyn Smith concludes) placed the sects on equal footing so that the establishment, however pale an imitation of its pre-Revolutionary self, lived on. The most revealing reservation by the Revolutionary legislature did not maintain a particular facet of Anglican supremacy but was buried in the last section of the 1776 religion bill (and essentially repeated annually until 1784):

And whereas great Varieties of Opinions have arisen touching the Propriety of a general Assessment or whether every religious society should be left to voluntary Contributions for the support and maintenance of the several Ministers and Teachers of the Gospel who are of different Persuasions and Denominations, and this Difference of Sentiments cannot now be well accommodated, so that it is thought most prudent to defer this matter to the Discussion and final Determination of a future assembly when the Opinions of the Country in General may be better known. To the End therefore that so important a Subject may in no sort be prejudged, Be it Enacted by the Authority aforesaid that nothing in ths Act contained shall be construed to affect or influence the said Question of a general Assessment or voluntary Contribution in any respect whatever.[176]

Nonestablishment Explained

Successful prosecution of the protracted War for Independence induced politically active Americans like Patrick Henry to seek civil enouragement and support of regular, effective Christian worship.[177] The displacements and ravages of battle on home territory had cut deeply into religious habits: churches damaged or destroyed by armies, combatants cut off from opportunity for regular worship, many of the clergy (particular Anglican) killed or exiled for supporting the British. Also, with full attention on social reconstruction at home, Henry and others saw the precariousness of the experiment in liberty without the redcoats as a galvanizing common enemy.[178]

Responding to newspaper editorials and citizen petitions from throughout the state, including one from the Presbyterian clergy, the Virginia Assembly in 1784 formally considered the Bill Establishing a Provision for Teachers of the Christian Religion.[179] After declaring its purpose and (significantly) its consistency with the Declaration of Rights, the bill required the county sheriff to collect a specified sum from each property holder for support either of a "minister" or "teacher" of the Gospel or "places of divine worship" of the taxpayer's choice, and "to none other use whatsoever." Quakers and Mennonites, who had no regular clergy and did not build churches, were excepted insofar as they retained discretion to further their particular mode of worship with the money. Individuals expressing no preferred Christian denomination were obliged to underwrite seminaries of learning in the county of collection.

Preliminary successes in the 1784 assembly gave way to eventual defeat of the bill in the 1785 session, when the delegates instead passed Jefferson's Bill for Establishing Religious Freedom.[180] This denouement may evidence a decisive popular rejection in Virginia of this particular species of direct aid to religion.[181] Whether it reveals anything else about even Virginian's church-state sensibilities, much more about the meaning of the First Amendment, are other matters. Assuming, as the Supreme Court did in *Everson*, that counting notable heads on each side of the issue is instructive, all we learn is that the general assessment was beneficial. First, one must add to Jefferson and Madison on the anti-assessment side George and Wilson Cary Nicholas,[182] George Mason,[183] and Andrew Moore[184] (a member of the First Congress). On the other side, in favor of the Bill for Supporting Teachers of the Christian Religion, were George Washington,[185] John Marshall,[186] Patrick Henry (the most powerful politician in Virginia at the time),[187] Governor Benjamin Harrison,[188] Edward Pendleton,[189] Edmund Randolph[190] (later attorney general in the Washington administration), John Page (a colleague of Madison in the First Congress),[191] John Frances Mercer (a delegate to the Constitutional Convention of 1787),[192] and one of Virginia's first senators, Richard Henry Lee.[193] Clearly in agreement with the bill's principle because of their contemporaneous support of an aid bill in the national Congress were Virginia's other first senator, William Grayson, and future president James Monroe. (Their specific views of the general assessment bill are not known.)

Senator Lee's reasons for supporting the assessment, expressed in a letter to Madison early in the controversy, illustrate the pro-assessment rationale:

Refiners may weave as fine a web of reason as they please, but the experience of all times shews Religion to be the guardian of morals—And he must be a very inattentive observer in our Country, who does not see that avarice is accomplishing the destruction of religion, for want of a legal obligation to contribute something to its support. The declaration of rights, it seems to me, rather contends against forcing modes of faith and forms of worship, than against compelling contribution for the support of religion in general.[194]

The second assumption of the *Everson* Court was that Madison's "A Memorial and Remonstrance" against the bill captured the meaning of the First Amendment's nonestablishment requirement. Historical facts reveal instead that Madison's opus did not even capture the thought of the Virginia majority who opposed the bill. Although it was the most comprehensive petition against the bill and assiduously circulated by its authors' allies, less than one-fifth of all Virginians who signed petitions against the bill signed the "Memorial."[195] Its comprehensiveness also diminishes its value as a guage of popular sentiment, for no one either could endorse all of its arguments (some were contradictory) or would (since others were obviously false or absurd). Madison contended that the state did not need publicly supported religion and that religion did not need the state's support; that public support of religion harmed the state; and that public support harmed religion. He persistently referred to the proposed bill as an "establishment" but offered varied accounts of its establishment qualities. The general assessment, he wrote, partook of the same authority as that which may establish one sect of Christians in preference to another, surely as much a non sequitur as saying that equality implies inequality but enough to trigger in dissenters' minds memories of the pre-1776 Anglican dominance. In the process, Madison at least relied on the prevailing definition of establishment as sect preference. Madison also said that sect inequality was introduced in favor of

Quakers and Mennonites, where in reality the bill was strenuously evenhanded in accommodating the internal organization of those relatively unstructured sects. Indeed the opposite of Madison's view is the more accurate: taxing Quakers, for example, and limiting disbursements to sects with regular clergy and separate houses of worship excluded Quakers from the benefits of the tax. Madison also suggested that the proposal was hostile to nonbelievers, where the bill in fact expressly accommodated their conscience. Revealingly, he never repeated one of his paramount private criticisms of it: that its limitation to Christianity was obnoxioius in itself and not for any tendency of it to hasten a return to pre-1776 practices. In a letter to Jefferson, Madison had even noted the "pathetic zeal" of the late Governor Harrison who had gained a majority for this "discrimination" (Madison's word in private) in favor of Christianity.[196]

A major thrust of the assault of the "Memorial" was along the line of conscience. Madison started by staking a claim to section 16 of the Declaration of Rights, though he knew that its ratifiers never thought it inconsistent with the Anglican establishment or a general asessment. This interpretation of section 16 was certainly not the accepted one in Virginia and was later authoritatively rejected by the U.S. Supreme Court in litigation over the Anglican glebe lands, where the justices (Virginians Marshall and Bushrod Washington among them) conclusively decided the compatibility of section 16 and a general assessment.[197] More curiously, just three years later Madison publicly proclaimed that section 16 would not even prevent compulsory contribution by all to one sect.[198] Madison's innovative reading of rights of conscience no doubt resonated with some of the bill's critics, especially Baptists, and here Madison probably struck his most telling blows. In several paragraphs, he tracked the Rhode Island critique of compulsory support of clergymen, emphasizing how the proposed bill would corrupt religion. But, as in Rhode Island, it is hard to connect such claims with the one equating nonestablishment with no aid, support, or encouragement of religion. Again, Madison failed to mention the section 16 violation seen by others in the bill's express preference for Christians.

The most remarkable feature of this "raw political document"[199] is its rhetorical excess. Following his conscience argument, Madison proclaimed that the bill was different only in "degree" from the Inquisition, thereby evincing an uncertain grasp of history, but perhaps a sound grip on a popular mind violently opposed to Roman Catholicism and well aware of the catholicity of the Anglican church. Madison also saw dissolution of trial by jury, freedom of the press, and no less than society itself in this bill supported by Washington, Marshall, Henry, and Lee. Ringing another unrelated chime of discontent in underrepresented western counties, Madison argued that popular support of the bill could not be accurately measured so long as the assembly was as unequally apportioned as it was at that time.

The remonstrance bears no trace of the reality that actually hastened the bill's demise[200] and that even Justice Rutledge conceded was a contributing factor: impoverished, already overtaxed, Virginians could not afford another assessment. Anglicans too felt the pain, for since the temporary suspension of taxation of Anglicans for their church in 1777, no one in Virginia had been compelled to support any clergyman. The true ground of antiestablishment hostility to the tax, as the Presbyterians saw it, was as a veiled attempt to revive universal support of Anglican clerics, that the tax was a stepping-stone on the return route to lost Anglican superiority.[201] To the extent that Madison claimed even a truly nondiscriminatory assessment, regardless of its "tendency," to be an establishment of religion, the point is curious. Without any compelled support at all, dissenters had vigorously battled the establishment since 1777, identifying Anglican privileges like those contained in the vestry and marriage laws as establishmentarian. Further, Jefferson's bill for establishing religious freedom,[202] which was no more than a declaration positively against the general assessment, did not disestablish Anglicanism. What was left of that regime after legislative tinkering between 1776 and 1785 was finally dismantled in 1786 by an act that declared an end to sect inequality.[203]

That the "Memorial and Remonstrance" is a grievously flawed measure of anything but Madison's considerable political abilities is really no matter, for doubtlessly evangelical religion defeated the assessment bill,[204] and nobody in Virginia opposed all aid and encouragement to religion. Madison himself did not believe everything he said in the "Memorial" and further evinced his devotion to political expediency by voting for the religious incorporation bill even though (unlike the assessment plan) it preferred the Episcopal church and did not even purport to be sect neutral.[205] (He explained the vote as a political sop, a "partial gratification" to the warmest votaries of the general assessment.)[206] Even while Jefferson prepared his bill for religious freedom, he did not contemplate anything like the separation of church and state for which the Supreme Court now cites him.[207] Of Virginia's organized religious groups, the Methodists had allied themselves with the Anglican establishment from 1776.[208] The Presbyterians agreed with Madison that religion did not need the state but, contra the "Memorial," asserted that the converse was not true.[209] That sect, much to Madison's chagrin, initially supported the general assessment, reasoning with the mainstream of Virginia society that without a stabilized regime of public worship, society might dissolve.[210] The Baptists characteristically condemned compelled support as violative of individual conscience and a corruption of religion not as establishmentarian, just as characteristically they reaffirmed their commitment to publicly sponsored and compelled religious behavior. In its petition denouncing the proposed assessment, for example, the Virginia Baptists' general committee suggested that the state's contribution to Christianity be expressed by "supporting those Laws of Morality, which are necessary for Private and Public happiness."[211]

Opposition to state aid, encouragement, and support of religion clearly was not among the animating principles of the Virginia General Assembly that defeated the assessment, passed Jefferson's bill, and subsequently disestablished Anglicanism. An Act for Punishing Disturbers of Religious Worship and Sabbath

Breakers passed in 1786 and extended the protecting hand of the state to ministers (provided they swore or affirmed their fidelity to the commonwealth) and religious assemblies. All nonhousehold labor was forbidden on penalty of 10 shillings.[212] Throughout the 1776–1786 period, the legislature granted a number of requests from religious organizations for lotteries to fund church construction, where lotteries were otherwise prohibited because they produced "vice, idleness, and immorality."[213] (The requests were apparently granted on a nondiscriminatory basis.) Before and after disestablishment in 1786, the legislature continued to proclaim fast and thanksgiving days and to pay for special sermons, and in 1777 it exempted the property, including slaves, of religious societies from taxation.[214]

Christianity continued to be, in Virginia as elsewhere, officially true. While the 1776 assembly repealed all previous parliamentary acts proscribing certain aspects of heresy, nothing was said of the common law, and Jefferson complained that a 1777 act gave the Virginia courts jurisdiction of heresy in assigning them general power "in all matters at common law."[215] Nor was anything said in 1776 or thereafter during the early national period of a 1705 Virginia statute punishing atheism, antitrinitarianism, polytheism, denial of Christianity, or the binding authority of the Scriptures.[216] Jefferson's express attempt to repeal that statute in 1776 was unsuccessful and (according to Elwyn Smith) caused him, "ever the lawyer [and free thinker], so much anxiety."[217] For that matter, nowhere was the explicit limitation of the general asessment to teachers of the Christian religion cited by evangelical opponents as an establishment of religion.[218]

General assessments received a warmer reception elsewhere in the South. The effect of the Protestant equality wrought by South Carolina's Constitution of 1778 was that other denominations could then be incorporated and supported with general tax funds.[219] In 1782 and again in 1784, bills were introduced in the Georgia legislature providing for public money to construct and repair churches and schoolhouses.[220] Sandwiched in between was Governor Lyman Hall, a transplanted New England Congregationalist who advocated partial return to the pre-Revolutionary system of regularized public worship.[221] Abraham Baldwin, holder of a Yale Divinity degree and subsequently a leading member of the First Congress, in 1785 introduced a Bill for the Regular Establishment and Support of Public Duties of Religion. The bill had a familiar preamble: "the knowledge and practice of the principles of the Christian Religion tends greatly to make good Members of Society as well as good Men." Baldwin's text opined that "the citizens of this State should be induced by inclination, furnished with opportunity and favored by Law to render public religious honors for the Supreme Being." The operative portion set apart a fraction of the property tax collected in each county for the "support of religion within such county." Congregations of at least thirty families "shall [choose] a Minister of the Gospel of approved Piety and Learning" who shall on "every Sunday publicly explain and Inculcate the great doctrines and precepts of the Christian Religion, and shall be paid out of the foregoing tax." This nonestablishment state, while limiting its largess to

Christians, went on to provide that "all the different sects and Denominations of the Christian religion shall have free and equal liberty and Tolerance in the exercise of their Religion within the State."[222] The bill passed on February 21, 1785, by a vote of 43 to 5.[223]

Leo Pfeffer denoted Maryland an establishment state,[224] and although he appears to find an establishment wherever there was a general assessment program, he failed to include Georgia and South Carolina. Perhaps surprisingly (at least to Pfeffer), Maryland did not, despite much agitation on the subject, enact a general assessment at any time after the Revolution. The beginning of the Maryland story is the 1776 constitution, which (in a clause drafted by a committee led by Charles Carroll) succeeded guarantees of religious liberty and Christian sect equality with:

Nor ought any person be compelled to frequent or maintain, or contribute, unless on contract, to maintain any particular place of worship, or any particular ministry; yet the Legislature may, in their discretion, lay a general and equal tax, for the support of the Christian religion.[225]

Anglican vestries sought implementing legislation in 1777,[226] and the Maryland Convention of the Episcopal Church later petitioned the general assembly to the same end.[227] In 1784, the council, in a message to the state senate, called for legislation, noting that "the Bill of Rights and Form of Government recognize the principle of public support for the ministers of the Gospel and ascertain the mode."[228] In that year, the legislature drafted a general assessment law but submitted it to the voters before acting on it with a strong recommendation of approval. This rather liberal provision, which excepted Jews, Muslims, and other nonbelievers entirely from its operation, was legislatively pronounced consistent with the Declaration of Rights because it aided all sects without discrimination. Among the many arguments of opponents some establishment criticisms surfaced, but their content reveals that only the sect-preferential tendency of it, and not nondiscriminatory aid itself, portended an establishment.[229] The assessment failed of enactment, but it was not until 1810 that the constitutional authorization for one was finally removed.

North Carolina's governor, Alexander Martin, urged in his 1785 annual message the legislature to support ministers of the gospel "without preference to any denomination," but the lawmakers ignored that plea. Nonestablishment scruples could not have figured much in the cool response, for months earlier, the legislators provided public funding for rebuilding the former Episcopal church in Hillsborough, invested title in the trustee of Hillsborough Academy (a public institution), and ordered that the church "shall on every Sunday in every year be open to the ministers of every sect or persuasion, being Christians, there to inculcate the truths of their holy religion." The legislature authorized the trustees to resolve all disputes over access to the pulpit and provided that Episcopalian ministers be preferred ("circumstances being otherwise equal") because the church was founded by Anglicans.

This exclusion of non-Christians from the pulpit was sociologically unimportant but was quite consistent with the 1776 disestablishment constitution. Article 32 of that document, authored by Presbyterian leader David Caldwell,[230] excluded from public office anyone who denied "The Being of God, or the Truth of the Protestant Religion, or the divine Authority of either the Old or New Testament."[231] That the Christian religion was aided thereby generated no constitutional concern. Chartering the Salisbury Academy in 1784, the legislature proclaimed that "the General Assembly are at all times disposed to give every proper encouragement for the promotion of learning, virtue and religion."[232] That disposition exercised itself in tax exemptions for religious bodies,[233] the granting of easements on surrounding private property sufficient to allow unfettered general access to churches (1784),[234] denying copyright protection to material dangerous to society's morals (1785),[235] and a statute providing for the solemnity of the Sabbath (1786)[236]

South Carolina's Constitution of 1778 similarly limited public office to members of the Protestant religion and "tolerated" only persons and societies "who acknowledge that there is one God, and a future state of rewards and punishments, and that God is publicly to be worshiped."[237] Roman Catholic congregations were denied the benefits of incorporation otherwise extended to all Christian churches by the requirement that all ministers of established (that is, incorporatable) churches be chosen by a majority of the faithful.[238] South Carolina further sponsored religion by constitutionalizing its blasphemy prohibition: "no person . . . shall use any reproachful, reviling or abusive language against any church."[239]

The assembly variously supplemented this fundamental law. The governor, by act of March 28, 1778, had to swear to "maintain and defend the laws of God, the Protestant religion, and the liberties of America."[240] Several laws passed during the 1780s preserved the Sabbath, including one requiring all white males eligible for militia duty to carry a gun and six rounds to church services (to guard "against the insurrections and other wicked attempts of negroes and other slaves.")[241] Church wardens and vestrymen continued to perform pivotal services in South Carolina through the 1780s, including care for the poor and enforcement of laws governing trade with slaves.[242]

A number of Georgia statutes of the late eighteenth century were prefaced with a belief in God and overflowed with requests for divine guidance and other expressions of religious faith.[243] In acts providing for public education, for instance, the legislature stated that promotion of education was second only to the promotion of religion[244] and that education and religion were necessary for a happy, prosperous society.[245] Specifically, although no student could be denied an education at the state university on account of religious beliefs, only Christians could serve on the board of trustees or as instructors.[246] A 1780 act governing the creation of towns and cities required that "two of the best lots in the center of the towns be reserved for houses of public worship,[247] and the revenue from the sale of other lots was, by act of 1783, made available for erecting the churches themselves.[248] A 1765 law, apparently in effect as late as 1800, channeled fines from illegal lottery promoters to churches for care of the poor.[249] Georgia was at least as protective of the Sabbath as its neighbor South Carolina, for it too required whites attending religious services to be armed.[250] Prohibited on the Lord's day were work, travel, and sports. Public houses were closed, and a master could not force a slave to work on Sunday.[251] Disturbing any religious congregation of white persons was punishable by a 5 pound fine.[252]

Only Protestants could hold state office in Georgia,[253] although a Catholic is said to have been a member of the first legislature.[254] (This proscription was deleted from the constitutions of 1789 and 1798.)[255] These two constitutions continued the free exercise and no-sect-preference regime of 1777[256] and added separate clauses governing direct financial aid to religion. The 1789 charter prohibited compulsory support of any religious profession besides one's own sect;[257] no compulsory support contrary to what the citizen "believes to be right, or hath voluntarily engaged to do" appeared in 1798.[258] Neither of these formulations, however, cut into the regime of state-fostered religion constructed under the 1777 constitution. Denying the existence of God or a future state of rewards and punishments was in 1816 deemed a crime against God, punishable by deprivation of the right to appear as a witness in court or to hold public office.[259] Sabbath regulation was enhanced in 1808 to prohibit liquor sales within a one-mile radius of any church[260] and in 1817 amended to close all retail establishments entirely.[261] Church wardens were empowered along with constables to enforce the Sunday blue laws.[262]

Most important, direct financial aid to churches continued apace even after the turn of the century. The town commissioners of Wrightboro, Georgia, were authorized in 1810 to use "any monies in their hands" to erect a church so long as all denominations of Christians were permitted to worshp there.[263] The general assembly still required towns to set aside lots for meetings houses, including one in Milledgeville, the antebellum capital, where the legislature reasoned that no "evil can result from the erection of a church on the state-house square."[264] In Georgia as elsewhere, church property was tax exempt.[265]

Although the Maryland General Assembly never implemented the general assessment authorized by the 1776 constitution, this "gentry-dominated, hierarchical society"[266] was, among the southern colonies, singularly supportive of the Christian religion. Unique among the United States and in contrast to the prevailing motif of town autonomy in New England and Georgia, the Maryland legislature governed most secular activity of churches to the end of the eighteenth century. The organic root of the power lay in the constitution's perpetuation of acts "already passed" for public funding of church building and repair, "unless the Legislature shall, by Act, supersede or repeal the same."[267] Also, the constitution voided "every gift, sale or devise of lands, and any bequest of goods or property, to any clergyman or sect" without the leave of the legislature (excepting up to two acres for a meeting house or cemetery).[268] The result was a legislative opus teeming with approvals of specific land transactions, ratifications of gifts and bequests, and acts authorizing subscriptions for particular church repair projects.[269] When a rebuilding project took an unexpected turn and more than the amount originally approved was needed, the vestry petitioned the assembly for a superseding act permitting a tax on the congregation, to be collected by the vestry.[270] Thus, specific assessments abounded in the absence of a general one.

Despite a well-founded reputation for hospitality to Roman Catholics in its early days, Maryland in the Revolutionary era was unsurpassed in its hostility to Romanists. The Maryland public school system was founded on a tax on "Irish Servants, being Papists, to prevent the growth of Popery" in the province.[271] In 1704, the assembly prohibited public celebration of the Mass.[272] As early as 1715, the legislature laid import duties on Negroes, hard liquor, and Irish servants.[273] Anti-Catholicism further distinguished itself by a subsequent increase to 20 shillings in the tax on "Irish servants, being Papists."[274] Any immigrant refusing to take the test oath—denying transubstantiation and promising to receive the sacrament in the Episcopal mode—was declared ipso facto Catholic and subject to the tax.[275] Schoolmasters in the public schools were required to take the oath; among those who did was the leading antifederalist and eventual Supreme Court litigator Luther Martin.[276] Indeed, the climate was so oppressive that even Charles Carroll, a powerful Catholic political figure and then the richest man in America, seriously considered emigrating with his entire family to escape discrimination.

While things were dismal for Catholics, they were worse for non-Christians. The constitution barred them from public office,[277] and a 1779 act limited the privilege of naturalization to Christians.[278] (Requiring aliens to forswear "allegiance or obedience" to any "king or prince" may have also effectively excluded Catholics.)[279] Only Protestant clergy or "Romish priests" were authorized to perform marriages; no secular or public official could join couples in wedded bliss.[280] Maryland's blasphemy law was especially foreboding. A first offense in denying the divinity of Jesus, the Holy Trinity, or the "Godhead of any of the three Persons, or of the Unity of the Godhead, or uttering any profane words concerning the Holy Trinity" required that the offender be "bored through the tongue" and fined. For the second offense, he or she was to be "stigmatized in the forehead with the letter B"; for the third, the penalty was death without benefit of clergy.[281]

The general sponsorship and encouragement of Christianity evident throughout the country was also evident in Maryland's Sabbath regulation,[282] its legislative incorporation of various sectarian groups as well as a society of Episcopal clergymen for the relief of widows and orphans,[283] and the liberal special assessments policy.[284]

THE MIDDLE STATES: PENNSYLVANIA, NEW JERSEY, DELAWARE, AND NEW YORK

In the thick of the Virginia general assessment controversy before authoring the "Memorial and Remonstrance," James Madison delivered a speech to the house of delegates covering the entire ground of opposition. In it Madison held up to the house familiar examples of genuine religious liberty and nonestablishment—New Jersey, Pennsylvania, Delaware, and Rhode Island—and urged imitation of their example.[285] Here Madison trod safe ground, for his listeners understood that those states were unquestionably nonestablishment polities and had never been anything else. Leonard Levy's conclusion is typical of historians' judgment. He flatly states that Pennsylvania, New Jersey, and Delaware "never experienced any establishment of religion."[286]

The universal perception of the three middle states—Pennsylvania, Delaware, and New Jersey—as pillars of religious freedom corresponded with reality. Before independence, the sect favoritism, compulsory church attendance, publicly enforced narrow orthodoxies, and other accoutrements of establishment found no favor there. After independence, no popular agitation for a general assessment surfaced, much less was one enacted. Yet, like Rhode Island, there is nothing in the experiences of these states, or in that of neighboring and analytically related New York, varying the definition of nonestablishment from no sect preference. Indeed, these four states were self-consciously nonestablishment from the day they were settled, yet all aided, encouraged, and sponsored Christianity, including providing direct material and financial assistance to religious institutions and societies. Like every other state, they were, by *Everson's* definition, establishment states. That no one in America would have so understood them further suggests that *Everson's* definition of establishment is an anachronism.

Pennsylvania: The Holy Experiment

William Penn had long suffered for his religious convictions, and, as Sanford Cobb put it, this addiction to freedom was the cornerstone of Penn's colonizing venture.[287] "We must give the liberty we ask," Penn wrote. "We cannot be false to our principles. We would have none to suffer for dissent on any hand. I abhor two principles in religion and pity them that own them," he continued. "The first is obedience to authority without conviction; and the other is destroying them that differ from one for God's sake. Such a religion is without judgment, though not without teeth."[288]

Desiring to furnish a precedent in government—a "holy experiment"—[289] Penn secured a colonial charter in 1681 and composed a "Frame of Government" for "Pennsylvania" in 1682. The first colonial assembly convened at Chester in that year and codified principles of religious freedom in harmony with Penn's plan. The first chapter, "Of Religion," proceeded from a preamble acknowledging the sovereignty of God and offered liberty to professing monotheists:

Be it enacted, That no person, nor or at any time hereafter, Living in this Province, who shall confess and acknowledge one Almighty God to be the Creator, Upholder and Ruler of the world; And who shall profess him, or herself, Obliged in Conscience to live peaceably and quietly under the civil government, shall in any case be molested or prejudiced for his, or her, conscientious persuasion or practice, Nor shall he or she at any time be compelled to frequent or maintain any religious worship, place, or Ministry whatever, contrary to his or her mind.[290]

Pennsylvania thus extended basic civil liberty to Jews and Roman Catholics. Apparently Catholics enjoyed political liberty as well, for the assembly required only a belief in Jesus Christ as "Saviour of the World" for voting and office-holding.[291] Further, and like Roger Williams's "lively experiment," Penn and his colonists proscribed compelled financial support of religion as an aspect of liberty of conscience,[292] not of nonestablishment, a term found nowhere in the laws. Liberty of conscience, however, did not extend to nonbelievers and, like Rhode Island, permitted compulsory observance of Christian moral norms in order to aid and encourage religion. In the laws forbidding compelled, direct financial support, the Pennsylvania legislature added:

But to the end, That Looseness, irreligion and Atheism may not Creep in under any pretense of Conscience in this Province, Be it further enacted, That according to the example of the primitive Christians, and for the ease of the Creation, Every first day of the week, called the Lord's day, People shall abstain from their usual and common toil and labor, That whether Masters, Parents, Children, or servants, they may the better dispose themselves to read the Scriptures of truth at home, or frequent such meetings for religious worship as may best suit their respective persuasions.[293]

In Penn's words, swearing, drinking, card playing, stage plays, and cockfights—all tending to "excite the people to rudeness, cruelty . . . and irreligion"—were forbidden because such "wildness and looseness of the people provoke the indignation of a God."[294] Lest there be any doubt of the nonsecular purpose of Pennsylvania's blue laws, the colonial legislature passed them in order to promote "religious and pious exercises" and to prevent wrongs against God.[295]

These unmistakably Quaker notions of liberty, which Cobb rightly points out were somewhat narrower than those of Roger Williams,[296] are clearly present in the Pennsylvania laws of the early national period (and bore fruit in neighboring states as well).[297] The Pennsylvania constitution of 1776, written by a convention of "common folks" and estimated the most radically egalitarian of its time by contemporaries and historians,[298] evidences the popular consumption of Penn's ideals. The constitution abjures sect preference and proclaims liberty of conscience, with its attendant proscription of compelled support contrary to "free will and consent."[299] It then notes: "Nor can any man, who acknowledges the being of God, be justly deprived or abridged of any civil right as a citizen'' on account of religion.[300] Members of the convention, having already declared their faith in the Holy Trinity,[301] required that state legislators acknowledge their belief in ''god, the creator and governor of the universe, the rewarder of the good and punisher of the wicked,'' as well as in the ''Divine inspiration'' of the New and Old Testaments.[302] A move in the constitutional convention of 1790 to delete this oath was defeated 47 to 13.[303]

Having declared itself a nonestablishment state and after proscribing direct compulsory support of the ministry, the constitution went on to authorize aid to religion. Section 45 provided that ''Laws for the encouragement of virtue, and prevention of vice and immorality, shall be made and constantly kept in force,'' thereby authorizing, for example, Sabbatarian laws.[304] The constitution also provided that religious societies previously incorporated shall be protected in the enjoyment of their customary privileges, thus ensuring the continuation of tax exemptions of churches.[305] These tax exemptions were retained by the constitution of 1790.[306]

Penn's original Sunday law was never repealed, and as late as 1825, churches in Philadelphia were permitted to place chains across streets in front of their buildings to keep traffic at bay during services.[307] Never repealed was a 1700 blasphemy proscription penalizing anyone who should ''wilfully, premeditatively, and despitefully blaspheme, or speak lightly or profanely of Almighty God, Christ Jesus, the Holy Spirit, or the Scriptures of Truth.''[308] In 1824, the state supreme court expressly affirmed the continuing validity of that law in the case of a man who said that the ''Holy Scriptures were a mere fable . . . a contradiction [which] contained a great many lies.''[309]

Financial aid to religion consistent with the constitution is evident in legislative endeavors to support higher education. By an act of November 27, 1779, the assembly amended the University of Pennsylvania's charter to make that ''seminary'' more ''catholic''—that is, more egalitarian. Confiscated lands were donated to the school and trusteeships established for Philadelphia's senior ministers in the following sects: Episcopal, Presbyterian, Baptist, Lutheran, German Calvinist, and Roman Catholic.[310] In 1783, the legislature established Dickinson College and opened trusteeships to all denominations of Christians. Because experience showed that people who study Christianity care ''zealously about youth education,'' the law ordained that vacancies in trusteeships be filled from among the clergy.[311] When endowing the German College in Lancaster in 1787, the legislature again required clerical trustees and further ordered preservation of the ratio of Lutheran and Calvinist trustees, with the proviso that the headmaster be chosen alternatively from the Lutheran and Calvinist churches.[312] These examples show that Pennsylvania lawmakers believed only that aid to religion be scupulously evenhanded in such a sectarian melting pot as theirs.

Given the (quite correct) judgment of Thomas Curry that from its beginning Pennsylvania ''established perhaps the broadest religious liberty in colonial America,''[313] this Christian commonwealth represents the fringe of plausible church-state settlements among the founding generation. *Everson* places the entire populace beyond it.

Delaware

The counties of New Castle, Kent, and Sussex "upon Delaware" enjoyed a measure of legislative autonomy beginning in 1702 but remained under the executive authority of Pennsylvania throughout the colonial era. More illustrative of the essential identity between Delaware and Pennsylvania in church-state matters is the overarching constitutional governance of William Penn's charter of liberties and privileges.[314] Carried into the fundamental legal existence of Delaware, for instance, was the limitation of public office to professing believers in Jesus's divinity, and particular colonial Delaware legislative acts reflected these basic norms. In addition to scattered material assistance (in the form of public land) to religious groups,[315] the assembly in 1744 extended the convenience of incorporation only to "religious societies of Protestants,"[316] required its members to forswear belief in transubstantiation, and declared "that the invocation or adoration of the Virgin Mary, or any other saint, and the sacrifice of the Mass, as they are now used in the Church of Rome, are superstitions and idolatrous."[317]

The fracturing of old loyalties in 1776 resulted in a constitution for what it described as "The Delaware State," comprising the same three counties "upon Delaware."[318] Article 29 forbade "establishment of any religious sect . . . in preference to another."[319] Section 2 of the declaration of rights said that "all men" have a right to worship God according to the dictates of their own consciences and that "no man" can be compelled to attend or maintain a ministry "contrary to or against his own free will and consent." Section 3 then limited civil rights and privileges to persons "professing the Christian religion," and article 22 of the constitution required all public officers to declare their faith in the Trinity and the divine inspiration of the Scriptures.[320] Both the declaration of rights and the constitution were primarily the work of George Read, president of the 1776 convention and later one of Delaware's first senators.[321]

In the period between independence and its ratification of the First Amendment's Establishment Clause, the Delaware Assembly consistently promoted, encouraged, and aided the Christian religion under the aegis of this nonestablishment constitution. A 1786 act to suppress "idleness, vice and immorality" outlawed horse racing, cock fighting, and the like because they "prejudiced religion, virtue and industry."[322] In 1787, the legislature, updating its incorporation provisions, expressly extended them to "Christians" (previously open only to Protestants).[323] No change in scope was effected; the "democratic" features of this encompassing charter of church organization were singularly Reformation and ecclesiologically alien to Roman Catholicism. (By act of 1777, the assembly repealed the anti-Catholic colonial oath of office.)[324] In 1790, the assembly took the power of performing marriages away from justices of the peace and located it exclusively in "ministers or preachers of the gospel."[325] That "holy institution" of "Almighty God" now also required the posting of bans on successive Sundays in places of public worship (no provision was made for posting on other public or civil buildings).[326] A Sabbath regulation dating from 1740 was finally remodeled in 1795. To "more effectually prevent the profanation of the Lord's day, commonly called Sunday," the usual assortment of worldly activities was stayed; the law held no relief for Saturday Sabbatarians or nonbelievers.[327] Like its Pennsylvania counterpart, the Delaware legislature left in effect (into the nineteenth century) its 1740 proscriptions of profane swearing and blasphemy, thus further cementing the official, public truth of Christianity.[328] Again similar to Pennsylvania, the Delaware Constitution of 1792 explicitly continued religious societies in the enjoyment of their "rights, privileges and communities," thereby preserving the tax exemptions they customarily enjoyed.[329]

Although there was no general asessment in Delaware or evidence of a sizable movement to secure one, the constitutional prohibition of establishments did not preclude nondiscriminatory aid to religion. That neither no sect preference nor freedom of conscience precluded a general assessment is apparent from the following correspondence between Delaware's foremost public men of the time, John Dickinson and George Read. Read had apparently forwarded a general assessment plan to Dickinson. Dickinson's sensitive, encompassing response is a classic expression of contemporary thought and shows that constitutional scruples conditioned only the way in which religion received direct, financial assistance. His comments are further illustrative of Quaker influences; though not a member of the Society of Friends, Dickinson was reared by Quaker parents and retained deep sympathy for the Friends throughout his life.[330]

It [Read's plan] carries with it the idea of levying contributions for the maintenance of ministers of the gospel upon all persons but such as shall disclaim the general religion of the country. But there are great numbers of Christians who regard the levying of such contributions as utterly unjust and oppressive. Let not that question be hastily, perhaps erroneously, decided. On the other hand, it is the duty of government, with the utmost attention and a caution, to promote and enforce the sublime and beneficial morality, as well as theology, of Christianity; and, considering them as connected with government, how can this be done better than by employing men of wisdom, piety, and learning to teach it,—and how can they be so employed unless they are properly supported,—and how can they be supported but by the government that employs them? Let impositions be laid for this purpose. If any man conscientiously scruples their lawfulness, let him be permitted to appropriate his share to the use of the poor, or any other public services. Thus government would strenuously carry on the grand work of teaching virtue and religion, without offering the least violence to the conscience of any individual,—a neglect and contempt of which last sacred right has been the disgrace and curse, and will infallibly be the destruction, of every human institution, however cunningly devised, on this momentous subject.[331]

New Jersey

Madison justifiably counted New Jersey an exemplar of religious freedom, for that colony originated as a haven for refugees fleeing New England's narrow orthodoxy, and it never had an established church of any kind.[332] The original proprietors, Lord John Berkeley and Sir George Carteret, published a scheme of government in 1664, which they called "Concessions"; among them was a guarantee of complete religious liberty to all "who do not actually disturb the civil peace of the province."[333] The colony, then divided into East and West Jersey, enjoyed thirty years of Quaker proprietary before becoming a royal colony in 1702.[334] Throughout the pre-Revolutionary era, New Jersey's polyglot Protestant population, heavily accented by Quaker roots and without a significant Anglican component, remained self-consciously nonestablishment. Indeed, whenever the few Episcopal ministers in the province lobbied for some of the privileged status elsewhere received, they were invariably greeted by hostility from the inhabitants.[335] Even their scheme to introduce an episcopacy with purely spiritual authority aroused intense antiestablishment hostility and had to be abandoned.[336] A discouraged Anglican missionary writing home to England in 1712 accurately portrayed his sect's status, remarking that "in New Jersey there are no laws in favor of the Church [of England]."[337] The state constitution of 1776 expressly decreed that there "shall be no establishment of any one religious sect in this Province in preference to another," proclaimed liberty of conscience, and forbade compulsory attendance and support of churches or ministries contrary to what the citizen "believes to be right, or has deliberately or voluntarily engaged himself to perform."[338]

Notwithstanding all these provisions and observations, at no time during the eighteenth and nineteenth centuries did New Jerseyans inhabit a regime that declined to aid, encourage, support, and sponsor religion, and there is no evidence that anyone in New Jersey wished otherwise. The Concessions and Agreement of 1664 authorized the legislature to appoint and maintain ministers.[339] Although this power was evidently never used, the assembly liberally bestowed substantial land grants on religious societies, and many towns established glebes for their ministers.[340] As the eighteenth century progressed and available land in populated areas disappeared, the New Jersey legislature, like that of Virginia, began granting dispensations from the general ban on lotteries to underwrite church construction. This practice survived the Revolution and was frequently relied on to rebuild meeting houses devastated by battle or by recriminating British troops. Although tax exemptions for churches and schools were not codified in New Jersey until 1851, before that time they were universally extended because, as a state court observed, it was "so obviously proper, and so entirely in accordance with public sentiment."[341]

As soon as they were established in the later seventeenth century, the two Jerseys separately provided for the civil enforcement of Christian morality, even while legislatively reiterating devotion to complete liberty of conscience. The

Quaker leaders of West Jersey were particularly devout in their professions of
freedom, but nevertheless they forbade cursing, swearing, and other "immoralities" in 1683.[342] They enacted stringent Sabbath regulations in 1693 because,
as historian Nelson Burr remarks, the Sabbath was as "sacred to the Quaker as
to the Calvinist."[343] In May 1694, the Quaker proprietors outlawed sexual prom-
iscuity because the "sin of uncleanness is one of the greatest in the eyes of a
pure God."[344] East Jersey was equally up to the task of requiring Christian
conduct of all its citizens.[345]

These Quaker influences survived unification of East and West, independence
from Britain, and the founding of the Republic. In a revision completed in 1800
by William Paterson, one of New Jersey's first senators and later an associate
justice of the U.S. Supreme Court, the assembly codified the colonial ban on
servile work and worldly amusements on the Sabbath.[346] Profane swearing carried
a 50 cent fine,[347] and blasphemy consisted of cursing, denying, or reproaching
Christ, the Holy Ghost, the Christian religion, or the Scriptures.[348] Exposing
any of the above to "contempt" or "scoffing" at them brought the identical
punishment of $200 or one year of hard labor.[349]

Quaker liberality did not extend to Roman Catholics. Intolerance was first
decreed in 1698 and was not removed until the constitution of 1844.[350] The 1776
constitution coupled its declarations of nonestablishment and freedom of conscience with limitations of civil right and public office to Protestants.[351] The
1799 act to incorporate trustees of religious societies addressed itself to Christians
and effectively excluded Roman Catholics, as elsewhere, by ordaining a governing structure that was uniquely Protestant.[352] A rider accommodated the more
hierarchical order of the Dutch Reformed church, but no dispensation for the
relatively few New Jersey Catholics was included.[353]

New York

In addition to geographical proximity, New York resembled the other great
middle states—Pennsylvania and New Jersey—in the heterogeneity of its population. Indeed, these three were the only states with substantial non-British
stock: the Germans (especially in Pennsylvania, where they constituted about
one-third of residents)[354] and the Dutch, whose influence in New York and New
Jersey bore the stamp of both time and numbers.[355] These melting pot qualities
help explain the absence—except for the four counties in and around New York
City—of any established church in the region.[356] Anglicans accounted for no
more than 10 percent of the state's total populace,[357] and the Church of England
was established in the city counties solely as a corollary of English colonial
administration.[358] The breach of imperial bonds thus left the Episcopalians easy
prey for the patriots' political and religious passions. Anglicanism was disestablished by the state constitution of 1777, thus offering a chance to examine

what disestablishment meant to a large, heavily populated northern state destined
to play a pivotal role in the ratification struggle of 1788.

The state constitution of 1777 embodied the principles of religious liberty and
separation of church and state as that generation of New Yorkers understood
them.[359] The drafters disestablished the Anglican church[360] and declared the "free
exercise and enjoyment of religious profession and worship, without discrimination or preference."[361] Disestablishment put Protestant sects on an equal footing and initiated a decade-long legislative endeavor to dismantle the system of
Episcopal privilege grown up since 1697. Separate acts passed in the 1780s
abrogated the tax on all residents for support of the Anglican church,[362] eliminated
the bishop of London's role in administration of Trinity Church,[363] put Columbia
(formerly King's) College on a footing of sect equality,[364] and extended the
privilege of incorporation to all sects.[365]

What was left was not a polity denuded of either the will or constitutional
means to aid and promote religion but what the most careful student of New
York religious history saw as the "pervasive certainty" that religion in general
be encouraged.[366] By "promoting" religion, one prominent contemporary meant
"that the State judges the fear of God and his service to be of great importance
to society and therefore determines to encourage and support their worship in
such a legal manner as shall render the poorest subject, or meanest sect, perfectly
secure in their spiritual privileges."[367]

This determination was collectively expressed by the New York legislature
on numerous occasions. The church incorporation law of 1784 stated that "it is
the duty of all wise, free and virtuous governments to countenance and encourage
virtue and religion."[368] To spur the founding of churches in frontier regions,
the state's land law reserved 400 acres in each township for support of the gospel
and 400 acres for schools.[369] Addressing the legislature on this subject in 1784,
Governor George Clinton linked education and religion with the good society
and remarked that there was "scarce anything more worthy of [their] Attention,
than the Revival and Encouragement of Seminaries of Learning."[370] During this
time, church property in New York was customarily exempt from taxation,[371]
and property with church buildings on it was excepted from foreclosure and
forced sale.[372] Scattered, discreet land grants to particular church groups—in the
nature of private bills—were also common in the 1780s.[373]

The truth of Christianity and Christian moral norms was publicly enforced.
The New York Assembly passed an otherwise typical Sabbatarian law in 1788
that provided a dispensation for Saturday Sabbatarians so long as they did not
disturb the Sunday worship of others.[374] Blasphemy proscriptions dated from the
era of Dutch administration[375] and continued in force into the nineteenth century.
In 1811, for example, some bodacious individual remarked that "Jesus Christ
was a bastard, and his mother must have been a whore."[376] Although the conclusion flowed irresistibly from the premise, the trial judge fined him $500 for
being in contempt of the Christian religion.[377] The appeals court responded to

the defendant's reliance on the constitutional guarantee of toleration and liberty of conscience:

The free, equal and undisturbed enjoyment of religous opinion, whatever it may be, and free and decent discussion on any subject is granted and secured; but to revile, with malicious and blasphemous contempt, the religion preferred by the whole community, is an abuse of that right.[378]

The Christian hegemony wrought by the New York lawmakers was, as elsewhere, effectively Protestant. That Roman Catholics were permitted to settle at all in New York State did not owe to John Jay, who proposed in the 1777 constitutional convention that no Catholic be permitted to hold land or enjoy civil rights unless he or she swore that no pope or priest could forgive sins.[379] As it was, the state constitution premised its guarantee of religious liberty with the need to "guard against that spiritual oppression and intolerance wherewith the bigotry and ambition of weak and wicked priests and princes have scourged mankind."[380] The constitution also practically precluded naturalization of Catholic immigrants through an oath requiring denial of allegiance to foreign powers "in all matters, ecclesiastical as well as civil."[381] (Adoption of the federal Constitution in 1789 deprived this statute of effect.) In 1788, the state legislature, without significant opposition, enacted a similar oath of abjuration for public officeholders[382] but rejected an effort to disenfranchise Catholics totally. While St. Peter's Catholic Church in New York City was incorporated under the act of 1784,[383] the common council of that city continued to refuse Catholics an opportunity to worship in the public exchange.[384] The political discriminations against Catholics persisted into the nineteenth century, when enterprising politicians finally appreciated the electoral potential of the ever-increasing Catholic population.[385]

MAPPING THE LANDSCAPE: THE SACRED CANOPY[386]

The national church-state landscape reveals significant divergences among state orderings of church and state. Beginning with Roger Williams's exile from Massachusetts Bay, the chronicle of interstate migration by spiritually minded freedom seekers conforms to at least that perception among the terrain's inhabitants. And, to be sure, there actually were significant distinctions between Quaker New Jersey and Baptist Rhode Island, on one hand, and Anglican Maryland and Congregational Connecticut, on the other, just as the views of James Madison varied deeply from those of John Jay and George Washington. The meaning of *establishment*, however, was not buffeted by this plurality of institutions and opinions. There were no discernable differences among states, among religious groups, and among individuals over what an establishment was or what nonestablishment entailed. From Georgia to Vermont, whatever one's view of the desirability of an establishment (and almost all were hostile to it by 1789),

virtually everyone agreed with future Chief Justice Oliver Ellsworth that establishment meant the legal supremacy of one sect, with all others laboring under
legal disabilities.[387] No sect preference was, by the time the First Amendment
was debated, drafted, and ratified, the settled meaning of nonestablishment.
Surely much was not settled in the church-state debate by that time, but the
definition of establishment partook of what was. Perhaps Jefferson supplied the
best evidence. While always in the vanguard of intellectual innovation regarding
religion and government, he nevertheless associated an establishment with tor-
ture, fines, and imprisonment of innocent men, women, and children.[388] A
contemporary example of an important but discretely defined constitutional provision might be the electoral college. Although ideas of proper and equal democratic representation have passed it by and there is much debate over its wisdom,
the Constitution leaves little doubt as to what it actually is.

Liberty of conscience was, by contrast, the more dynamic term in the prevailing
church-state lexicon, and it housed many of the divergences mentioned. Nevertheless, a workable—that is, sufficient to resolve the status of aid and encouragement of religion generally—core meaning of conscience liberty is evident
from the foregoing materials. Direct compelled subvention of a sect other than
one's own was an idea whose time had passed, as the prevalence of the certificate
system in New England attests. But even that guarantee did not flow from
unadorned liberty of conscience; it was expressly and additionally set out in the
relevant constitutional or statutory provisions alongside the general protection
of conscience. (This accommodation was typically denied to nonbelievers, even
outside New England, since no one cared to patronize irreligion.) On the other
hand, compulsory taxation to benefit one's own sect was a widespread practice
and obviously consistent with the liberty of conscience guaranteed by the state
constitutions. All the southern disestablishment constitutions, for example,
clearly permitted such public tithes even while proclaiming liberty of conscience
and disdaining establishments.[389] This is perhaps the most compelling evidence
of the bankruptcy of no-aid history. At the moment southern disestablishmentarians achieved their objective, they simultaneously recognized the need to
compel support of religion. Moreover, where direct, compelled support of one's
own clergy was prohibited, that required explicit expression, as in the cases of
Rhode Island and Pennsylvania. As a legally operative guarantee, then, liberty
of conscience by itself did not forbid a general asessment. And it would not
forbid modern aids much less coercive. That conscience should be understood
to outlaw general assessments was an idea circulating in 1789. That the prevailing
legal definition of the term, though, was consistent with assessments is apparent
from the conscience arguments against them. The usual assertion was that real
or genuine or true liberty of conscience forbade general assessments, implying
that the existing or ordinary version of it did not. Most important, there is no
evidence that freedom of conscience was inconsistent with all aid, support, and
promotion of religion.

Free exercise of religion was a less frequently employed term, but available evidence shows that it was a lesser included guarantee of freedom of conscience and was thus even less a menace to sect-neutral aid. The 1777 New York Constitution, for example, guaranteed the "free exercise and enjoyment of religious profession and worship."[390] Antifederalist critic Robert Yates (who walked out of the Philadelphia convention) criticized the constitution for omitting this protection against "persecution in religious matters," and the New York portion of the "sacred canopy" uniquivocally attests that free exercise was consistent with aid and encouragement of religion. Virginia provides another illustration of free exercise. The 1776 constitutional craftsmen accepted Madison's proposed guarantee of free exercise of religion but clearly believed that to be compatible with a genuine establishment of religion, for they plainly declared that Anglicanism was to remain the state church there. I have argued extensively elsewhere that the core of "free exercise" is captured by what the Founders regarded as a cognate phrase: "no molestation" on account of religious belief.[391]

More compelling than the differences among states, groups, and individuals of the early national era is what they held in common. Put most forcefully, the Supreme Court's interpretation of the Establishment Clause does not represent even the fringe of historical opinion; literally no one advanced the view now ascribed by the justices to the entire American people. Much less did anyone say that nonestablishment required it. No state exhibited a no-aid policy. Quakers and Baptists alike were firmly committed to public Christian orthodoxy, however hostile they may have been to public stipends for their preachers. Neither Roger Williams, who prided himself on the integrity of the Sabbath in Rhode Island,[392] nor Isaac Backus, the early national Baptist leader, shared the Court's view.[393] Nor did James Madison, who supported the Virginia bill for incorporating religious congregations and who in 1787 helped draft terms of sale for the Northwest Territory that required that parts of each township "be given perpetually for the purposes of religion."[394] Not even Thomas Jefferson, to whom Christianity was both the most sublime and the most perverse system known to the world,[395] went as far as the Court says all of his contemporaries did. Jefferson, for example, suggested in 1781 that American liberty depended on a popular perception that it was the gift of God and thought it politically beneficial if Americans privately decided that there was "only one God, and he all perfect" and that there was a future state of rewards and punishments.[396] At about the same time, he drafted a bill for the Virginia Assembly authorizing punishment of ministers who failed to preach sermons at the legislators' command.[397] Later, President Jefferson negotiated a treaty with the Kaskaskia Indians whose terms included government provision of Catholic missionaries to the tribe.

In *Everson v. Board of Education*, the Supreme Court contemplated much of the terrain covered here by the sacred canopy and correctly perceived the early American practices were overwhelmingly at odds with the Court's own historical reading of the Establishment Clause. Justice Rutledge's oft-quoted dissenting opinion also correctly concludes that by 1789 the meaning of establishment was well settled.[398] Nevertheless he agreed with the majority that nonestablishment meant no aid, encouragement, or support. For the Court's historical analysis to survive the realities of the early national period surveyed here, the Court need locate in the amending process itself a revolution in both popular sentiment and the accepted meaning of nonestablishment. That these unlikely events did not occur can be proved.

NOTES

1. *Everson v. Board of Education* 330 U.S. 1, 42 (1961).
2. Quoted in Joseph F. Thorning, *Religious Liberty in Transition* 6 n. 14 (1931).
3. Ibid.
4. L. Pfeffer, *Church, State and Freedom* 141 (1953).
5. Sanford H. Cobb, *The Rise of Religious Liberty in America* 513–15 (1902).
6. M. Forkosch, "Religion, Education, and the Constitution—A Middle Way," 23 *Loy. L. Rev.* 617, 632 (1977).
7. W. Van Alstyne, "Comment: Trends in the Supreme Court: Mr. Jefferson's Crumbling Wall—A Comment on Lynch v. Donnelly," 1984 *Duke L.J.* 770, 773 n. 8 (1984).
8. *Wallace v. Jaffree*,———. U.S.———, 105 S. Ct. 2479, 2512 (1985).
9. L. Levy, *Judgments*, 169–218 (1972).
10. See J. Nowak, R. Rotunda, and N. Young, *Constitutional Law* 1117 (2d ed. 1983). Vermont was the tenth state to ratify.
11. E. Smith, *Religious Liberty in the United States* 24 (1972).
12. George C. Groce, Jr., *William Samuel Johnson, A Maker of the Constitution* 31 (1937).
13. P. Conley, *Democracy in Decline* 11 (1977).
14. 2 *Federal and State Constitutions of the United States, 1857* Ben Perley Poore comp. 2d ed. 1924) (hereafter cited as *Poore's 1* or *2*).
15. *Poore's 1* at 957.
16. Ibid. at 257.
17. Ibid. at 957 (Massachusetts), and *Poore's 2* at 1281, (New Hampshire), 1859 (Vermont). The Connecticut Constitution referred to is the Organic Act of 1784, governing church-state relations in the state. It can be found in its entirety in *The First Laws of the State of Connecticut* (John D. Cushing, comp. 1982) 21–22 (hereafter cited as *Ct. Laws*).
18. *Ct. Laws* at 43.
19. *The First Laws of the Commonwealth of Massachusetts* 240 (John D. Cushing Comp. 1981) (hereinafter cited as *Mass Laws*).
20. *Poore's 1* at 957 (Massachusetts) and *Poore's 2* at 1281 (New Hampshire), 1865 (Vermont). *Ct. Laws* at 20.
21. *Poore's 2* at 1286–87.
22. Ibid. at 1861 (constitution of 1777).
23. Ibid. at 1859.
24. *Poore's 1* at 951 (Massachusetts) and *Poore's 2* at 1281 (New Hampshire), Ct. Laws at 21–22.
25. *Mass. Laws* at 238.

26. *Ct. Laws* at 214.

27. Ibid. at 215.

28. Ibid. at 67.

29. Ibid.

30. *Mass. Laws* at 235.

31. Ibid.

32. Thorning, *Religious Liberty*, at 157.

33. *Ct. Laws* at 258–59.

34. Ibid., at 134.

35. Ibid. at 116.

36. Ibid. at 11, 131.

37. *Poore's 1*, at 957.

38. Thorning, *Religious Liberty*, at 20 n. 7. For a brief description of the life of Caleb Strong, see *Memoir of the Hon. Caleb Strong, LLN.* (originally published in the *American Quarterly Registrar*), 10–12, for a description of a solid New England Congregationalist.

39. See Charles Lippy, "The 1780 Massachusetts Constitution: Religious Establishment or Civil Religion," 20 *J. Church & St.* 533, 536 (1978).

40. *Poore's 1*, at 957.

41. Thorning, *Religious Liberty*, at 33.

42 . *Poore's 2* at 1281.

43. P. Lauer, "Church and State in New England," 10 *Johns Hopkins University Studies in Historical and Political Science* 51. (1891).

44. *Ct. Laws* at 21.

45. Ibid. at 21–22.

46. C. Wingate, 2 *Life and Letters of Paine Wingate* 487 (1930).

47. This composite is drawn from *Ct. Laws* at 21–22, the Massachusetts Constitution of 1780, and the New Hampshire Constitution of 1784, unless otherwise indicated.

48. C. Kinney, Jr., *Church and State, The Struggle for Separation in New Hampshire 1630–1900* 97 (1955).

49. Ibid. at 36–38.

50. *Poore's 1*, at 957; see also Jacob C. Meyer, *Church and State in Massachusetts from 1740–1833* (1930) at 142–44.

51. *Ct. Laws* at 22.

52. Thorning, *Religious Liberty*, at 170, n. 70.

53. Ibid.

54. Meyer, *Church and State*, at 201–20. The certificate movement is but one illustration of the general acceptance by the late eighteenth century of toleration, at least for all Protestants, as a basic principle of church-state relations. See T. Curry, *The First Freedoms: Church and State in America to the Passage of the First Amendment* 78–80 (1986).

55. *Everson* at 42 n. 33.

56. *Poore's 1* at 958 (Massachusetts), and at 1281 (New Hampshire).

57. *Poore's 2* at 1859 (1777), 1867 (1786).

58. *Ct. Laws* at 21.

59. *Poore's 2* at 1859 (1777 Constitution).

60. Ibid., at 1281.

61. *Poore's 1* at 957.

62. *Ct. Laws* at 21.

63. Lippy, *Mass Convention*, at 534.

64. Thorning, *Religious Liberty*, at 33.

65. *Ct Laws* at 21–22. What Connecticut did was grace the law of inertia with a state imprimatur by using "established" with a lower case "e," as in "already organized."

66. Kinney, *Church and State*, at 36–38.

67. M. Louise Greene, *The Development of Religious Liberty in Connecticut* 338–39 (1905).

68. Ibid. at 339; *Poore's 1* at 957; Thorning, *Religious Liberty*, at 26–27.

69. Thorning, *Religious Liberty*, at 35.

70. Ibid. at 34.

71. Wingate, *Life and Letters*, at 487.

72. Curry, *First Freedoms*, at 171.

73. Smith, *Religious Liberty*, at 11–12.

74. Curry, *First Freedoms*, at 170.

75. *Poore's 1* at 956.

76. The vote was 5654 to 2047. Thorning, *Religious Liberty*, at 33. A few towns called for an amendment providing no exemptions; many more wished to make clear that support of another sect's ministers would not be compelled. Even Boston, however, which had long enjoyed an exception to general norms that permitted voluntary church maintenance in the city, approved the principle of tax-supported religion. Curry, *First Freedoms*, at 167.

77. Thorning, *Religious Liberty*, at 35.

78. *Poore's 2* at 1280.

79. Kinney, *Church and State*, at 127.

80. *Journal of Convention Held in 1791* (1792).

81. Kinney, *Church and State*, at 93–95.

82. Ibid. at 128.

83. *Poore's 2*, at 1857, 1866, 1873.

84. *Ct. Laws* at vi.

85. Wingate, *Life and Letters*, at 486.

86. Conley, *Democracy in Decline*, at 8.

87. Arnold, *History of Rhode Island*, quoted in *Poore's 2* at 1600.

88. Conley, *Democracy in Decline*, at 15.

89. Ibid. at 14.

90. Cobb, *Rise of Religious Liberty*, at 430.

91. Thorning, *Religious Liberty*, at 139.

92. Ibid. at 8.

93. *The First Laws of the State of Rhode Island* 83 (John D. Cushing comp. 1983) (hereinafter cited as *RI Laws*).

94. Conley, *Democracy in Decline*, at 8.

95. Ibid. at 11.

96. Ibid. at n. 16.

97. *RI Laws* at 81–82.

98. Ibid. at 595.

99. Ibid.

100. Ibid. at 394.

101. Ibid. at 577–79.

102. Smith, *Religious Liberty*, at 108.

103. Ibid.

104. Ibid.

105. Curry, *First Freedoms*, at 91.

106. Conley, *Democracy in Decline*, at 13.

107. Ibid. at 34.

108. Ibid. at 13. For an overview of Rhode Island behavior during the confederation period, see Conley, *Democracy in Decline*, at 57–144. For further critical comments, refer to 3 *The Debates in the Several State Constitutions* 183 (Jonathan Elliot ed. 1937) Richard Henry Lee: "Rhode Island has so rebelled against justice, and so knocked down the bulwarks of probity, rectitude, and truth, that nothing rational or just can be expected from her." Ibid. at 28. Edmund Randoph: "Rhode Island—in rebellion against integrity— Rhode Island plundered all the world by her paper money; and, notorious for her uniform opposition to every federal duty."

109. *Pennsylvania and the Federal Constitution, 1787–1788* 108 (B. McMaster and F. D. Stone eds. 1970).

110. Richard E. Welch, Jr., *Theodore Sedgewick, Federalist: A Political Portrait* 65 n. 22 (1965).

111. R. Isaacs, "Evangelical Revolt: The Nature of the Baptists' Challenge to the Traditional Order in Virginia, 1765 to 1775," 31 *Wm. & Mary Q.* 345–68 (3d series 1974).

112. Ibid.

113. Smith, *Religious Liberty*, at 9.

114. S. Bolton, *Southern Anglicanism* 5 (1982).

115. Quoted in *Everson* at 11.

116. Isaacs, "Evangelical Revolt," at 347.

117. Paul Conklin, "The Church Establishment in North Carolina," 42 *N.C. Hist. Rev.* 11, 22 (1955).

118. N. Rightmeyer, *Maryland's Established Church* 23 (1956); K. Coleman, *The American Revolution in Georgia, 1763–1789* 12 (1958); George C. Rogers, *Church and State in Seventeenth Century South Carolina* 11 (1959).

119. Bolton, *Southern Anglicanism*, at 142.

120. Coleman, *American Revolution*, at 5.

121. Bolton, *Southern Anglicanism*, at 142.

122. Ibid. at 148.

123. Ibid. at 142.

124. Ibid.

125. Harold E. Davis, *The Fledgling Province: Social and Cultural Life in Colonial Georgia, 1733–76* 212 (1976).

126. See, e.g., Coleman, *Revolution in Georgia*, at 5; Bolton, *Southern Anglicanism*, at 147; Edward McCrady, *History of South Carolina in the Revolution* 210 (1909).

127. Vestrymen in South Carolina did not collect a specific tax from parish inhabitants to pay the Anglican minister; instead the established clergyman was paid out of a general tax collected at the provencial level from all inhabitants. Bolton, *Southern Anglicanism*, at 147.

128. Thomas E. Buckley, *Church and State in Revolutionary Virginia* 67 (1977).

129. Bolton, *Southern Anglicanism*, at 149–50.

130. Ibid. at 149.

131. Smith, *Religious Liberty*, at 30.

132. Fletcher M. Green, *Constitutional Development in the South Atlantic States, 1776–1860* 108 (1971).

133. *First Laws of the State of Maryland* (John D. Cushing comp. 1981) (hereinafter cited as *Maryland Laws*).

134. Bolton, *Southern Anglicanism*, at 159.

135. Conklin, "Church Establishment," at 17.

136. Ibid.

137. Ibid. at 18.

138. Harold G. Davis, *The Fledgling Province: Social and Cultural Life in Colonial Georgia, 1733–76* 227–28 (1976)

139. McCrady, *History* at 209.

140. Ibid., at 210.

141. P. Clarkson and R. Jett, *Luther Martin of Maryland* 20 (1970).

142. Isaacs, "Evangelical Revolt," at 366–67.

143. McCrady, *History*, at 206; Stephen Weeks, *Church and State in North Carolina* 53–54, in Johns Hopkins University Studies in Historical and Political Science, vol. 11 (1893); Bolton, *Southern Anglicanism*, at 14.

144. See Weeks, *Church and State*, at 11, 54–5; Conklin, "Church Establishment," at 27.

145. Conklin, "Church Establishment," at 27.

146. Ibid. at 27–28.

147. Weeks, *Church and State*, at 55–56.

148. *Poore's 2*, at 1413.

149. Ibid.

150. McCrady, *History*, at 206.

151. Green, *Constitutional Development*, at 109.

152. McCrady, *History*, at 209–10.

153. See, e.g., G. Rogers, *Church and State in Seventeenth Century South Carolina* 22 (1959); Bolton, *Southern Anglicanism*, at 163; *Constitutional Development*, at 110; Charles Singer, *South Carolina in the Confederation* 9 (1931).

154. See Pfeffer, *Church*, at 141.

155. Levy, *Establishment Clause* at 51.

156. Curry, *First Freedoms*, at 191.

157. Bolton, *Southern Anglicanism* at 9. See Davis, *Fledgling Province*, at 193–232.

158. *Poore's 1* at 383.

159. Bolton, *Southern Anglicanism*, at 14.

160. *Poore's 1* at 819.

161. As to the participants' understanding of their accomplishments, the unanimous verdict is borne out by events described in notes 163–203 and accompanying text. Historical accounts placing disestablishment at 1785–86 include Bolton, *Southern Anglicanism*, at 14; H. Beeman, *The Old Dominion and the New Nation, 1788–1801* 93 (1972); R. Meade, *Patrick Henry* 277 (1969); Green, *Constitutional Development*, at 141. Even Cobb apparently concludes as much (*Religious Liberty* at 495). Isaacs speaks of disestablishment "from 1776 to 1785" (*Evangelical Revolt* at 349).

162. *Poore's 2* at 1909.

163. Smith, *Religious Liberty*, at 36–38. Moncure Conway, *Edmund Randolph*, 150, 161–62 (1889); Buckley, *Church and State*, at 17–18.

164. Buckley, *Church and State*, at 18.

165. Conway, *Randolph*, at 161–62 n. 1.

166. Pfeffer, *Church*, at 108.

167. Buckley, *Church and State*, at 19.

168. Ibid. at 18–19. Buckley explains that disestablishment was Madison's intention, not Henry's. See also Conway, *Randolph*, at 158.

169. Smith, *Religious Liberty*, at 37; Conway, *Randolph*, at 161–62.

170. Buckley, *Church and State*, at 19–20.

171. Ibid. at 20.

172. Conway, *Randolph*, at 162.

173. Buckley, *Church and State*, at 22.

174. Ibid.

175. Pfeffer, *Church*, at 114.

176. Buckley, *Church and State*, at 21.

177. Ibid. at 35.

178. The year 1784 seems to have marked a kind of catharsis on the subject of the political necessity of religion, as countless public men took stock of the prevailing state of religious laxity and endeavored to promote religiosity through legislation. See, e.g., Buckley, *Church and State*, at 72–74 (Virginia); Kate Mason Rowland, *Life and Correspondence of Charles Carroll of Carrollton* 67 (1898) (Maryland); Henry C. White, *Abraham Baldwin* 88 (1926) (Georgia); Richard McCormick, *Experiment in Independence* 46–50 (1950) (New Jersey).

179. See appendix 2.

180. See appendix 1.

181. See M. Malbin, "The Supreme Court and the Definition of Religion" (Ph.D. diss. Cornell University, 1973).

182. M. Singleton, "Colonial Virginia as First Amendment Matrix: Henry, Madison and Assessment Establishment," 8 *J. Church & St.* 344, 357 (1966).

183. Kate Rowland, *Life of George Mason* 88–89 (1853).

184. Buckley, *Church and State*, at 199.

185. Conway, *Randolph*, at 199; Rowland, *Life of Mason*, at 404; 12 *Correspondence of Washington* (J. Sparks ed. 1853): Washington wrote of the general asessment in response to Mason's appeal to support his opposition to it: "Although no man's sentiments are more opposed to any kind of restraint upon religous principles than mine are, yet I confess, that I am not amongst the number of those who are so much alarmed at the thoughts of making people pay towards the support of that which they profess."

186. A. Beveridge, 1 *The Life of John Marshall* 22 (1916); Buckley, *Church and State*, at 194.

187. Henry's sway over Virginia politics was witnessed by George Washington, who remarked to Madison in 1788 that Henry's "edicts . . . are enregistered with less opposition [in the Virginia Assembly] than those of the Grand Monarch are in the Parliament of France. He has only to say, let this be law, and it is law." Quoted in W. Crosson, *Writings of James Monroe* 103 (1946).

188. Buckley, *Church and State*, at 193.

189. 2 *The Letters and Papers of Edmund Pendleton, 1734–1803* (D. Mays ed. 1967).

190. Rowland, *Life of Mason*, at 90.

191. Buckley, *Church and State*, at 195.

192. Ibid. at 194–95.

193. James Curtis Ballagh, 2 *The Letters of Richard Henry Lee* 304–5 (1911).

194. Ibid.

195. Buckley, *Church and State* at 175.

196. Letter of January 9, 1785, in 1 *Writings of James Madison* 131 (1865).

197. *Terrett v. Taylor*, 13 U.S. (9 Cranch) 43 (1815). The Court opined that the free exercise of religion codified in section 16 "cannot be justly deemed to be restrained by aiding with equal attention the votaries of every sect to perform their own religious duties, or by establishing funds for the support of ministers, for public charities, for the endowment of churches, or for the sepulture of the dead." At 49.

198. See 3 *Elliot's* at 330.

199. Buckley, *Church and State*, at 133.

200. Singleton, "Colonial Virginia," at 262–63.

201. Buckley, *Church and State*, at 151.

202. See appendix 1.

203. Cobb, *Rise of Religious Liberty*, at 495.

204. This position is that posited by Buckley, *Church and State*.

205. Conway, *Randolph*, at 164.

206. Letter to Jefferson, January 9, 1785, in 1 *Writings of Madison* at 129–30 (1865).

207. See notes 395–97 and accompanying text.

208. Singleton, "Colonial Virginia," at 348.

209. Buckley, *Church and State*, at 95.

210. Ibid.

211. Ibid. at 140.

212. Sadie Bell, *The Church, the State, and Education in Virginia* 156 (1930).

213. Ibid. at 157; *The First Laws of the State of Virginia* 7 (John D. Cushing comp. 1982) (hereinafter cited as *Va. Laws*).

214. Bell, *Church*, at 156.

215. Smith, *Religious Liberty*, at 42.

216. Ibid. at 42–43.

217. Ibid. at 43.

218. The only criticism on this score was in the bill's supposed implication that the same power that could compel contributions to one's own sect could compel one to support another's worship. Buckley, at 151.

219. Bolton, *Southern Anglicanism*, at 84.

220. Reba Strickland, *Religion and the State in Georgia in the Eighteenth Century* 165–66 (1939).

221. White, *Baldwin*, at 88.

222. Ibid. at 89–90.

223. Strickland, *Religion and the State*, at 166.

224. Pfeffer, *Church*, at 141.

225. *Poore's 1* at 819.

226. Rightmeyer, *Maryland's Established Church*, at 118.

227. Ibid at 123.

228. Rowland, *Charles Carroll*, at 67.

229. Curry, *First Freedoms*, reports at 156–57 that the authors of a petition to the assembly, opposing the bill, portrayed the bill, probably accurately, as reflecting primarily the desire of some of the Episcopalian clergy for public support:

No fierce resentment of the Episcopalians built up as a result of the assessment bill, but the persistent suspicion that it represented a covert way of helping them contributed substantially to its defeat. Presbyterian minister Patrick Allison did not object in principle to state support for religion, but he opposed this particular measure vigorously as an Anglican plot. Catholics adhered to the same position. In 1785 John Carroll, soon to become the first Catholic bishop in the United States, wrote to a friend in Europe:

> Where the [assessment] law truly formed upon the principles of the constitution, we R.C. should have no very great objection to it: but from certain clauses in it, and other circumstances, we, as well as the Presbyterians, Methodists, Quakers, and Anabaptists are induced to believe, that it is calculated to create a predominant and irrestible influence in favor of the Protestant Episcopal Church.

A decade later, William Duke, an Episcopalian, confirmed Carroll's observation when he wrote that the Church of England did not know how to cope without government support and so "laid hold of the provision in the constitution" allowing the state to pass an assessment.

230. Louise I. Trenholme, *The Ratification of the Federal Constitution in North Carolina* 20 (1932).

231. *Poore's 2* at 1413.

232. Conklin, "Church Establishment," at 29.

233. *Waltz v. Tax Commission*, 397 U.S. 664 (1970).

234. *N.C. Laws* at 562.

235. Ibid. at 564.

236. Ibid. at 686.

237. *Poore's 2* at 1620.

238. Ibid. at 1627.

239. Ibid.

240. *The Public Laws of South Carolina* 297 (J. Cushing, compiler, 1981) (No. 1211, 1778).

241. *Public Laws of South Carolina* 185 (No. 726, 1743, "made perpetual " by the Revival Act of 1783). See also at 168 (No. 695, 1740) (5 pound penalty for ordering a slave to work on Sunday); at 490 (Act No. 1579, 1789) (County courts open every day but Sunday); at 376 (Act No. 1395, 1785) (Sheriff could not serve writ on the Sabbath).

242. *Public Laws of South Carolina*, at 154, 176, 490.

243. White, *Baldwin*, at 87.

244. *The First Laws of the State of Georgia* 286 (John D. Cushing comp. 1981) (hereinafter cited as *Ga. Laws*).

245. Ibid. at 299.

246. Ibid. at 301.

247. Ibid. at 234.

248. Ibid. at 284; see Coleman, *Revolution in Georgia*, at 198–99.

249. *Ga. Laws* at 111–13.

250. Ibid. at 157.

251. Ibid. at 80–83.

252. Ibid. at 457.

253. *Poore's 1* at 379.

254. Strickland, *Religion and the State*, at 164.

255. See *Poore's 1* at 384–87 (1789), 388–95 (1798).

256. Ibid.

257. Ibid. at 386.

258. Ibid. at 385.

259. Ida M. Martin, "Civil Liberties in Georgia Legislation, 1800–1830," 45 *Ga. His. Q.* 329, 331 (1961).

260. Ibid. at 332.

261. Ibid.

262. Ibid.

263. Ibid. at 331.

264. Ibid. at 332.

265. Ibid. at 331.

266. Ronald Formisano, "Federalists and Republicans: Parties, Yes-System, No," in *The Evolution of American Electoral Systems* 33, 56 (P. Kleppner ed. 1981).

267. *Poore's 1* at 819–20.

268. Ibid. at 820.

269. See, e.g., *Maryland Laws*, ch. 22 (1779), ch. 8 (1781), ch. 14 (1783), ch. 13 (1783), ch. 19 (1784), ch. 40 (1784), ch. 44 (1785), ch. 31 (1789), ch. 4. (1790), ch. 47 (1790).

270. Rightmeyer, *Maryland's Established Church*, at 110.

271. Paul S. Clarkson and R. Samuel Jett, *Luther Martin of Maryland* 19 (1970).

272. Rightmeyer, *Maryland's Established Church*, at 54.

273. Clarkson and Jett, at 19.

274. Ibid.

275. Ibid.

276. Ibid. at 21.

277. *Poore's 1* at 820.

278. *Maryland Laws*, ch. 6 (1779).

279. Ibid.

280. Ibid., ch. 12 (1777).

281. Ibid., ch. 16 (1723).

282. Ibid.

283. See e.g. ibid., ch. 58 (1797) (Presbysterian incorporation); ch. 55 (1792) (Roman Catholic incorporation); ch. 13 (1782) (allowing Methodist preachers to preach); ch. 78 (1784) (for relief of widows and orphans of Anglican clergy).

284. See notes 272 and 273 and accompanying text.

285. 1 *Writings of Madison* at 166–67.

286. Levy, *Judgments*, at 192.

287. Cobb, *Rise of Religious Liberty*, at 441.

288. Ibid.

289. Ibid.

290. Ibid. at 443.

291. Ibid. at 444.

292. Ibid. at 441.

293. Ibid. at 443–44.

294. Curry, *First Freedoms*, at 75.

295. 2 *Pa. Stats. at Large* 175–76 (1706). See ibid. at 3–4 (1700), both found in Note, "State Sunday Laws and the Religious Guarantees on the Federal Consttituion," 73 *Harv. L. Rev.* 729 (1960).

296. Cobb, *Rise of Religious Liberty*, at 441.

297. See Quaker influence upon laws of Delaware and New Jersey in the text.

298. R. Brunhouse, *The Counter-Revolution in Pennsylvania, 1776–1790* 12–16 (1942); B. Bruce Thomas, *Political Tendencies in Pennsylvania, 1783–1794* (1939), at 26–27.

299. *Poore's 2* at 1541.

300. Ibid.

301. Thomas, *Political Tendencies*, at 26.

302. *Poore's 2* at 1543.

303. Thomas, *Political Tendencies*, at 26.

304. *Poore's 2* at 1547–48.

305. Ibid. at 1548.

306. Ibid. at 1554.

307. Chester J. Antieau et al., *Religion Under the State Constitutions* 73 (1965).

308. Cobb, *Rise of Religious Liberty*, at 516.

309. Antieau et al., *Religion*, at 81.

310. 1 *Pennsylvania Laws* 474 (November 27, 1779).

311. 2 *Pennsylvania Laws* 500 (September 9, 1783).

312. Ibid. at 398 (March 10, 1787).

313. Curry, *First Freedoms*, at 75.

314. First Senator (and draftsman of Delaware's 1776 Constitution) George Read called Penn's Charter the "constitution" of Delaware until 1776.

315. Rightmeyer, *Maryland's Established Church*, at 172–73.

316. Ibid. at 172.

317. *The First Laws of the State of Delaware* 155 (John D. Cushing comp. 1981).

318. *Poore's 1* at 273.

319. Ibid. at 277–78.

320. Ibid. at 276.

321. William T. Read, *Life and Correspondence of George Reed* 182–87 (1870).

322. *Del. Laws* at 866.

323. Ibid. at 879–84 passim.

324. *Del. Laws* at 155.

325. *Del. Laws* at 972–76.

326. Ibid.

327. Ibid. at 1209.

328. *Del. Laws* at 173–74. There is no evidence in the laws up to 1800 of any repeal.

329. *Poore's 1* at 287.

330. M. Flower, *John Dickinson: Conservative Revolutionary* 285 (1983).

331. Dickinson to Read, April 20, 1786, in Read, at 412–13.

332. See Cobb, *Rise of Religious Liberty*, at 399–400, 406, 408; Nelson Burr, *The Anglican Church in New Jersey* 1–3, 152 (1954).

333. Cobb, *Rise of Religious Liberty*, at 400.

334. Ibid. at 401.

335. See Burr, *Anglican Church*, at 359–71.

336. Ibid. at 359 et seq.

337. Cobb, *Rise of Religious Liberty*, at 409.

338. *Poore's 2* at 1313.

339. Burr, *Anglican Church*, at 2.

340. Ibid.

341. Antieau et al., *Religion*, at 135.

342. Burr, *Anglican Church*, at 3.

343. Ibid.

344. Ibid.

345. Ibid.

346. *Laws of New Jersey* (1800) (hereinafter cited as *Paterson Laws*).

347. Ibid. at 331.

348. Ibid. at 211.

349. Ibid.

350. Burr, *Anglican Church*, at 1.

351. *Poore's 2* at 1313.

352. *Paterson Laws* at 412.

353. Ibid. at 413.

354. Brunhouse, *Counter Revolution*, at 2.

355. McCormick, *Experiment*, at 44; J. Pratt, *Religion, Politics, and Diversity: The Church-State Theme in New York History* 3–25 (1967).

356. Rudolph J. Pasler and Margaret Pasler, *The New Jersey Federalists* 32 n. 25 (1975).

357. G. Wilder Spaulding, *New York in the Critical Period* 32 (1932).

358. Pratt, *Religion*, at 30–78.

359. Ibid.

360. Curry explains that some New Yorkers denied the presence of an Anglican establishment during the colonial period and that this sentiment explains the constitution's failure to mention Anglicanism explicitly. Curry, *First Freedoms*, at 161. Both sides, however, agreed that the Church of England was established if it enjoyed preferential status and (most important) that no establishment existed if the 1693 law was read to permit compulsory financial support of other Protestant sects as well.

361. *Poore's 2* at 1338.

362. 1 *First Statutes of New York 1778–1789*, 131.

363. 1 *First Stats.* at 128.

364. 2 *First Stats.* at 145.

365. 1 *First Stats.* at 104.

366. Pratt, *Religion*, at 114.

367. Ibid. (quoting Rev. John Livingston).

368. 1 *First Stats.* at 104.

369. Ibid. at 330; Spaulding, *New York*, at 16.

370. Pratt, *Religion*, at 115.

371. Antieau et al., *Religion*, at 135; see Pratt, *Religion*, at 116 n. 33.

372. 1 *First Stats.* at 178.

373. See, e.g., ibid. at 322, 325, 334; 2 *First stats.* at 137.

374. 2 *First Stats.* at 257.

375. Pratt, *Religion*, at 30.

376. Antieau et al. *Religion*, at 81.

377. Ibid.

378. Ibid.

379. Pratt, *Religion*, at 85; Spaulding, *New York*, at 89. Jay's anti-Catholicism was perhaps unrivaled in his time. Pratt said that the first chief justice was consumed "by the 'old anti-popery' tradition," and Jay's behavior during the early national period earns him that sobriquet.

380. *Poore's 2* at 1338.

381. Ibid. at 1339.

382. Pratt, *Religion*, at 107.

383. Spaulding, *New York*, at 34.

384. Ibid.

385. Pratt estimates that by 1790 there were approximately one thousand Catholics in the state, most of them in New York City. Pratt, *Religion*, at 107. For an excellent account on New York sectarian politics in the nineteenth century, see ibid. at 117–256.

386. The "sacred canopy" is a phrase borrowed from Peter Berger's book of that name. P. Berger, *The Sacred Canopy* (1967). It is used here to denote the edifice of publicly supported and maintained religion just discussed. The metaphor usefully suggests that just as God sends rain upon the just and the unjust alike, everyone in America (not just believers) inhabited a universe whose canopy—an overreaching sheet stitched out on legal materials—was undeniably sacred. Religion (here Christianity) pervaded the public, not just the private, realm in a way the Supreme Court's account of the founders simply denies.

387. Thorning, *Religious Liberty*, at 96 n. 13.

388. See notes 146, 151, 158, 160, and 161–178, and accompanying text.

389. Curry, *First Freedoms*, at 211.

390. *Poore's 2* at 1338; 467C. *Ford Essays* at 313.

391. See G. Bradley, "The 'No Religious Test' Clause and the Constitution of Religious Liberty: A Machine That Has Gone of Itself," in *Case Western Reserve Law Review* 37 (forthcoming).

392. Curry, *First Freedoms*, at 135.

393. Cobb, *Rise of Religious Life*, at 439.

394. See chapter 5, note 21, and accompanying text.

395. *The Life Correspondence of Rufus King* 50 (Charles King ed. 1894).

396. W. Berns, *The First Amendment and the Future of American Democracy* 31 (1976).

397. See chapter 3, note 23, and accompanying text.

398. *Everson* at 42.

3

Ratification of the Constitution: The Whale's Demands

"Mr. Madison has introduced his long expected amendments," Massachusetts Congressman Fisher Ames wrote Thomas Dwight on June 11, 1789. "He has hunted up all the grievances and complaints of newspapers, all the articles of conventions, and the small talk of their debates, and placed them before the House."[1] Madison biographer Irving Brant confirms the reliance and adds that Madison relied on amendments requested by the ratifying (of the federal Constitution) conventions of Massachusetts, South Carolina, New Hampshire, Virginia, New York, North Carolina, as well as by minorities in Pennsylvania and Maryland.[2] Independent examination of Madison's congressional proposals verifies these claims and further reveals that Madison drew even more than the content of the amendments from the demands of the 1788 state conventions. The evils to be remedied were clearly identified there and, most important, the political strategy deployed in the conventions became the raison d'être of Madison's amending labors. That the Bill of Rights was produced by political intrigue indifferent to the amendments themselves—Leonard Levy refers to it as a "lucky political accident"[3]—is quite clear. In his initial address to the newly assembled national legislature, President Washington appealed for those amendments "rendered expedient" by the "nature of objections which have been urged against the system, or by the degree of unrest which has given birth to them."[4] Madison himself had already admitted to Jefferson that he never viewed a bill of rights "in an important light" but might favor one for no other reason than that "it is anxiously desired by others."[5] In fact, he publicly embraced the amendment movement for the first time by publishing his intent to preserve those "essential rights, which have been thought in danger [and] as may banish the party heats which have so long and so imperiously prevailed."[6] Of the Establishment Clause in particular, Madison remarked on the House floor that he questioned whether the amendment was necessary but reminded that it "had been required by some of the State Conventions."[7] Congressman George Clymer, among others, responded that Madison was merely throwing a "tub or a number of tubs" to the whale, a metaphor derived generally from seafaring lore, and from Jonathan Swift in particular, meaning a diversion to avoid real danger[8] and connoting in this context that Madison's personal liberty amendments would short-circuit demands for structural alterations in the new government, which were the real objectives of the pro-amendment or antifederalist adversaries of the Philadelphia Constitution. Or as "Centinel," an antifideralist scrivener, put it in 1788: "Like a barrel thrown to the whale, the people were to be amused with fanciful amendments, until the harpoon of power should secure its prey, and render resistance uneffectual."[9]

David Anderson rightly notes that in instances such as these, the intentions of the whale (the antifederalists) are more important than those of the ship's crew (the First Congress, especially Madison).[10] What does the whale demand? What will satisfy him and make him go away? The religion clauses, like the whole Bill of Rights, were concessions, a "tub to the whale," and self-consciously so. Interpretation of them must take full account of the demands to which the drafters bowed in submitting them to the states in 1789 for ratification by legislatures.[11]

That the Bill of Rights in fact addressed and satisfied the demands of 1788 (insofar as those demands pertained to personal liberty guarantees) is fully discussed in subsequent chapters. For now, what I call the "Bill of Rights synthesis" in U.S. constitutional history, grievously obscuring historical reality, needs attending. Because constitutional questions like due process, free speech, and unreasonable search and seizure have become vessels for our most expansive, forward-looking philosophical discourse about the substance of American society, the tendency is to conscript the framers into this army of theoretical speculators. This compensates not so much for the framers' failure to articulate liberal answers to the whole problem of church-state; in fact, they were not concerned with the whole problem of church and state, only with a portion of it called sect equality. *Everson* is a classic case in point. Thomas Curry is another, more understated, example. Despite considerable research and much success in breaking free of the synthesis, his discussion of the whale's demands reveals that he too cannot escape its sway. He faithfully reports that all the discussion leading up to adoption of the First Amendment was about eliminating sect preferences, but he views that as paradoxical because the debate did not involve what he regarded as the most contentious issue of church and state: general assessments. Why is this paradoxical, unless one presupposes, like the *Everson* Court, that nonestablishment was a comprehensive settlement of religion and the law? Of course, it was not, and once one adduces proof that the Bill of Rights contained no more than affirmations of what was taken for granted, the paradox disappears. General assessments were not mentioned in connection with nonestablishment because they presented no sect partiality concerns.

That the amendments were not at all the product of philosophical speculation will be shown shortly; that they could not have been is apparent once an acquaintence with the political process that gave them life is made. That process affects substance should not surprise us, for we have decades of political science research at hand, but the Supreme Court consistently (perhaps willfully and therefore dishonestly) ignores the Bill of Rights process when declaring the historical meaning of the terms. That process forced the meaning of proposed amendments to the political center or, more exactly, to convergence upon a common denominator of popular sentiment broad enough to attract hill-country Baptists, New England Puritans, and tidewater Anglicans. Put differently, the process itself was inconsistent with both extant fringe or wholly novel interpretations of settled norms like nonestablishment and freedom of conscience. Instead the political structure and strategies that resulted in adoption of the Bill of Rights could result in only standard, commonly entertained definitions of (for example) nonestablishment being adopted as well.

The seedtime of amendments precluded speculation due to a variety of pressures. The most obvious structural limit was that ordained by the new Constitution—the large majorities in Congress and among the states necessary for success.[12] The important historical fact is that the states recommended amendments along with, not instead of, their ratification of the Constitution (North Carolina excepted), thus clamping upon themselves that document's strenuous formula for fruitful alteration. Less obvious but perhaps more important is what the amendment advocates initially were trying to do: defeat the proposed Constitution. Since defeat meant rejection by a sufficient number of popularly elected state ratifying conventions, theirs was essentially an effort in popular political coalition building. There is, in historical fact, ample evidence of a nationwide antifederal network of activists borrowing ideas and stratagems from neighboring as well as distant states.[13] Indeed the personal liberty amendments proposed by the state conventions were remarkably similar, frequently identical.[14] The effect was to tame the whale's demands by homogenizing them through politically necessary interstate, intersectional cooperation.

A corollary centripetal force flowed from the popular component of the political coalition under construction. Compelling evidence indicates that antifederal leaders actually desired either the wholesale defeat of the Constitution or such far-reaching structural amendments as to make it what they originally expected of the Philadelphia convention: Articles of Confederation with a little more bite.[15] A bill of rights was at least secondary to them (if it mattered at all), but it served, in Leonard Levy's words, to "dramatize" opposition to the Constitution among those unable to appreciate the subtle but more dangerous threats posed by the new order.[16] As the struggle matured, antifederalists stepped up what their adversaries frankly labeled as demagogic uses of the omitted bill of rights. Indeed, most federalists were quite satisfied that the real source of oppostition to the

Constitution had nothing to do with endangered freedoms. Rather, antifederalists were holders of state sinecures threatened with obsolescence or by replacement with federal officers,[17] people who did not want to pay their debts and were afraid federal judges would make them pay,[18] and just plain cranks.[19] That the essential rights of freedom trumpeted by antifederal elitists were intended at least primarily for popular consumption is clear, and it meant that the norms had to appeal to, and be understood by, large numbers of relatively unsophisticated people from all parts of the country.

The meaning of the words was further homogenized in the state conventions. In some of the meetings, the actual drafters, if not the sources of amendments, were federalists, not the Constitution's opponents.[20] Madison adopted the same tactic in Congress: recognizing the need to do something to conciliate, he felt it better that friends of the new government suggest alterations that stopped short of endangering its essential features. In all the state conventions, amendments therefore walked a political tightrope: enough to satisfy amenable opponents of the Constitution without alienating supporters. Thus the formulations adopted by Madison in the initial Congress were truly the product of centrist bipartisan sentiment.

The final constraint on possible readings of the religion clauses stems from the uncertain legal status of "declarations" or "bills" of rights. As a relatively recent innovation, only some states had them, and even in these states, they were not uniformly part of the constitution.[21] That amendments were a judicially enforceable constraint on the legislature was unclear; at least, that did not exhaust the effective uses of a bill of rights. "Repeated violations of these parchment barriers have been committed by overbearing majorities in every State," Madison wrote in 1788 to Jefferson.[22] Their efficacy in a democracy, if any, lay more in their declaratory effect: public officials and the populace may feel bound by them, and the people may better judge the performance of their elected representatives by their light. Also, where the governors overstepped their delegated authority, a bill of rights would, in Madison's words, "be a good ground for an appeal to the sense of the community."[23] To serve these purposes, the meaning of a bill of rights had to be popularly accessible. As Madison in Congress said of his own propositions, "I would limit it to the plain, simple, and important security that has been required."[24]

Madison then made a further connection between bills of rights and the sense of the community that helps explain his conduct in the First Congress. Well before committing himself in any way to amendments and before he formulated any specific proposals, he told Jefferson that the rights protected must closely track the sense of the public; otherwise they would lose (because of repeated violations) "even their ordinary efficacy."[25] Thus Madison divorced a federal bill of rights from his own latitudinal views, views that he admitted in the same letter to Jefferson were quite alien to the sense of the community.

The Supreme Court in *Everson* specifically contemplated and unequivocally estimated the political complexion of the amendment movement just outlined.

The "freedom-loving colonials" were "shock[ed] into a "feeling of abhorrence" at the prevailing illiberality of their times.[26] Justice Black cited only a 1774 letter of James Madison to support this startling popular reversal.[27] "The imposition of taxes to pay ministers' salaries and to build and maintain churches and church property aroused their indignation," he wrote, citing the Virginia "parson's cause" of 1763 championed by Patrick Henry.[28] In 1785 Henry proposed the general assessment and the parson's cause was, in any event, an episode in anticlericalism, not in opposition to the existing Anglican establishment. The kernel of Henry's objection was that the church was not performing its establishmentarian functions well enough.[29] It was these feelings of "shock and indignation" that found expression in the First Amendment, Justice Black concluded."[30] Nothing is cited in support of this claim.

The claim is unsupportable. While entire populations may impersonate the stumble-drunk gone cold turkey, it does not happen often, and the Court surely has provided no evidence that the Ameican people revolutionized their church-state order in adopting the First Amendment. That no less than a revolution was necessary the Court implicitly conceded, since the justices portray pre–Bill of Rights America as a rather nasty place. The problem is that the amendment process did not purport to educate or uplift the citizenry or to break them of established patterns and habits. The process not only was not revolutionary, it was not even a reform movement. The nature of the contest required that agitation for religious amendments to the Constitution be rooted in, and an endeavor to perpetuate, mainstream colonial and early national practices, which were all anybody wanted. In this light, the Bill of Rights movement was a grand popular affirmation of the liberty and liberality abroad in the states, the precise opposite of the Court's portrayal of righteously indignant reformers.

More pertinent to the Court's synthesis is the surviving evidence of what did happen, evidence that reveals not a single advocate of separating church and state or of anything like the no-aid regime the Court created. That omitting a bill of rights from the 1787 Constitution rallied their antifederal adversaries no doubt surprised the framers, for only in the waning days of the Philadelphia conclave were express declarations in favor of individual liberty even suggested.[31] Concern for religious liberty was not among these afterthoughts, and those regarding standing armies, civil jury trial, and liberty of the press were quickly dispatched by the delegates.[32] Indeed, besides Madison's proposed nondenominational national university—also given short shrift by the founding fathers[33]— Article VI's[34] ban on religious tests was the only religious item on the convention agenda. The delegates' acceptance of the article was another dangerously unreflective decision, for this failure to make the Constitution sufficiently Christian was probably the single most agitated religious issue in the ensuing ratification struggle.

North Carolina and Connecticut voted against the ban, and the Maryland delegation divided.[35] At least one source of Maryland's indecision was the viewpoint of Luther Martin, the most powerful and outspoken critic of the Constitution in that state. In his antifederal magnum opus, the "Genuine Information" he imparted to the Maryland legislature on November 29, 1787,[36] Martin attacked Article VI, sarcastically relating that some delegates were "so *unfashionable*" as to think an oath desirable. Martin believed that "in a Christian country, it would be *at least decent* to hold out some distinction between the professors of Christianity and downright infidelity or paganism."[37] Dr. Benjamin Rush, the Philadelphia physician and devotee of higher education, stated the objection more broadly in a letter to John Adams: "Many pious people wish the name of the Supreme Being had been introduced somewhere in the new Constitution. Perhaps an acknowledgment may be made of his goodness or of his providence in the proposed Amendments."[38]

That the proffered Constitution was a pagan document, or at least insufficiently infused with Christian orthodoxy, was a theme resounding throughout the Union and accounted for perhaps half of all the popular criticism of the new government's relationship with religion. The discussion on both sides was premised on a distinction between two species of oaths. Oliver Ellsworth (among others) described a "particular" oath in his "Landholder" series, one that discriminated among denominations of Christians, as the tests in England did in favor of Anglicans.[39] Such a provision would, Ellsworth argued, be "to the last degree absurd" in the United States for it would necessarily exclude a great majority of Protestants from national office.[40] This first senator correctly concluded that a majority of Americans rejected this "indignity."[41] Indeed, few among even the most zealous desired, or were wiling to risk, a sectarian litmus for federal office.

The Constitution's defenders were not nearly so in tune with the majority on a general oath requiring a belief in a Supreme Being, a future state of rewards and punishments, and the divine authenticity of Scriptures.[42] That a test so defined corresponded with popular desires is apparent enough from the presence of one in almost all the state constitutions. And the reason for including them in the state constitutions was immediately advanced against the federal document: public office in the United States ought to be limited to orthodox Protestant Christians. One New Hampshire antifederalist fulminated that a "Turk, a Jew, a Rom[an] Catholic, and what is worse than all, a Universal[ist] may be President of the United States."[43] Similar arguments were made in the Virginia, Massachusetts, South Carolina, and North Carolilna ratifying conventions.[44] "Pagans,"[45] "deists,"[46] "heathens,"[47] and "Mahometans"[48] were sometimes added to the list of undesirables, but the focal point of fear was undoubtedly Rome. Antifederalist Zachias Wilson of North Carolina wished the Constitution had excluded "Popish priests"[49] from office; others thought it enough to keep them out of the presidency.[50]

Anti-Catholicism was the dominant feature of antifederalist religious complaints in North Carolina. Opposition to the treaty power, for instance, rested in part on fears that one made with foreign powers might compel adoption of the Catholic religion in the United States.[51] Article VI was exhaustively discussed in that state's convention, and among the antifederalists railing against it was the same Reverend Caldwell who was most responsible for disestablishment in 1776.[52] The Constitution's ablest defender, later Supreme Court Justice James Iredell, climaxed his speech on the subject by showing that it was practically impossible for the pope to become president (a broadside suggesting its possibility was circulating at the time). Given the constitutional qualifications for presidential office, Iredell reasoned, one person could not realistically ascend the "Romish" hierarchy and have time to secure the confidence of his own countrymen. "It would be still more extraordinary if he should give up his popedom for our presidency," he reassuringly concluded.[53]

Iredell's response typified the first line of the federalists' Article VI defense: given America's social composition, there was no realistic prospect of a non-Protestant's gaining national elective office. But the deepest antifederal claim made an end-run around Iredell, and scored effectively. As "an invitation for Jews and pagans of every kind to come among us," Reverend Caldwell foresaw that at "some future period . . . [Article VI] might endanger the character of the United States."[54] "Several gentlemen" in the Massachusetts convention urged that Article VI departed from "the principles of our forefathers who came here for the preservation of their [Protestant] religion."[55] Caldwell added that even irreligious persons admitted that Christianity is "best calculated " to make "good members of society, on account of its morality," thus linking the extant Protestant character of the nation with its continued existence.[56] "Colonel" James, a Massachusetts antifederalist, was satisfied to note simply that "a person could not be a good man without being a good Christian," by which he clearly meant Protestant.[57]

Some federalist responses alleged that excluding test oaths was a fair expression of religious freedom and that oaths were ineffective anyway since unscrupulous men would feign the requisite piety.[58] Nowhere, however, did they deny the present existence or desirability of an indefinitely maintained Christian republic. Governor Samuel Johnston of North Carolina attempted to reassure Caldwell and his supporters by suggesting that Christian immigration would always outstrip that of Jews and pagans. In all probability, Johnston continued, the children of even such people would be Christians and thus ensure "the progress of the Christian religion among us."[59]

The formal amendment that percolated its way through the South Carolina convention proposed that the word *other* be inserted between *no* and *religious* in Article VI.[60] The intuition there was not lost on federalist leader Roger Sherman, writing as "A Citizen of New Haven."[61] Sherman insisted that no alteration of meaning was thereby accomplished because its omission in the original amounted to a clerical error.[62] A "Carolina Citizen" flushed out Sherman's point: A "general" religious test was implied in the oath of office itself, and the framers intended to exclude only "particular" test oaths.[63]

This was the only religion amendment demanded by the South Carolina convention. When Madison looked there, he saw only evidence of what one South

Carolina delegate branded as the Constitution's "too great latitude allowed in religion."[64] Even more disturbing to Madison, the leader of the opposition was Rawlins Lowndes, who led the fight against disestablishment in 1778.[65] The only alteration concerning religion demanded by New Hampshire was that "Congress shall make no Laws touching Religion, or to infringe the rights of Conscience."[66] That amendment grew out of antifederalist fears that the national government was insufficiently devoted to Christianity, and it sought protection from congressional intermeddling with New Hampshire's regime of publicly maintained orthodoxy.[67] Formulated by a committee chaired by eventual federalist and Senator John Langdon,[68] it was adopted to placate these antifederalist anxieties.[69] That opposition included, according to federalist Governor Sullivan, the "pious deacon" who would close the public office door to Universalist, some who were "blinded through excess of zeal for the cause of religion, and some who put on the "masque of sanctity" to win converts.[70]

Massachusetts debated Article VI to the virtual exclusion of other aspects of religious liberty[71] and tracked the New Hampshire proceedings by locating religious zeal in the antifederalist camp. In other words, those opposed to the Constitution because of church-state concerns were those who desired a tighter fit between Christianity and the federal government. In any event, no religion amendment at all was proposed by the Massachusetts delegates.[72]

Maryland followed the same pattern. The Constitution encountered relatively little opposition there, and the ratifying convention itself recommended no amendments.[73] A committee of thirteen appointed by the convention to draft proposed alterations considered, and rejected, one that said "that there be no national religion established by law; but that all persons be equally entitled to protection in their religious liberty."[74] First Congressman George Gale was among those against recommending that provision to the full body of delegates.[75] After some complicated, heavy-handed political maneuvering, the convention later declined even to consider other amendments approved by the committee.[76] A small, disaffected but articulate minority of the convention thereafter adopted the no national religion clause, among others unrelated to church-state, as their ground of opposition.[77] The clause itself connoted, as Madison recognized on the House floor during the amendment debate, a system like that of England or perhaps of pre-Revolutionary Maryland. Any temptation to read the clause more expansively is cut off by the publicly declared views of its chief proponents. Maryland's leading antifederalists, all of whom attended the convention and signed the minority report, were Luther Martin, Governor William Paca, future Supreme Court Justice Samuel Chase, and John Francis Mercer. When Madison viewed this portion of the disquieted public restless for amendments, he saw what was even by Maryland's conservative standards the less enlightened side of the church-state controversy. Martin's views are illustrated in his "Genuine Information" and in his earlier career in Maryland's Protestant common schools.[78] Mercer, a recently transplanted Virginian, opposed Madison in 1785 and voted in the Virginia Assembly for the general assessment.[79] Paca and Chase were seasoned political veterans who (along with Charles Carroll) had expressly rejected draft language in the 1776 state constitution that would have prohibited, as in Pennsylvania and Rhode Island, compelled support for any ministry. Instead they helped secure constitutional authorization of a general assessment.[80] In 1783 Governor Paca asked the legislature to activate the latent assessment by providing equally for all Christian ministers.[81] More recently, as vestrymen of the Annapolis Episcopal Church, they administered the legislatively enacted state aid to their parish.[82]

Amendments demanding express protection for freedom of conscience and prohibition of establishments were adopted by only four ratifying conventions: those of New York,[83] Virginia,[84] North Carolina,[85] and Rhode Island[86] (a minority in Pennsylvania published a list of grievances citing insufficient protection of conscience).[87] But the volume of opposition amounted to much less than that. Rhode Island's ratifying convention did not convene until after Madison performed his congressional act,[88] and Rhode Island remained at this time a clear example of how not to run a government.[89] The North Carolina antifederalists were hardly eager to separate church and state, in either the Madisonian or modern Supreme Court reading of that phrase. In all events, Virginia played the pivotal role. First, as the largest state and home of many distinguished patriots, it could subvert any union simply by staying out of it. Second, the convention debates there were within Madison's personal knowledge and might have more heavily weighed in his congressional preparations. Third, Madison's actions in the First Congress never escaped the influence of Virginia state politics. Fourth, and most important, both North Carolina and Rhode Island adopted precisely the same wording as did Virginia. This common denominator was the oft-contested section 16 of Virginia's Declaration of Rights, with a no-sect-preference rider:

That religion or the duty which we owe to our Creator, and the manner of discharging it can be directed only by reason and conviction, not by force of violence, and therefore all men have an equal, natural and unalienable right to the free exercise of religion according to the dictates of conscience, and that no particular religious sect or society ought to be favored or established by Law in preference to others.[90]

New York's convention adopted an indistinguishable formula, tracking the non-establishment phrasing almost verbatim,[91] thereby making no sect preference the only nonestablishment demand articulated by the ratifying conventions. This was the whale's demand, and it requires no historical crystal ball to understand it.[92]

The freedom of conscience language adopted no more supports the Court's reading of the nonestablishment than the no sect preference directives. First, section 16 of the Virginia Declaration of Rights was adopted in 1776 with the universal understanding that it did not impair the Anglican establishment,[93] much less prohibit even a general assessment. In addition, the U.S. Supreme Court later declared section 16 consistent with nondiscriminatory aid.[94] Second, what was not adopted by the Virginia ratifying convention was Jefferson's Bill for

Establishing Religious Freedom,[95] which was universally understood to outlaw general assessments (but not other forms of aid, encouragement, and support). Similarly omitted by all the state conventions were other verbal formulas—like that in the laws of Rhode Island and Pennsylvania—known to invalidate general assessment schemes (again, but not other less intimately coercive aid programs). Third, any innovative reading of these well-settled phrases is again precluded by the structure of the process itself and by the identities of those responsible for their adoption. Besides the unenligthened opposition in North Carolina, Madison well knew that the leading antifederalist in the New York convention, and one of the movement's national leaders, was Governor George Clinton.[96] His record as governor reveals a decided preference for state aid to religion within the confines of a nonestablishment constitution.[97] Virginia's antifederal champion was Patrick Henry, also the champion of the general assessment. His able lieutenant was future first Senator Richard Henry Lee, another proponent of the general assessment. The committee that actually drafted the amendments included many other veterans of the assessment struggle, with Henry, Marshall, Randolph, and Harrison among the majority who had favored that measure.[98] Thomas Jefferson, one of the separationist champions, was in France when Virginia's seminal amendments were formulated, and Madison had opposed all amendments as federalist floor leader.

The convention debates and enveloping newspaper discussions unequivocally reveal that the proposed religion amendments meant what they said—most particularly for our purposes that nonestablishment consisted of sect equality and that, taken as a whole, the universal practice of state aid, sponsorship, and promotion of religion was not in the least threatened by the proposed amendments. Elaborations of the religion amendments fall into two categories: general comments on the whole, especially in relation to prevailing norms and state constitutional practices, and pointed expressions of the particular evil each component of the amendment addressed and remedied. The former class of comments reveals that the religious liberty endangered, and for which protection was sought, was that liberty the people had long enjoyed, which was currently enshrined in all state constitutions and accorded with contemporary popular views on the subject. The freedom at issue in Pennsylvania was held among the "most sacred and invaluable privileges of man";[99] in New York "one of the inestimable blessings of a free government";[100] included within "the residium of human rights"[101] and among the "most inestimable gifts of the great Creator"[102] in North Carolina"; and described by Patrick Henry in the Virginia convention as this "sacred right,"[103] one of the "great rights,"[104] and one of the "great objects" of government.[105] All these characterizations were by antifederalists pressing for amendments to the Constitution.

Added to the lineage was popular support for the religious liberty contemplated. Characteristic was Roger Sherman's response to the perceived need to expressly secure this liberty from encroachment: "The prevailing liberality" would not permit any invasion, regardless of constitutional language.[106] Referring to the entire Union as an asylum of freedom, James Monroe, who voted against the Constitution, told the Virginia convention that "freedom of conscience is enjoyed here in the fullest degree. The states are not disturbed by a contrariety of religious opinions."[107] Madison echoed, "Happily for the states, they enjoy the utmost freedom of religion."[108] Numerous delegates and commentators opined that because of the conscience of the American people, there was no genuine danger of a federal establishment.[109]

Finally distinguishing the genus of religious liberty the founders cherished from that which the Supreme Court would have them cherish was the oft-repeated link to extant state constitutions. In what was by all accounts the first call for personal liberty amendments to the new Constitution, Richard Henry Lee tied them to the "various Bills or declarations of Rights whereon the Governments of the greater number of the States are founded.[110] Samuel Spencer, probably the most articulate antifederalist in the North Carolina convention, made the point more clearly: a clause that expressly reserved to the states powers not delegated (effectively what is now the Tenth Amendment) "would render a bill of rights unnecessary."[111] Patrick Henry embraced this option during the Virginia conclave,[112] and George Mason, in the same setting, sought a barrier against the federal government like that in Virginia's Declaration of Rights.[113] Antifederalist concern in North Carolina was similarly focused on the prospect of losing rights secured under the North Carolina Constitution.[114] It was, in sum and in the words of many antifederalists, because the national government overrode the state constitutions—one antifederalist said the Supremacy Clause was the entire problem—that they feared for their liberties. A clearer refutation of the Court's revolutionary uprooting would be difficult to imagine, for all these antifederalists wanted was the assurance that existing state practices would be preserved from federal encroachment.

It is of no wonder, then, that in phrasing the constraints appropriate to the federal government, the various state conventions simply lifted entire provisions from their own or another state's constitution. The Pennsylvania antifederal minority took an obvious short cut that captured the sentiment of the entire movement: "The rights of conscience shall be held inviolable, and neither the legislature, executive nor judicial powers of the United States shall have authority to alter, abrogate or infringe any part of the constitutions of the several states, which provide for the preservation of liberty in matters of religion."[115]

The particular evil feared was in one part persecution, that is, being molested on account of religious sentiment or infringement of the right to worship the Supreme Being as one pleased. The other, and larger, concern was sect domination. One North Carolina delegate inquired whether a national establishment would be Episcopal or Presbyterian.[116] The federalists argued in response that sect equality was already ensured by both the absence of any enumerated power to interfere in religion and by the multiplicity of sects in the United States.[117] William Spaight, a drafter of the Constitution and later a senator from North Carolina, urged that "no sect is preferred to another."[118] Madison argued that "no one sect will ever be able to outnumber or depress the rest."[119] North Carolina Governor Samuel Johnston insisted that there was no basis to fear "that any one religious sect shall be exclusively established"; indeed, he knew "but two or three states where there is the least chance of establishing any particular religion," noting Massachusetts and Connecticut.[120] Edmund Randolph assured Virginia's antifederalists that the variety of beliefs "will prevent the establishment of any one sect, in prejudice to the rest. Zachariah Johnson similarly counselled that "the difficulty of establishing a uniformity of religion in this country is immense." The classic, and seminal, expression of this theme was doubtlessly Madison's. His Tenth Federalist Paper was a number in the *Publius* series of pro-Constitutional essays published in New York newspapers, a series widely circulated about the states. Quite possibly the most important piece of political theory ever propounded by an American, and thus hardly an obscure effort, Madison's commitment to sect-equality there is often overlooked, probably because it is subsumed within his general recipe for "curing the mischief of faction." It bears emphasizing that Madison squarely confronted the danger of spiritual tyranny by the national government, a danger very high on antifederalists' grievance list. He conceded that "a religious sect may degenerate into a political faction in a part of the Confederacy," and at least *try* to subordinate others. The remedy? "A variety of Sects dispersed over the entire face of [the Confederacy] must secure the national councils against any danger from that source." That a multiplicity of sects, by checking the political aggressions of each other, would secure religious liberty was Madison's theme, both in the Federalist and at the Virginia Convention.[121]

But the worries persisted. One broadside circulating in Pennsylvania asked whether, if a majority of the "continental legislature" established "a form of religion . . . which all the pains and penalties which in other countries are annexed to the establishment of a national church, what is there in the proposed constitution to hinder their doing so? Nothing; for we have no bill of rights."[122] Patrick Henry cut deeply into the federalists' assurance; he asked, Why leave such important objects to implication? Why not expressly declare what it is the national government ought not to do?[123]

The ratifying conventions did just that and so informed Congress of the amendments they wished proposed to the states for ratification. The conventions sought freedom of conscience as known to the state constitutions, especially Virginia's, which Madison argued in the Virginia convention would not prohibit even compulsory contributions by all to one Protestant sect.[124] They also demand equality of sects (which would prohibit such a discriminatory assessment). Not a word was spoken during the ratifying process, so far as surviving evidence indicates, in support of *Everson*'s claim that "shocked" colonials sought to revolutionize the relationship between church and state. On the contrary, the ratifying process was deeply conservative in its celebration of the present and immediate past and in its insistence that the prevailing regime need be preserved inviolate. Not a single word was spoken that, even liberally construed, suggested that nonestablishment "meant at least this": neither a state nor the federal government can aid, foster, or encourage religion, even on a nondiscriminatory basis.

NOTES

1. S. Ames, ed., *Works of Fisher Ames* 52–53 (1854).

2. Irving Brant, *The Life of James Madison* 264 (1954).

3. L. Levy, "The Legacy Reexamined," 37 *Stan. L. Rev.* 767 (1986).

4. 1 *Annals of Cong.* 29 (J. Gales ed. 1834).

5. Madison to Jefferson, October 17, 1788, in 1 *Writings of Madison* 423 (1865 by order of Congress).

6. Letter of January 13, 1789, *Massachusetts Centinel*, March 4, 1789, at 1.

7. *Annals* at 758.

8. See D. Anderson, "The Origins of the Press Clause," 30 *UCLA L. Rev.* 455 n. 251 (1983); Julius Goebel, Jr., 1 *History of the Supreme Court of the United States* 433 n. 105 (1971).

9. *Independent Gazetteer*, October 17, 1788, quoted in Anderson, "Origins," at 497, n. 251.

10. Anderson, "Origins," at 485.

11. Ibid. at 497.

12. See U.S. Const. art. V.

13. See e.g., *The Life and Correspondence of Rufus King* 50 (Charles R. King, ed. (1894); James Curtis Ballagh, 2 *The Letters of Richard Henry Lee* 438, 444, 468–69 (1911); 2 *Elliot's Debates* 276 (1836) (statement by Willie Jones); E. McPherson, ed., "Unpublished Letters from North Carolina to James Madison and James Monroe," 14 *N.C. Hist. Rev.* 156, 166 (1937).

14. See notes 83–92 and accompanying text.

15. See generally J. Main, *The Antifederalists: Critics of the Constitution, 1781– 1788* 119–67 (1961).

16. L. Levy, *Legacy of Suppression* 217, 227 (1960).

17. B. McMaster and F. Stone, eds., *Pennsylvania and the Federal Constitution, 1787–1788* 83, 114 (1970) (opposition in Pennsylvania basically that of political jobbers); Paul L. Ford, ed., *Essays on the Constitution of the United States* 402 (1892) (North Carolina's Hugh Williamson to same effect), and 144 (Oliver Ellsworth expressing same view); H. Beeman, *The Old Dominion and the New Nation, 1788–1801* 93 (1972).

18. See, e.g., *Debates and Proceedings in the Convention of the Commonwealth of Massachusetts* 406 (1788); L. Renzulli, *Maryland: The Federalist Years* 66 et seq., (1972); 8 *Letters of Members of the Contintental Congress* 581 (E. Burnett ed. 1936) (statement of William Grayson); J. Conley, *Democracy in Decline* 117 (1977) (James Madison).

19. 3 *Farrand's Records of the Federal Convention* 291 (letter from George Nicholas to James Madison of April 5, 1788, in which Nicholas described George Mason's antifederal disposition to "the irritation he feels from the hard things that have been said of him, and second to a vain opinion he entertains . . . that he has influence enough to dictate a constitution for Virginia, and through her to the rest of the Union"). Ford, *Essays*, at 161 (Oliver Ellsworth as "The Landholder" portrayed Richard Lee's opposition as factious,"rooted in his implacable hatred to George Washington, [and] his attempts to displace him and give the command of the American Army to General Lee").

20. Massachusetts and Virginia, for example. See 3 *Elliot's Debates* 191 (1836) (speech of Edward Randolph).

21. 1 *Writings of Madison* at 181; See speech of Benjamin Rush, McMaster and Stone, *Pennsylvania*, at 294; 3 *Elliot's* 583 (1836), (speech of James Madison), 191 (speech of Edmund Randolph); 4 *Elliot's* at 66 (speech of William Davie), 130 (speech of James Iredell).

22. 1 *Writings of Madison* at 426 (Madison to Jefferson, Oct. 17, 1788).

23. *Annals* at 775.

24. Ibid.

25. 1 *Writings of Madison* at 427 (letter of October 17, 1788).

26. *Everson v. Board of Education* 330 U.S. 1, 11 (1962).

27. Ibid.

28. Ibid. at 10.

29. See Rhys Isaac, "Religion and Authority: Problems of the Anglican Establishment in Virginia in the Era of the Great Awakening and the Parson's Cause," *Wm. & Mary Q.*, 3d ser., 30, 3–36 (1973).

30. *Everson* at 11.

31. J. Madison, *Notes of Debates in the Federal Convention of 1787* 630 (Norton ed. 1966).

32. Ibid. at 630 (civil juries), 639 (standing armies), 640 (liberty of the press).

33. Ibid. at 639.

34. "The Senators and Representatives before mentioned and the Members of the several State Legislatures, and all executive and judicial Officers, both of the United States and of the several States, shall be bound by Oath or Affirmation, to support this Constitution; but no religious Test shall ever be required as a Qualification to any Office or public Trust under the United States."

35. Madison, *Notes*, at 561.

36. 3 *Farrand's Records* at 172 et seq.

37. Ibid. at 227.

38. Letter of June 15, 1789, in *Letters of Benjamin Rush*, 515–17 (Lyman Butterfield ed. 1951).

39. Ford, *Essays*, at 169. See 16 NLHR 486, at 52.

40. Ford, *Essays*, at 169.

41. Ibid. Ellsworth hastened to deny any implication that he believed the civil government had no right to "interfere in the matters of religion." "It [the government] has a right to prohibit and punish gross immoralities and impieties, because the open practice of these is of evil example of our laws against drunkeness, profane swearing, blasphemy, and professed atheism." Ibid. at 171.

42. Ibid. at 169; "A North Carolina Citizen on the Federal Constitution, 1788," 16 *N.C. Hist. Rev.* 36, 53 (1939).

43. C. Wingate, 2 *Life and Letters of Paine Wingate* 487 (1930), Sullivan to Belknap, February 26, 1788.

44. See, e.g., 3 *Elliot's* 635 (1836) (Virginia); 4 *Elliot's* 191–205 (1836) (North Carolina); *Mass. Debates* at 351; see notes and text (this chapter) for South Carolina (records of South Carolina debates are those of the legislature deliberating over whether to call a convention, unless otherwise indicated).

45. *Elliot's* 198 (speech of Governor Johnston).

46. *Debates and Proceedings in the Convention of the Commonwealth of Massachusetts* 219 (1788) (hereinafter cited as *Mass. Convention*).

47. 4 *Elliot's* 199 (speech of Reverend Caldwell).

48. Ibid. at 194 (speech of James Iredell).

49. Ibid. at 212.

50. *Life of Wingate* at 221.

51. 4 *Elliot's* at 192.

52. Ibid. at 199.

53. Ibid. at 195–96.

54. Ibid. at 199.

55. *Mass. Convention* at 219.

56. 4 *Elliot's* at 199.

57. *Mass. Convention* at 221.

58. See, e.g., Ibid. at 220 (Rev. Shute); Ford, *Essays*, at 170 (Oliver Ellsworth as "Landholder").

59. 4 *Elliot's* at 220.

60. 2 *Documentary History of the Constitution of the United States* 140 (1894, 1965).

61. Ford, *Essays*, at 231.

62. Ibid. at 235.

63. NLHR at 53.

64. 4 *Elliot's* at 312 (speech of Patrick Calhoun).

65. L. McCrady, *History of South Carolina in the Revolution* 213 (1909).

66. 2 *Documentary History* at 143.

67. *Life of Wingate* at 220–21.

68. L. Mayo, *John Langdon of New Hampshire* 214 (1937).

69. See Sullivan to Belknap, February 26, 1788, in *Life of Wingate*, at 220–21.

70. Ibid.

71. See *Mass. Convention* for a complete overview.

72. See ibid. at 83–84 for list of amendments.

73. The vote was 63 to 11 for ratification. Renzulli, *Maryland*, at 86.

74. 2 *Elliot's* at 553.

75. See Gale's votes on amendments (ibid. at 554), and vote to adjourn without considering amendments (at 555).

76. See Renzulli, *Maryland*, at 82–93.

77. 2 *Elliot's* at 533.

78. Paul S. Clarkson and R. Samuel Jett, *Luther Martin of Maryland* (1970), at 143–44.

79. T. Buckley, *Church and State in Revolutionary Virginia* 195 (1977).

80. *The First Laws of the State of Maryland* (J. Cushing comp. 1981) (hereinafter cited as *Maryland Laws*, proceedings of convention for November 1, 1776).

81. T. Curry, *The First Freedoms: Church and State in America to the Passage of the First Amendment* (1986).

82. See *Maryland Laws*, ch. XI (1774), ch. 44 (1785).

83. 2 *Documentary History* at 191.

84. Ibid. at 380.

85. 4 *Elliot's* at 244.

86. Ibid. at 311.

87. McMaster and Stone, 2 *Pennsylvania* at 461.

88. It met in March 1790 at South Kingston and adjourned, without ratifying the Constitution, until May of the same year, where the Constitution was ratified by a vote of 34 to 32.

89. Madison was a member of the convention and the committee that drafted proposed amendments.

90. 3 *Elliot's* at 656.

91. Thomas Curry also considered that sect preference was the "evil" sought to be remedied in the Establishment Clause. Curry, *First Freedoms*, at 197.

92. 2 *Documentary History* at 380.

93. See chapter 7, notes 161–81, and accompanying text.

94. *Terrett v. Taylor* 13 U.S. (9 Cranch) 43 (1815).

95. See chapter 2, note 202.

96. See E. Wilder Spaulding, *His Excellency George Clinton: Critic of the Constitution* (1938) ("George Clinton . . . was the foremost opponent of the Constitution of 1787").

97. See chapter 2, notes 361–75, and accompanying text; chapter 6, note 36, and accompanying text.

98. 3 *Elliot's* at 656.

99. McMaster and Stone, 2 *Pennsylvania* at 256 (Smilie).

100. 2 *Elliot's* at 400 (Treadwell).

101. 4 ibid. at 138 (Spencer).

102. Ibid at 154 (Spencer).

103. 3 *Elliot's* at 317.

104. Ibid. at 587.

105. Ibid. at 462.

106. Madison, *Notes*, at 561.

107. *Elliot's* at 211.

108. Ibid. at 330.

109. See e.g., *Pamphlets on the Constitution of the United States* (1888) (Paul Ford ed.), at 135, 137 (Tench Coxe writing as "An American Citizen"); 3 *Elliot's* at 330 (James Madison); 4 *Elliot's* at 199 (Governor Johnston).

110. J. Ballagh, 2 *The Letters of Richard Henry Lee* 442–43 (1911).

111. 4 *Elliot's* at 163.

112. 3 ibid at 150.

113. Ibid. at 266.

114. 4 ibid. at 191 (Reverend Henry Abbott).

115. McMaster and Stone, 2 *Pennsylvania* at 421.

116. 4 *Elliot's* at 191–92.

117. 3 ibid. at 104 (Governor Randolph).

118. 4 ibid. at 208.

119. 3 ibid. at 330.

120. 4 ibid. at 199.

121. 3 ibid. at 204 (Randolph); 3 ibid. at 645 (Johnson); 3 Ibid at 330 (Madison). Quotations are from the Mentor edition of *The Federalist Papers* (1961) at 84.

122. "An Old Whig," printed from *Independent Gazetteer*, in Evans's American Imprint Series I, entry 20380.

123. 3 *Elliot's* at 149–50.

124. Ibid. at 330.

4

In Congress: Throwing a Tub, or Tubs, to the Whale

"INTENT": THE MEANING OF THE WORDS

When James Madison rose from his House seat in the late afternoon of May 4, 1789, and told his colleagues that "he intended to bring on the subject of amendments to the constitution" on May 25,[1] he signaled the end of a tortuous political odyssey. That on the next morning fellow Virginian (and Patrick Henry lieutenant) Theodorick Bland laid before the House the Virginia Assembly's call for a second constitutional convention[2]—a conclave that might have gutted the Philadelphia document—helps explain Madison's conversion from unrepentant adversary of amendments to eager champion. Madison evidently followed a political stratagem suggested to him by Henry "Lighthorse" Lee, who urged that federalists like Madison "derail [antifederalists] by complying with the rational views of the advocates for amendments spontaneously."[3] But more than the timing of Madison's proposal was dictated by political needs; his enlistment in the amendment ranks itself resulted from electoral necessity. Madison's epic journey began when Patrick Henry denied Madison his first ambition—a Senate seat—because of Madison's conspicuous nationalism and hostility to constitutional alteration.[4] Although Madison sat on the committee that drafted the amendments recommended by the Virginia convention, it was common knowledge, as Madison admitted,[5] that he saw them as only the necessary meant to secure ratification of the Constitution. Indeed, Henry so distrusted Madison that he gerrymandered him into a difficult House contest with the young James Monroe, waged primarily on turf dominated by Henry and Monroe sympathizers.[6] Monroe, an antifederalist supporter of significant amendments, appeared headed for vic-

tory until Madison, in January 1789 and goaded by political advisers, finally
announced in favor of amendments.[7] (In a November 1788 letter, Madison falsely
claimed to have favored amendments during the Philadelphia convention, where
he proposed none and did not support the few delegates who did.)[8] Citing
"changed circumstances" in a letter to Baptist minister George Eve,[9] he finally
endorsed a "bill of rights,"[10] which a published version of the Eve letter described as "the fullest provision on the rights of conscience, general warrants,
etc., etc."[11] As Virginia historian Harold Beeman notes, the addressee was not
randomly selected but was part of enduring Madisonian strategy to cultivate the
large Baptist population in his section of Virginia. As Beeman further concludes,
Madison had not been willing to support amendments, though many Americans
sought that reassurance, until his own political career was on the line.[12]

Madison's congressional colleagues commented abundantly on his predica-
ment. "Poor Madison," Pennsylvania Senator Robert Morris wrote, "had taken
a wrong step in publishing the letter on amendments, and was now forced to
bring them on."[13] South Carolina Senator Pierce Butler saw Madison's congressional proposals as merely a promise to his constitutents made good and opined
that the Virginian was "not hearty in the cause of amendments."[14] Or, as Fisher
Ames succinctly put it, the amendments "may get the mover some popularity,
which he wishes."[15]

Madison's May 4 initiative, however unwilling or unenthusiastic, was also a
beginning, the start of a historical misperception that continues to this day to
govern, if not haunt, the life of each American. Justice Rutledge wrote in
Everson: "All the great instruments of the Virginia struggle for religious liberty
thus became warp and woof of our constitutional tradition, not simply by the
course of history, but by the common unifying force of Madison's life, thought
and sponsorship. He epitomized the whole of that tradition in the [First] Amendment's compact, but nonetheless comprehensive, phrasing."[16] *Everson* is just
one of many judicial and scholarly treatments of the Establishment Clause as
virtually the pristine expression of Madison's church-state philosophy.[17] Contemporary political and editorial commentary frequently harken back to the founders and framers, and most often it is Madison who is summoned from the grave.

The historical fallacy with the most severe consequences is the implication
that to the extent Madison "authored" or "sponsored" the Establishment Clause,
it represents what Madison personally believed was the proper alignment of
church and state. That fallacy thus makes inquiries into the thought of James
Madison relevant, and a scholarly cottage industry has sprouted up around just
that.[18] Therefore, one is obliged to speculate, which is the real Madison? The
president who in 1811 vetoed an act incorporating the Alexandria Episcopal
Church as violative of the Establishment Clause[19] or Virginia representative
Madison who in 1785 voted for the bill incorporating religious societies? Was
it the Madison of 1811 who vetoed a reservation of land to a Baptist meeting
house in Mississippi Territory (worth about $10) as an establishment[20] or who
between 1787 and 1789 voted four times in the national legislature in favor of

such reservations?[21] Or was it President Madison who repeatedly issued pungently pious Thanksgiving Day proclamations (but who later regretted it),[22] or the Madison on 1780 who introduced into the Virginia legislature a bill, drafted by Jefferson, enabling the general assembly to declare days of fast and Thanksgiving on which every "minister of the gospel shall . . . perform devine service and preach a sermon, or discourse, suited to the occasion . . . on pain of forfeiting fifty pounds for every failure, not having a reasonable excuse."[23] Are these contradictions a product of maturation? Did Madison's personal views consistently evolve over time, so that there is an early Madison and a late Madison? If so, which is the appropriate touchstone? Or instead, were his philosophical views relatively static but inconsistently—or expediently—applied? Was Madison's thinking on church and state simply confused and erratic?

A second unnecessary scholarly debate spawned by the basic misperception is who really wrote the First Amendment.[24] Was it Madison after all or the deeply conservative New England federalist Fisher Ames? If Ames, then a second scholarly cottage industry—Ames on church and state—may be expected. Is the final language more reflective of the version proposed by the New Hampshire ratifying convention and its representative in Congress, Samuel Livermore? Does the final draft in any event bear, as one historian safely put it, a distinctly Madisonian flavor?[25] What if it should turn out that the Establishment Clause in fact is a compromise between Fisher Ames's language and an even more conservative Senate formulation and that Madison's own version was decisively rejected? Does Madison's legacy, then, play no role in the search for the amendment's meaning? How, in any case, can authorship determine the meaning of a collective compromise in Congress, whose operative significance resides in the actions of thirteen highly differentiated state legislatures?[26]

The truth is that Madison's personal philosophy, whatever it may have been, has nothing to do with the meaning of the Establishment Clause, and we should never regard, for example, "Madison on school prayer," as a surrogate for the "Constitution on school prayer." Not only was the fact of his involvement, and the timing of it, dictated by external pressures, it is clear that the text and meaning of his proposals were drawn from sources other than his own reflection. His initial proposal, and the only one that can be linked to him, was that proffered on June 8 and that historians agree (with Fisher Ames) was founded on the work of the state conventions: "The civil rights of none shall be abridged on account of religious belief or worship, *nor shall any national religion be established*, nor shall the full and equal rights of conscience be in any manner, or on any pretext, infringed (emphasis added)"[27] Fortunately, Madison expressly defined on the House floor what he meant by the highlighted provision. He said it responded to the fear that "one sect might obtain a pre-eminence, or two combine together, and establish a religion to which they would compel others to conform."[28] When the wording was pared down to "no religion shall be established by law, nor shall the equal rights of conscience be infringed," Madison again provided a public interpretation. He "apprehended the meaning of the words to be, that Congress should not establish a religion, and enforce the legal observation of it by law, nor compel men to worship God in any manner contrary to their conscience.''[29] Nowhere in either published or private debate during this period did Madison deviate from these pronouncements. They, and not any undisclosed thoughts developed before or after, constitute Madison's interpretation of the Establishment Clause.

The explanation for the distance between the First Amendment and Madison's personal philosophy is not hard to locate. His was a highly specific political enterprise with no room for unorthodox views—his own or anyone else's. It was a project that had to succeed and whose sole measure of success was the achievement of bipartisan, bicameral congressional approval succeeded by transectional state ratification. ''They are restrained to points on which least difficulty was apprehended,'' Madison wrote of his initial propositions. ''Nothing of a controvertible nature ought to be hazarded by those who are sincere in wishing for the approbation of of each House, and of the State Legislatures.'' As if to justify himself, he also wrote to Jefferson at about the same time that ''every thing of a controvertible nature'' was ''studiously avoided.''[30]

''Noncontroversial'' understates the banality of the liberties championed by Madison. As Julius Goebel correctly notes, if Madison had been ''under and academic mandate to shun controversy, his choice could not have been more politically temperate.''[31] His colleagues were much less charitable. South Carolina Senator Ralph Izad wrote Jefferson that the amendments were a waste of time.[32] Pierce Butler, the state's second senator, referred to them as a ''few milk and water amendments,''[33] an epithet echoed by powerful Virginia antifederalist George Mason.[34] Pennsylvania Congressman George Clymer appropriately called them a ''tub or a number of tubs to the whale.''[35] To Senator Robert Morris, they were ''nonsense''[36] and to Fisher Ames ''trash.''[37] Fellow Virginian Edmund Randolph described their effect as an ''anodyne to the discontented.''[38] South Carolina's Aedanus Burke portrayed the select committee's version of Madison's amendments as ''little better than whip-syllabub, frothy and full of wind, formed only to please the palate.'' Fisher Ames picked up Burke's epicurean metaphor: the proposals ''will stimulate the stomach as hasty pudding . . . rather food than physic. An immense mass of sweet and other herbs and roots for a diet drink.''[39]

To these and other congressional colleagues, Madison's amendments were more than inoffensive; they were restatements of such obvious, taken-for-granted essentials that only the belabored discussion of them was offensive. Georgia Congressman James Jackson said the amendments were not worth a ''pinch of snuff; they went to secure rights never in danger.''[40] This tepidness did not owe to Madison's personal views, for he was the first to admit that his ideas were far more exotic than those of his contemporaries.[41] Rather, the amendments sprang from political necessity comprised of a number of particulars. Some alteration need be accomplished to honor Madison's campaign commitments and ensure his political survival. Indeed, at least one House colleague recorded that

Madison was preoccupied by his political fortunes in Virginia and literally in fear for his professional life.[42] Madison also was concerned to quiet popular fears elsewhere of the new system and to entice North Carolina into the Union. Federalists besides Madison sympathized with at least these objectives. But federalists could not "lop off essentials" or introduce any genuine modifications weakening the constitutional structure system at the outset. (They detected such a design in Patrick Henry's choice of two vigorous antifederalists, Richard Henry Lee and William Grayson, for the first Senate.) Added to the turbid political equation was the antifederalists' relative indifference to a bill of rights; they indeed wanted "essential" changes. Madison walked a dangerously fine line in limiting his offering to personal liberty guarantees, neglecting entirely the much more numerous structural alterations proposed by the people. And from among the individual rights cited by the states, he chose the least offensive. In selecting the Maryland minority formulation—"no national church"—he struck a chord with resonance throughout the Union. Few, if any, Americans desired a system of privilege and disability for themselves like that prevailing in England. That such a prospect was remote underwrote the widespread derision greeting Madison's formula. Nevertheless, nothing more was possible; Madison knew it and moved forward.

As Madison privately noted, federalists predominated in both houses of Congress, and they were mostly familiar faces.[43] He needed agreement on religious liberty from two-thirds of them, and they were, virtually to a man, quite hostile to his personal viewpoint. Madison biographer Irving Brant reports that the New England senators were most active in reworking Madison's proposals in that chamber,[44] and they were a formidable bunch of church-state traditionalists. Paine Wingate of New Hampshire,[45] Massachusetts's Caleb Strong,[46] Connecticut Senator William Samuel Johnson,[47] and New York's Rufus King[48] were all actual drafters of public aid to religion legislation. Oliver Ellsworth, a personally observant and orthodox Congregationalist, was thoroughly committed to the public enforcement of the truth of Christianity.[49] The remaining New Englanders—Tristram Dalton (Massachusetts), John Langdon (New Hampshire), and Phillip Schuyler(New York)—were all seasoned politicians steeped in the church-state regime of the Northeast.[50]

Southern prospects were not much brighter for Madison. Charles Carroll[51] and John Henry[52] of Maryland were publicly committed to aid to religion, as was William Few[53] of Georgia, William Paterson[54] of New Jersey, and George Read[55] of Delaware. Read's colleague Richard Basset, a wealthy lawyer and landowner, was a remarkably devout Methodist, who built the denomination's first church in Delaware. He later was devoted to the state Bible Society. Georgia's second senator, James Gunn, presents the opposite extreme. Gunn arrived in Georgia with the military expedition that relieved Savannah in 1782 (he was a native Virginian) and died under a moral cloud in 1801 due primarily to his central role in the infamous Yazoo land sale fraud of the 1790s. All accounts portray him as a thoroughly unprincipled, abrasive, ambitious figure, one unlikely either to articulate or defend unconventional philosophic views on church and state or on any other subject. The contemptuous South Carolinians Izard and Butler doubtless saw in Madison's proposal no more than the sect equality enjoyed throughout the states. Each was a steadfast member of the previously established Anglican church; Butler served on the vestry of St. Michael's in Charleston during the 1780s, and Izard's great-grandfather introduced in 1704 the bill that established the church in South Carolina. Each was a stalwart of the deeply conservative low-country obligarchy that controlled South Carolina.[55] Neither they nor the federalist Robert Morris would have joked about a serious proposition to prohibit all aid, encouragement, and support of Christianity. Perhaps most important of all, at least for Madison, the Virginia senators—Lee and Grayson— were most active in the Senate amendment debate, and each was opposed to Madison on the general assessment issue. The only senator whose views might have imitated Madison's, the irreverent Pennsylvanian William Maclay, was ill throughout the Senate debate and confined to bed.[57] The considerable historical evidence reveals not a single senator whose personal views were even close to Madison's (much less those attributed to them by the Supreme Court) and no one who thought nonestablishment meant anything more than sect equality. To put the point a little differently, a proposal that prohibited all aid, encouragement, or support of religion would not have been milk and water to them; it would have scandalized them. Such an amendment would not have garnered two votes, much less two-thirds.

A House of Representatives composed of fifty-five members cannot be treated exhaustively. Although there may have been a few, like Thomas Sumter of South Carolina, whose personal opinions resembled Madison's, there were not many, and no such person participated in the religion clauses debate. In the light of publicly expressed views on church and state or of the constituency that elected them to Congress, the vast majority of the House certainly held distinctively un-Madisonian views. Unquestionably among the un-Madisonian are Elbridge Gerry[58] and South Carolina's Thomas Tucker,[59] the leading antifederalists in the House.

Notably those House members who actually shaped the religion clauses, and the meaning they gave them in proposing the Bill of Rights, are readily identifiable. Madison's initial proposal—no national religion—was publicly defined by him and was postponed for future consideration by a committee of the whole House.[60] On July 21 Madison moved for discussion by that committee, but instead his proposals, along with all other amendments proposed by the State ratifying conventions, were sent to a select committee of one member from each state, chaired by John Vining of Delaware.[61] Vining was on record as a member of the confederation congress in favor of publicly supported religion,[62] and his committee included Madison, George Clymer, Elias Boudinot of New Jersey (who later became president of the American Bible Society),[63] New York's Egbert Benson (who along with Madison helped draft Confederation era ordinances reserving western lands for churches),[64] Abraham Baldwin of Georgia,[65]

George Gale of Maryland,[66] the dyspeptic Aedanus Burke, and three New Englanders. Vining's committee modified Madison's original proposal and reported that "no religion shall be established by law, nor shall equal rights of conscience be infringed."[67] Discussion of this version—similar to the existing clause—on August 21 amply reveals what the House meant by it. Sylvester of New York spoke first and "feared it might be thought to have a tendency to abolish religion altogether."[68] Gerry wanted to contract the language by substituting *no religious doctrine* for *religion*,[69] in what Curry describes as an attempt to place the national government on a solidly New England track.[70] Next up was Maryland's Daniel Carroll, whose biographer records his support for all religious groups,[71] followed by Madison's reassurance that it simply prohibited a national religion.[72]

The most revealing exchange of congressional deliberations then took place between Benjamin Huntington of Connecticut and Madison, one unfortunately misunderstood by Justice Rutledge in *Everson*. Huntington echoed Sylvester's fear, which he presumed assuaged by "the gentlemen from Virginia." Then Huntington related:

He [Huntington] understood the amendment to mean what had been expressed [by Madison]; but others might find it convenient to put another construction upon it. The ministers of their congregations to the Eastward were maintained by the contributions of those who belonged to their Society; the expense of building meeting-houses was contributed in the same manner. These things were regulated by by-laws. If an action was brought before a Federal Court on any of these cases, the person who had neglected to perform his engagements could not be compelled to do it; for a support of ministers, or building of places of worship might be construed into a religious establishment.[73]

Justice Rutledge understood Huntington's fear to be that "this might be construed to prevent judicial enforcement of private pledges,"[74] where no one listening to Huntington misunderstood the compulsory tax support, regulated by public enactments or bylaws, prevalent in New England. Huntington was asking Madison whether the New England system, much more coercive than even the general assessment opposed by Madison in 1785, might be an establishment. (Huntington's preface implies that neither he nor Madison thought so.) Madison alleviated this fear, clearly indicating that there was no conflict:

Mr. Madison thought if the word national was inserted before religion, it would satisfy the minds of honorable gentlemen. He believed that the people feared one sect might obtain a pre-eminence, or two combine together, and establish a religion to which they would compel others to conform. He thought if the word national was introduced it would point the amendment directly to the object it was intended to prevent.[75]

Justice Rutledge here misfired, badly and momentously. He correctly read Madison as reassuring Huntington but concluded that Madison "unmistakably stated that 'establishment' meant public 'support' or religion in the financial sense. Madison concluded precisely the opposite and thereby aligned himself with the settled view of establishment. Nonestablishment, Madison reasoned, simply meant aid to religion must avoid sect preeminence and compelled conformity of belief. Put differently, aid to religion must be accomplished on a nondiscriminatory basis, according to Madison in the First Congress.

But there is another element to his reassurance that the Supreme Court had never addressed but that, properly interpreted, cuts deeply into its no-aid reading of the Establishment Clause. This "federalism" strand, evident from Madison's emphatic use of *national*, is rescued from mere implication by the next speaker, Samuel Livermore of New Hampshire. Livermore "thought it would be better if it was . . . made to read . . . that *Congress* shall make no laws touching religion.[76] This was precisely the alteration sought by the religious zealots in the New Hampshire convention.[77] The committee of the whole promptly passed Livermore's substitute, 31 to 20.[78]

In completely disabling Congress, the House version says nothing about what an establishment was, or was not, but it speaks volumes of the underlying motive of the legislators. The intention thus manifested tracked the federalist view that Congress had no enumerated authority over religion in the first place, as well as the basic antifederalist endeavor to preserve existing state constitutional regimes from intermeddling federal legislation. That is precisely what the Pennsylvania minority recommended and effectively what the other conventions wanted as well. The New Hampshire language adopted by the House amounted to the same thing: protection from federal interference in the enjoyment of existing state practice. That the motion passed during a discussion centered in the concerns for New England public orthodoxy stands the Supreme Court's "revolutionary" "uprooting of as such [church-state] relationships" on its head. The manifest intention of the farmers in Congress was to do nothing that burdened, much less uprooted, the sacred canopy.

Before the House could vote on Livermore's formula, Fisher Ames moved that it be replaced by "Congress shall make no law establishing religion, or to prevent the free exercise thereof, or to infringe the rights of conscience."[79] Ames's language was adopted without apparent discussion and constituted the House version forwarded for Senate consideration.[80]

Madison did not speak in connection with Ames's version, but it is indistinguishable from that which occasioned the August 15 discussion. That discussion in turn reveals Madison's understanding of the final House bill: sect equality, an interpretation questioned by no one present. Moreover, the temper of the entire House may be gauged by the conjunction of the Livermore and Ames's version on August 20. In passing Ames's proposal instead of Livermore's without extended debate, the motivation of Livermore's proposal to leave state regimes undistrubed no doubt underlay the Ames language. That the last two versions were offered by members from that section along with southern federalists like Carroll and Madison reinforces initial observations that what was noncontroversial among that audience amounted to no more than, as Pierce Butler wrote, "one or two general things already well-secured."[81] The leading northern antifederalist, Elbridge Gerry, wished to narrow the amendment further,[82] and his foremost southern colleague, Thomas Tucker, contributed an additional amendment to permit religious tests for federal office (as his state ratifying convention demanded).[83]

Contemporaneous private correspondence confirms the unexceptional content of the amendments. South Carolina federalist representative William Loughton Smith wrote Edward Rutledge on August 9 that the amendments "are thought inoffensive to the Federalists."[84] Pennsylvania Congressmen Clymer and Fitzsimmons described the House product to Senator Robert Morris as "perfectly innocent."[85] Madison explained his obvious caution to Edmund Randolph the day after Ames's language passed: "two or three contentious additions would even now frustrate the whole project."[86]

Madison's sense of foreboding was well founded. The Senate was not only deeply federal but distinctly un-Madisonian in its church-state views. Indeed, the leading antifederalist there, Virginia's Lee, candidly admitted that Madison's idea of amendments was not that of the Virginia conventioners whose cause Lee and his colleague Grayson were prepared to press.[87] Senator William Maclay recorded the senator's first encounter with amendments, on August 24 when the House articles were sent over, as one of open contempt.[88]

The senators immediately set to work cutting into Ames's religious freedom guarantee. On September 3, they struck out the free exercise clause and inserted, in lieu of religion," "one Religious Sect or Society in Preference to others."[89] Tinkering with the language continued, as one proposal to scrap the House version entirely was defeated[90] and another to affirm that version as it stood was rejected as well.[91] The Senate seems to have hit on a solution in passing, by the end of the day, the Ames language shorn of "nor shall the equal rights of conscience be infringed." This initial settlement on "Congress shall make no law establishing Religion, or prohibiting the free exercise thereof" was short-lived, even if destined to return as essentially the present wording.[92] On September 9, two-thirds of the senators adopted their final version: "Congress shall make no laws establishing articles of faith or a mode or worship, or prohibiting the free exercise of religion."[93] The sparse Senate *Journal* records the author of neither this nor any other alteration nor the votes cast. Since Maclay was indisposed during this phase of the debate,[94] there is no other account of it. We know generally that Lee and Grayson were most active in the amendment proceedings, and at least one historian, Irving Brant, discerns especial New England influence on the religion clauses.[95] The bare official record does show that the Senate language is essentially that proposed by Elbridge Gerry of Massachusetts in the House on August 15, which was responsive to Sylvester's concern that saying "no religion shall be established" "might be thought to have a tendency to abolish religion altogether." The Senate's final formulation is of the same color. The words themselves undoubtedly constricted the unintended connotations of the House language—no one could think the senators tended to abolish religion altogether—and prodded the federal guarantee along New England lines. There, doctrinal conformity was never enjoined, although religion was aided and, some would say, Congregationalism preferred. Given the complexion of the Senate, the words were intended at least to pin the guarantee down to what all apparently agreed was an acceptable idea: prohibiting a national church. While the senator's intentions may thus have not differed from those of House members like Fisher Ames (whose language the Senate was gutting), their verbal formula connoted, if anything, a sect-equality soft version. This same linguistic caution underlay the Senate's rejection of "freedom of conscience" in favor of "free exercise." The latter phrase also pointed the norm directly at the problem: freedom to worship without recrimination. Eliminated were any implications engendered by the increasing philosophical speculation enveloping "liberty of conscience." Again, the New Englanders, aided by Virginia's two senators, were probably behind the change. That the Senate language cut into an already narrow House version is further apparent. At least one senator sought to add religious tests to the Constitution,[96] and New Hampshire Senator Paine Wingate, truly a pillar of New England orthodoxy and the antithesis of the modern Court's framers profile, reported the amendments to the equally orthodox Timothy Pickering with no comment on the religious liberty guarantees.[97] If it had meant much more than banning a national church, Wingate would have commented at length.

Richard Henry Lee struck the same chord. A supporter of the general assessment in 1785, Lee wrote to Patrick Henry on September 14 that the House amendments "were far short of the wishes of our Convention, but as they are returned by the Senate they are certainly much weakened."[98] In a letter to Francis Lightfoot Lee, the senator complained that the amendments were "much mutilated." "It is too much the fashion now to look at the rights of the People, as a Miser inspects a Security to find out a flaw."[99] More eloquently, Lee complained that "the English language has been carefully culled to find words feeble in their nature or doubtful in their meaning."[100] One observing newspaper editor concluded that the senator's doctoring had killed the patient; they had gone so far that agreement with the House was now impossible.[101]

Madison seemingly agreed. Paine Wingate wrote to his absent colleague John Langdon that "Madison says he had rather have none than those agreed to by the Senate."[102] Madison's own hand, however, reveals an exasperated but nevertheless undaunted champion. On September 14 he bemoaned "the difficulty of meeting the minds of men accustomed to think and act differently."[103] By September 21, with the Senate refusing to budge on the religion clauses, Madison, Sherman, and Vining[104] were appointed to a conference committee balanced by Ellsworth, Paterson, and Carroll.[105] Out of this committee of six came the present version of the First Amendment, passed by each house in the waning days of September. "Laws respecting an Establishment of religion" was a new formulation, which certainly represented some kind of verbal middle ground between Senate and House. That it passed without comment confirms its close identification with its predecessor in either chamber. The composition of the committee of six permits no other conclusion. The three senators were deeply committed to the type of principles articulated by the entire Senate. Roger Sherman was strictly New England orthodox, while Madison's view of the House language as compromised is clear. Vining's commitment to nondiscriminatory aid was public record.

The Supreme Court sometimes reads "respecting an" to demonstrate the framers' intention to "uproot" the traditional order by prohibiting laws "tending" toward, or "anything like," an establishment of religion. If true, that would mean "tending toward" sect inequality, which is not to say "no discriminatory aid or support." In any event, the Court's view contends that a compromise between (for lack of better terms) a "conservative" House version and a "reactionary" Senate formula turned out to be a truly "revolutionary," if not unthinkable, notion clearly repudiated (at this juncture) by Madison himself. The other conferees led public lives wholly at war with the revolution the Court says they wrought. Indeed pouring *Everson*'s entire brew into "respecting an" is no more than the wishful thinking that underlay *Everson* itself. If "respecting an" imputes anything new, it is, as some commentators have argued, a return to the Livermore formula by preventing Congress from interfering with existing state establishments. The amalgam perhaps intended was that the national government may neither effect an establishment nor interfere with states that do.

This "federalist" interpretation of "respecting an" is squarely grounded in the text. A fair reading of the words reveals that they ordinarily mean "in regard to," "with reference to," or "interfering with," suggesting, if not clearly conveying, the "state enclave" purpose. Such a notion, in contrast to the "anything like" interpretation, is supported by the historical record. It unequivocally addresses the central fear of antifederalists that the federal government would invade state regimes. Second, the typical federalist (people like Madison) response was that Congress had no power over religion in the states. Third, Livermore's formula obviously had ample support—it passed the House 31 to 20—and it met the fears of New Englanders, which were evident throughout the congressional debate.

To the extent "respecting an" is thus accurately emphasized, incorporation of the Establishment Clause (via the Fourteenth Amendment) becomes logically impossible; it would be like trying to apply the Tenth Amendment to the states. How does one translate "Congress shall not interfere with state practices " into a command to state governments?

Leonard Levy has cobbled together disparate elements of this discussion into a rather intriguing interpretation of the religion clauses. He says: "At bottom the [first] amendment expressed the fact that the Framers of the Constitution had not empowered Congress to act in the field of religion.[106] The derailment here is multifaceted. One element is the (again) dizzying notion that this residual emptiness can be "incorporated" by the Due Process clause and thus fastened upon the states. "At bottom the Fourteenth Amendment expressed the fact that the Framers of the Constitution (or of the Due Process Clause?) had not empowered the states to act in the field of religion" is, literally, senseless. State governments do not (with very rare, and no relevant, exceptions) take power from the Federal Constitution at all; they just endure limitations. Another element is its inconclusiveness: even so, what does that tell us about state aid to religious schools? Government can do that with its taxing or spending powers, or its power over education. "Power over religion," as such, is unnecessary. Indeed, Levy is telling us that the First Amendment actually tells us nothing new at all—it merely reflects what had previously been said, perhaps only implicitly, in the Constitution. Here he builds upon a formulation (ironically) actually rejected at Philadelphia: the federal government has "no power over the subject of religion" was Charles Pinckney's offering in the summer of 1787. Why then do we persist in looking to the First Amendment for guidance at all, especially when one appreciates the deformity in Levy's use of Pinckney? Levy would have us believe that Pinckney's represents a positive declaration that government should, as a normative matter, remain separate from religion, and thus mutually exclusive domains are reserved by law for the two. In fact, Pinckney's was more a descriptive observation that a national government of enumerated powers in a union of states possessing plenary authority over most local, domestic matters simply did not—as a matter of fact—have anything to do with the sacred canopy. In any event, if Levy is correct up to this point, why then did the First Congress ultimately *reject* Livermore's proposed "no laws touching on religion"?

Yet, the point that bears most careful note in light of our discussion is the twofold sense in which Levy's historical conclusions, forming the key premises of his argument, are false. As a matter of constitutional and legal fact, he is wrong. The federal government had power "over religion" and no one doubted that it did in the territories, in the military, in Indian relations, and in the District of Columbia. Sherman's Convention comment upon Madison's nondenominational university evidences this, as do the actions of the First Congress and its successors who consistently exercised these powers. The plentiful comments regarding "no power" had as their point of reference the states, as if to say, Congress has no power over religious practices in the states, where state governments retain full authority over the matter. Here, Levy's conclusion-drawing is incomplete, and simply misapprehends the "no power" theme: it was, at bottom, a federalism claim and not a blanket disability in the national government. In any event, it is not true that the federal government has no power over religion in the states, and experience has shown that only a very short-sighted view of the "necessary and proper" clause, as well as other federal powers such as naturalization, sustains that error. That does not really matter, however, nor does it matter that antifederalist boogey-men treaties embracing Catholicism were exaggerated, though literally possible. What matters is this: the First Amendment is simply inexplicable except against a background in which the federal government is *believed* to have power over religious practices in the states. Further, it was the joint accomplishment of both federalists and antifederalists to finally convince the ratifying generation that this was the case. The First Amendment just *cannot* be interpreted in a medium, like Levy's, which would begin with a complete absence of power. At an irreducible minimum, even Levy's argument leads only to the conclusion that the First Amendment was hypothetical or conjectural, setting limits on non-existent powers. It does not change the meaning of it, which remains sect equality.

That the language chosen was just another formulation for the same nonestablishment idea of sect equality is manifest in the post-mortem comments of participants in the struggle. Richard Henry Lee continued to criticize the niggardly treatment of personal liberty by Congress, as did his colleague William Grayson.[107] Theodore Sedgwick, another deeply conservative Massachusetts representative who was more enamored of the Senate's formulation than his own House's, nevertheless thought the finished product unobjectionable, "proper and sufficient."[108] Further, the state legislatures—especially those in Virginia and Rhode Island—said that they ratified a nonestablishment norm.[109] But the most powerful testament to the Congress's understanding of the religion clauses is that found in conduct, the language which, according to Edmund Burke, never lies.

PRAXIS

"This [Supreme] Court," wrote Chief Justice Taft for a unanimous bench in *Hampton Co. v. United States*,[110] "has repeatedly laid down the principle that a contemporaneous legislative exposition of the Constitution when the founders of our Government and framers of our Constitution were actively participating in public affairs, long acquiesced in, fixes the construction to be given its provision."[111] This rule of construction is most often articulated (as in *Hampton*) where the First Congress implemented the 1787 Constitution. Because of the substantial overlap in membership, the 1789 legislative meeting is frequently treated by the Supreme Court as if it were a rump session of the Philadelphia convention.[112] Even more persuasive is this rule of construction where the overlap is total, as it is with the First Congress and the Establishment Clause. At the very least, the legislative behavior of the First Congress should help locate their understanding of what they wrought. And the record leaves no doubt that the First Congress understood government aid, support, and encouragement of religion to be perfectly consistent with the religion clauses.

The record consists only in small part of the chaplaincies[113] and pious Thanksgiving proclamation[114] that the First Congress passed without apparent dissent and that have recently drawn the Supreme Court's attention. Each act inaugurated a system of governmentally sanctioned and supported religious expression that persists to the present day,[115] and the pungent religiosity of Washington's first Thanksgiving address,[116] delivered at the behest of a joint resolution, goes well beyond the kind of polite nod to the Supreme Being, in, for example, Jefferson's Declaration of Independence. That the entire Congress assembled for worship at St. Paul's Episcopal Church, along with Washington, after the president's inaugural suggests the same genuine personal conviction.[117] Washington issued another Thanksgiving message,[118] John Adams issued two,[119] and President James Madison at least four.[120] The First Congress also created the military chaplain's system acquiesced in by Americans of all persuasions up to the present moment.[121]

Various members of the court and the academic community harmonize these actions with a no-aid reading of the Establishment Clause, even if the harmony is purchased by simply treating them as exceptions to the rule.[122] If these enactments do not persuade such observers that the first congressmen just were not men who believed in the complete separation of church and state, their action of July 21, 1789, ought to. On the same day that they debated the Establishment Clause, the House of Representatives, without noticeable opposition, passed an ordinance of governance for the western territory.[123] Previously passed by the Senate, it became law with the president's signature on August 7.[124] The act effectively continued arrangements ordained by the Northwest Ordinance of 1787, passed by the Confederation Congress on July 14, 1787.[125] The importance of the 1789 provision goes beyond its frequently noted provision that "religion, morality and knowledge, being necessary to good government and the happiness of mankind, schools and the means of education shall forever be encouraged,"[126] although that unquestionably was a belief shared by the entire founding generation, including the first congressmen.[127] The territorial regime established during the Confederation, expressly validated and continued by the First Congress and its successors, was suffused with aid, encouragement, and support for religion. The territories, governed ultimately by Congress, immediately by its appointees, and subject to the limits of the Establishment Clause, were indistinguishable from the sacred canopy erected to the east, and the first congressmen knew it when they reenacted the ordinance.[128]

The 1787 ordinance expressly repealed a temporary measure for territorial governance passed on April 23, 1784,[129] and became the constitution, or organic law, of the territories until statehood was attained. The land so organized was still largely unsettled, but the method of ongoing land distribution was set in 1785.[130] A committee headed by Senator William Grayson reported an ordinance that reserved a section of each township for the support of religion, the profits arising from it to be applied forever according to the will of a majority of male residents within the town. A motion to strike this transplantation of the New England town system succeeded even though the vast majority of delegates— seventeen of twenty-three and including Senators Rufus King and William Johnson—favored its retention.[131] Only Maryland and Rhode Island voted to strike, while the New York and North Carolina delegations divided. The remaining states present—Pennsylvania, Delaware, and Virginia among them—approved, but Grayson's proposal still fell short of the seven that the Articles of Confederation required to enact legislation.[132] Upon hearing of this near miss, Madison (who was not a delegate) wrote to James Monroe (who was): "How a regulation so unjust in itself, and smelling so strongly of an antiquated Bigotry could have received the countenance of a Committee, is truly a matter of astonishment."[133]

Madison was hardly preaching to the choir. Monroe had voted for the religious reservations, as had Virginia's other two delegates, Senators Lee and Grayson.[134]

In fact, the delegates accomplished the same end for most of the territory through subsequents acts, so that when the First Congress reenacted the Northwest Ordinance, it addressed a population that resided largely in towns with publicly supported churches. Much of the Ohio territory was sold by the confederation in chunks of several million acres to speculators for resale to individual buyers. In July of 1787 the Confederation Congress stipulated in a contract of sale to the Ohio Company that "lot No. 16" in each township be reserved for schools, and "lot No. 29" "be given perpetually for the purposes of religion."[135] Additionally two complete townships were held "for purposes of a university."[136] These recommendations, drafted by a committee of four, including Madison and First Congress colleague Egbert Benson, were also incorporated in another large purchase by a consortium headed by John Symmes.[137] In this there was little novelty for territorial residents, for prior to reoreganization under the Confederation, Ohio residents were subject to parish taxes, just as residents of the states—chiefly Connecticut—claiming the territory were.[138] Moreover, Connecticut reserved jurisdiction over a large piece of Ohio—the Western Reserve—and thus continued its own New England style of administration until 1802.[139]

Among those present and evidently voting for these sale provisions were Senators Lee, Grayson, and William Few of Georgia and Congressmen James Schureman (New Jersey) and Daniel Huger (South Carolina).[140] Grayson explained the reservation's rationale in a letter to George Washington: "The idea [public support of religion and education] holds forth an inducement for neighborhoods of the same religious sentiments to confederate for the purpose of purchasing and settling together."[141] Grayson might have added the view, elsewhere expressed,[142] that among the initial settlers would be a large percentage of rough-and-ready characters who needed a dose of religion to civilize them. The promoters capitalized on Grayson's notion. In newspaper advertisements during 1789 and 1790, the Ohio Company included a description of reserved lots for schools, religion, and a university as an incentive to relocate there.[143]

Illinois residents came into their publicly supported churches through a different route, although also via the offices of James Madison. In September 1788, just after the Virginia ratifying convention, Madison headed a committee of three that rectified an "omission" in previous acts governing "Illinois and Post St. Vincennes."[144] Omitted were "grants of land for Supporting Religion and for Schools" as had been done in western land sales. A tract of land adjoining each village "was reserved forever" for the "sole and only use of supporting the ministry of Religion in such Village."[145] Another tract was designated for schools.[146]

Land distribution policy converged with another strand of territorial administration in grants to missionary societies to underwrite conversion of the frontier Indians. Paying missionaries, including by 1803 Catholic priests,[147] to "propagate the Gospel among the heathens'' was a continuous feature of federal Indian relations from 1785 until at least 1896, when Congress was appropriating $500,000 annually in support of sectarian missions to the Indians. During the first decade after the Establishment Clause took effect, successive Congresses appropriated approximately 12,000 acres of land for one society, the United Brethren, for its efforts among the Indians in the Northwest Territories.[148]

This policy began with the initial distribution ordinance of May 20, 1785, which reserved three townships for the use of "Christian Indians" formerly settled there.[149] In July 1787, Congress enacted, along with the Northwest Ordinance, a reserve of 10,000 acres adjoining the towns and vested it in the United Brethren for "civilizing the Indians."[150] On September 3, 1787, Madison implemented the arrangement by reporting a recommendation that the geographer survey the designated tracts "as speedily as possible" and convey to the Brethren the "intermediate spaces" at the prevailing rates.[151] While not granting new lands, the Fourth, Fifth, Sixth, and Seventh Congresses all endorsed this arrangement with the United Brethren.[152]

The Unitas Fratrium, also known as the Moravians, was, and is, a communitarian Christian sect customarily cited as the first Protestant church. Its founder, John Hus of Bohemia, earned the title Reformer before the Reformation by being burned at the stake in 1415 for protesting abuses of the Roman Catholic church (a full century before Martin Luther's revolt).[153] In 1749 the British Parliament granted the Brethren privileged status in the colonies, recognizing it as an "ancient Protestant Episcopal Church," and the Moravians established a settlement in North Carolina by 1753.[154]

More important than its compelling pedigree was the sect's unique qualifications to be sent at public expense among the heathens: the United Brethren epitomized the aspirations of a nonestablishment Christian republic. It publicly professed a strict avoidance of sectarian controversy, disdaining points of difference among the various Protestant denominations. The Brethren espoused the "great truths held in common" and viewed the Bible, without sectarian gloss, as the standard of faith and practice. A sect without any hierarchy or formal structure, as well as a church without a creed, it was Scripture grounded and Christ centered. Moreover, except for conscientiousness objection to violence, the Brethren preached extreme submission to duly elected popular authority.[155] Living examples of nondenominational Protestantism, it is no wonder they were the first Protestant sect to undertake a mission to the Indians or that a Congress hampered by a nonestablishment stricture perceived no difficulty in paying them to do it.

The most interesting, but not the first,[156] instance of treaty obligations regarding sectarian missions came in 1803 when President Jefferson asked the Senate to ratify a treaty with the Kaskaskia Indians. The treaty required the United States to pay a Catholic priest $100 annually for ministrations to the tribe.[157] The document, which the Senate ratified,[158] also appropriated $300 for erection of a Catholic church.[159] Jefferson was hardly unique among presidents in employing religion for public purposes, especially among the Indians, but if he did so, who among the founding generation believed the Establishment Clause forbade aid to religion?[160]

The Northwest Ordinance of 1787 itself enjoined the "utmost good faith" on those dealing with the Indians. The text is further revealing of congressional sentiment in its inclusions of both a general and a specific guarantee of religious liberty alongside its exhortation to promote religion, morality, and schools.[161] Generally the 1787 act presumed to extend to the territories the "fundamental principles of civil and religious liberty" guaranteed by the state constitutions,[162] essentially what the First Amendment proposed to engraft on the national government itself. The first congressmen, even while debating the Establishment and Free Exercise clauses, did not hesitate to reenact the ordinance with its declaration of the necessity of religion and morality. After ratification of the Bill of Rights, Congress again did not hesitate to endorse the 1787 action in its entirety. During the incumbencies of Adams and Jefferson, Indiana (1800)[163] Michigan (1805),[164] and Illinois (1809)[165] territories were organized by simple application of the Northwest Ordinance. President Madison signed the bill organizing Missouri territory on basically the same footing, an act that explicitly incorporated the religion and morality clause of 1787.[166] Only the Eighth Congress, which divided the Louisiana purchase into Orleans and Louisiana territories, departed from form. It prohibited abridgment of civil liberties on account of religious belief and further declared void all territoral enactments that conflicted with the Constitution or laws of the United States.[167]

That each of the first four presidents and a majority of the first ten Congresses should specifically reenact a 1787 ordinance that harmonized religious liberty with the necessity of promoting religion and morality reveals that the First Amendment was, in their understanding of it, in harmony with the 1787 ordinance. What should establish beyond doubt that these federal actors—Jefferson and Madison among them—viewed aid, encouragement, and support of religion as consistent with the religious clauses are the territorial regimes themselves. The frontier lawmakers, subject to federal constitutional restraints, took the necessity of religion and morality to heart and established a legal panoply of public supports of religious institutions and Christian morality.

Orleans territory, which constituted the present state of Louisiana, is the most revealing instance. Specifically enjoined to respect the Constitution by President Jefferson and the Eighth Congress, the territorial legislature promptly proceeded to sponsor religious institutions. The territorial university was founded in 1805 on the cornerstone of "learning," "the ablest advocate of genuine liberty and the best supporter of rational religion."[168] In the 1806 incorporation of an Episcopal church in New Orleans, the assembly required appointment of a "faithful minister of Jesus Christ."[169] Neither this incorporation during Jefferson's administration nor that of a Catholic church shortly after Madison's inaugural[170] drew a response from the White House, despite Madison's 1811 veto of an incorporation act as an establishment. Nor did President Jefferson or Secretary of State

Madison protest when all religious property was exempted from taxation,[171] when Sabbath observance was enjoined,[172] when (as was common in Virginia) church construction was underwritten by a legislative exception to the ban on lotteries,[173] or when the legislature appointed the governor and the "person exercising the function of chief of the Catholic church" in the territory as superintendents of the New Orleans charity hospital.[174] President Madison lodged no objection to these practices in accepting Louisiana State into the Union or in subsequently setting up Missouri territory (formerly Louisiana territory) on the same footing as Orleans.[175]

One cannot assume that Madison was unaware of what the territorial legislatures were doing. His 1811 veto of the Mississippi appropriation for a Baptist church proves that he was aware, although his tolerance of similar practices in Orleans and his leadership in permitting precisely such assistance in the Northwest, make the Mississippi episode inexplicable. Obscured by Madison's veto was the underlying approval by both houses of the Eleventh Congress of aid to the church.

Central to the significance of the 1789 reenactment is the reality, undoubtedly known to Congress, that the territories were beginning to look like New England. James M. Varnum, formerly Rhode Island's representative to the Confederation Congress and by 1788 a supreme judge of the Northwest Territory, boasted in an Independence day address at Marietta, Ohio, that, mindful of "our" dependence on the "Supreme Will," territory residents "have not neglected the great principles and institutions of religion."[176] Indeed they had not. In addition to the public lots on which their churches stood, profane swearing, blasphemy, and Sunday labor were already prohibited.[177] Governor General Arthur St. Clair, along with Varnum and Samuel Parsons, also a supreme judge, spoke most forcefully to the former issues:

Whereas idle, vain and obscene conversation, profane cursing and swearing, and more especially the irreverently mentioning, calling upon, or invoking the sacred and supreme being, by any of the divine characters in which he hath graciously condescended to reveal his infinitely beneficial purposes to mankind, are repugnant to every moral sentiment, subversive of every civil obligation, inconsistent with the ornaments of polished life, and abhorrent to the principles of the most benevolent religion.[178]

Nor was Sunday just a convenient day of rest. The trio remarked of Sabbath observance:

Whereas mankind in every stage of informed society, have consecrated certain portions of time to the particular cultivation of the social virtues, and the public adoration and worship of the common parents of the universe: and whereas a practice so, rational in itself, and comfortable to the divine precepts is greatly conducive to civilization as well as morality and piety; and whereas for the advancement of such important and interesting purposes, most of the Christian world have set apart the first day of the week, as a day of rest from common labours and pursuits; it is therefore enjoined that all servile labour, works of necessity and charity only excepted, be wholly abstained from on said day.[179]

The rulers hoped to avoid the necessity of passing laws with specific penalties by simply "enjoining" observance.[180] This experiment in self-discipline failed. Eleven years later, the territorial legislature added penalties of between fifty cents and two dollars for each offense, with those unable to pay committed to two days of hard labor on town highways.[181]

Congress in 1800 carved Indiana Territory out of the Northwest,[182] leaving behind what became the state of Ohio, and until 1809 the territory comprised the present states of Indiana and Illinois.[183] The now-distinct Indiana legislature immediately imitated its predecessor. In 1807 while Jefferson was president, Indiana prohibited blasphemy, profanity, and wordly behavior on Sunday, with precisely the same $2 or two days penalty.[184] The territory, under Governor William Henry Harrison, was a prolific church incorporator. Granting one in 1807 to a group that in the legislature's words was devoted to propagating the "gospel of our blessed Savior Jesus Christ,"[185] the lawmakers at the same time absolutely prohibited the cutting of trees on land reserved, appropriated, or intended for the care and support of schools or religion.[186] On no other property did the prohibition apply. A rash of incorporations during the Madison administration,[187] about which, unlike the one in Alexandria, the president remained silent, included one containing a legislative preamble revealing the intentions behind the practice:

Whereas it is by the said general assembly believed that the propagation of the gospel contributes in an eminent degree to civilization, and that republican legislatures have, and ever ought to extend their constitutional aid to every institution, whose basis is religion, and whose object is general philanthropy, and improvement of the human species; that the incorporation of churches with proper restrictions, will be the sure means of diffusing the great and important truths contained in the Divine revelations.[188]

If Madison truly believed incorporation of churches violated the First Amendment, his conduct did not generally accord with his views. More important, his views did not accord with those of his contemporaries, for as the preamble explains, incorporation was granted by legislators acutely conscious of constitutional restrictions. The Indiana incorporation acts further reveal this awareness, for at least two of those surviving from Madison's tenure grant trustee power to "make such by-laws, ordinances and regulations in writing, not however, inconsistent with the constitution and laws of the United States" or of territorial laws.[189] Not only do these authorizations suggest a literal transplantation of the New England religious society in which civil authority enforced the tithes set by the trustees (and which Madison assured Huntington was consistent with the Establishment Clause); they reveal a collective body aiding religion and scrupulously avoiding constitutional prohibitions. The Supreme Court would deny the existence of these legislators, for the justices say the founding generation rendered "aid to religion" and "constitutionally valid" mutually exclusive categories.

NOTES

1. 1 *Annals of Congress* 257 (J. Gales ed. 1834)
2. Ibid. at 258–60.
3. H. Beeman, *The Old Dominion and the New Nation, 1788–1801* 93 (1972). Lee thus proved himself a resilient friend. In late 1786, he wrote Madison after hearing that he had been dropped from the Virginia congressional delegation in favor of Madison: "Your abandonment of a man who loved your character to excess and who esteemed your friendship among the first blessings of life connected with the circumstances of your election to the office from which he was dismissed, together with many other considerations which are unnecessary to repeat wound one deeply." Henry Lee to James Madison, December 20, 1796, in 8 *Letters of Members of the Continental Congress* 524 (E. Burnett 1936). Lee was later reinstated due to the resignation of another delegate.
4. Beeman, *Old Dominion*, at 23–24.
5. 3 Elliot's at 656.
6. Beeman, *Old Dominion* at 24 quoting Madison to Jefferson, October 17, 1786. See J. Goebel, 1 *History of the Supreme Court of the United States 413–14 (1975)*.
7. Beeman, *Old Dominion*, at 25.
8. Madison to George L. Turberville, November 2, 1788, in Goebel, 1 *History* at 426 n. 72.
9. Ibid. at 25.
10. Beeman, *Old Dominion*, at 25.
11. See, e.g., *Boston Independent Chronicle*, February 26, 1789.
12. Beeman, *Old Dominion*, at 26.
13. Robert Morris to Richard Peters, August 24, 1789, in Goebel, 1 *History*, at 446.
14. Pierce Butler to James Iredell, August 11, 1789, in *Life and Correspondence of James Iredell* 263–65 (Griffith McRee ed. 1857).
15. Ames to Timothy Dwight, June 11, 1789, in *Works of Fisher Ames* 52–53 (Seth Ames ed. 1854).
16. *Everson v. Board of Education* 330 U.S. 1, 39 (1962).
17. See, e.g., reiterations of Madison's centrality to First Amendment interpretation in W. Van Alstyne, "Trends in the Supreme Court: Mr. Jefferson's Crumbling Wall— A Comment on *Lynch v. Donnelly* 1984," *Duke L.J.* 770, at 773, 777–79; Richard E. Morgan, *The Supreme Court and Religion* (1972), at 24; Note, "Religion and Morality Legislation: A Reexamination of Establishment Clause Analysis," 59 *N.Y.U. Rev.* 301, 317–18, 358–60 (1984).
18. I. Brant, *The Life of James Madison* (1954); Brant, "Madison: On the Separation of Church and State," *Wm. & Mary Q.* 3d ser. 8 (January 1951), at 12; Robert L. Cord, *Separation of Church and State: Historical Fact and Current Fiction* (1982), at 20–36; and review essay by Dennis G. Stovers, 17 *Am. Pol. Sci. Rev.* 1030 (1983).
19. Cord, *Separation*, at 33.
20. Ibid. at 34.
21. See notes 135–47 and accompanying text.

22. Cord, *Separation*, at 34–35.

23. Drakeman, "Religion and the Republic: James Madison and the First Amendment," 25 *J. Church & St.* (1983), at 427–41.

24. That Madison did is most forcefully propounded (in addition to the *Everson* Court) by Irving Brant. The most forceful counter is C. Kruse, "The Historical Meaning and Judicial Construction of the Establishment of Religion Clause of the First Amendment," 2 *Washburn L.J.* 65 (1965). For a balanced discussion of the issue see Drakeman, "Religion," 429–434.

25. Morgan, *Supreme Court*, at 24.

26. In other words, ratification by the states, not Congressional proposal, makes it "law."

27. 1 *Annals* at 451.

28. Ibid. at 758.

29. Ibid.

30. Madison to Pendleton, June 21, 1789, in 5 *Documentary History of the Constitution of the United States* 179 (1894, 1965).

31. Goebel, 1 *History*, at 429.

32. 15 *Works of Jefferson* 22 (J. Boyd, ed. 1958).

33. Life of Iredell, at 263, 265 (Pierce Butler to James Iredell, August 11, 1789).

34. L. Levy, *Emergence of a Free Press* 264 (1985).

35. Goebel, 1 *History*, at 436–37.

36. Ibid. at 446.

37. Fisher Ames to George Richards Minot, July 23, 1789, in *Works of Ames* at 65–66.

38. Randolph to Madison, June 30, 1789 quoted in 2 A. Beveridge, *Life of Marshall* 59 (1917).

39. Ames to George Richards Minot, June 12, 1789 in 2 *Works of Ames* at 53–54.

40. Curry, *First Freedoms*, at 206. Leonard Levy suggests (*Emergence*, at 261) that some of this rhetorical trashing owed to the greater desirability of amendments altering the structure of the Constitution along the states' rights lines the speakers preferred. This is unlikely. Many of the most caustic commentators—Morris and Ames, for instance—were enthusiastic trashers. In other words, they thought the amendments trite regardless of their views on the constitutional structure. Second, Madison's proposals were inoffensive restatements of ideas whose time had arrived. Third, Levy fails to appreciate the effect of political strategies on the content of change; the purpose of amendments was to make a grand show of securing rights never in danger. Madison was keenly aware of this.

41. See Goebel, 1 *History*, at 432; 1 *Annals* at 449.

42. Fisher Ames wrote to George Richards Minot on July 2, 1789, of "the people of Virginia (whose murmurs, if louder than a whisper, make Mr. Madison's heart quake). 1 *Works of Ames* at 678, 680; to William Tudor on March 8, 1790: Madison "is so afraid that the mob will cry out, crucify him; sees Patrick Henry's shade at his bedside every night." Id. at 729; see also letter to Minot dated March 23, 1790, in id. at 729.

43. Madison to Pendleton, April 8, 1789, in Goebel, 1 *History*, n.76.

44. Brant, *Life*, at 267.

45. C. Wingate, 2 *Life and Letters of Paine Wingate* 221 (1930) (letter regarding Congressional chaplains); Ibid., at 438 (letter addressing public support of church construction); Ibid., at 485 (letter detailing his general devotion to New England orthodoxy).

46. J. Thorning, *Religious Liberty in Transition* 20 n. 26, (1931) (Strong helped draft Massachusetts Article III); William Dunne, *What Happened to Religious Education* 66–67 (1958). In 1801, Massachusetts Governor Strong made an impassioned plea to support the regime of public-supported orthodoxy noted earlier.

47. See *The Life and Correspondence of Rufus King* 50 (Charles R. King ed. 1894). See generally George Groce, *William Samuel Johnson: A Maker of the Constitution* (1937), at 13, 44, 45 (1937).

48. *Life of King* at 50.

49. See chapter 3, note 41, and accompanying text.

50. For background on Langdon, see L. Mayo, *John Langdon of New Hampshire* 214 (1937); on Schuyler, see B. Lossing, *The Life and Times of Maj. General Philip Schuyler* (1873). Dalton enjoyed a long, distinguished career in Massachusetts politics, holding several elected offices during the 1780s when various components of that state's sacred canopy were enacted. See the brief sketch in 1 *The Journal of the Senate* 5 (M. Claussen ed. 1977). Elbridge Gerry's biographer remarks that Dalton, like Izard and Morris, desired no amendments to the Constitution. James T. Austin, *The Life of Elbridge Gerry* 89 (1829).

51. See chapter 2, note 225, and accompanying text. See also K. Rowland, *Life and Correspondence of Charles Carroll or Carrollton* 182 (1898) (Carroll evidently introduced a bill to support Roman Catholic priests).

52. Rowland, *Life of Carroll*, at 115 (Henry, a pillar of Maryland's aristocratic regime, introduced in the same Maryland legislative session that sent him to the U.S. Senate a bill to incorporate religious societies). Henry, however, voted against the reservation of land for religious uses in the territory. See Ronald Smith, "Freedom of Religion and the Land Ordinance of 1785," 24 *J. Church & St.* 589, 596 (1982). The reason for this vote is unknown.

53. Few was continuously a member of the Continental Congress from 1777 until its dissolution and was present for many of the votes there concerning organization of the territories and the land sale contracts reserving land for religion. See Henry C. White, *Abraham Baldwin* 101, 113 (1926). Few later became mayor of New York City.

54. See chapter 2, notes 346–49, and accompanying text. See generally J. O'Connor, *William Paterson: Lawyer and Statesman, 1745–1806* (1979).

55. See chapter 2, notes 318–21, and accompanying text.

56. See L. Sikes, "The Public Life of Pierce Butler" (Ph.D. diss. University of Tennessee, (1973).

57. *The Journal of William Maclay* (Boni ed. 1927), at 145–48. The only member of the Senate not yet mentioned is New Jersey's Jonathan Elmer, a distinguished physician who served several terms in the Confederation Congress and in the state legislature, whom McCormick described as a "Federal Character," like Paterson and Elias Boudinot. R. McCormick, *Experiment in Independence* 289 (1980). Elmer descended from a long line of distinguished Presbyterians noted, according to a New Jersey historian, for their devotion to the cause of religion, and is perhaps the most elusive member of the First Senate.

58. See note 70 and accompanying text.

59. See note 83 and accompanying text.

60. 1 *Annals* at 468.

61. Ibid. at 685–88.

62. Smith, "Freedom of Religion," at 596.

63. See G. Boyd, *Elias Boudinot Patriot and Statesman* (1952).

64. See note 136 and accompanying text.

65. See chapter 1, notes 222–24, and accompanying text.

66. See chapter 3, note 74, and accompanying text.

67. 1 *Annals* at 757.

68. Ibid.

69. Ibid.

70. Curry, *First Freedoms*, at 202.

71. Ibid. at 758; Mary Virginia Geiger, *Daniel Carroll: A Framer of the Constitution* 83 (1943).

72. 1 *Annals* at 758.

73. Ibid.

74. *Everson* at 42, n. 34.

75. 1 *Annals* at 731.

76. 1 *Annals* at 759.

77. Ibid.

78. Ibid.

79. Ibid. at 796.

80. Ibid.

81. Butler to Iredell, August 11, 1789 in 2 *Life of Iredell*, at 265.

82. See 1 *Annals* at 757.

83. Ibid. at 807.

84. William Smith to Edward Rutledge, August 9, 1789, in 69 *S.C. His. Mag.* 1, 14 (1968).

85. Goebel, *History*, at 446.

86. Ibid. at 440.

87. Lee to Patrick Henry, May 28, 1789, in J. Ballagh, 2 *The Letters of Richard Henry Lee* 487 (1911).

88. *Maclay's Journal*, at 131. Among the named contemnors were Izard, Morris, and Langdon. Maclay remarked that the ''six-year'' class ''hung together on this business, or the most of them.'' Id. The other six-year senators were Johnson, Henry, and Gunn.

89. 1 *The Journal of the Senate* 116 (Martin P. Claussen ed. 1977).

90. Ibid. at 116–17.

91. Ibid.

92. Ibid. at 117.

93. Ibid. at 123.

94. *Maclay's Journal* at 140–48.

95. Brant, *Life of Madison*, at 264.

96. 1 *Senate Journal* at 116.

97. Wingate to Pickering, September 14, 1789, in Wingate, *Life and Letters* at 334.

98. Lee to Patrick Henry, September 14, 1789, in Ballagh *Letters* at 501.

99. Lee to Francis Lightfoot Lee, September 13, 1789, in ibid. at 500.

100. Ibid. at 524.

101. *Massachusetts Centinel*, September 26, 1789.

102. Wingate to Langdon, September 17, 1789, in Wingate, *Life and Letters*, at 334–35.

103. Madison to Pendleton, September 14, 1789, in Goebel, 1 *History*, at 454.

104. For a brief sketch of John Vining's life and career, see William Read, *Life and Correspondence of George Read* 501–6 (1870).

105. 1 *Annals* at 939; 2 *Senate Journal* at 142.

106. Levy, *Esablishment Clause* at 84.

107. See Lee and Grayson to Speaker of Virginia House of Representatives, September 28, 1789, in 5 *Documentary History of the Constitution of the United States* 217 (1894, 1965) (hereinafter cited as *Doc. History*).

108. R. Welch, *Theodore Sedgwick, Federalist* 77 (1965).

109. See chapter 5, notes 46–64, and accompanying text.

110. *Hampton Co. v. United States* 276 U.S. 394 (1928).

111. Ibid. at 412.

112. Sixteen members of the First Congress were signers of the 1787 Constitution: John Langdon, Nicholas Gilman, Rufus King, William Samuel Johnson, Roger Sherman, William Paterson, Robert Morris, George Clymer, Thomas Fitzsimmons, George Read, Richard Bassett, Daniel Carroll, James Madison, Pierce Butler, William Few, and Abraham Baldwin.

113. 1 *Annals* at 242.

114. Ibid. at 949, 959–60.

115. See, e.g., *Lynch v. Donnelly*, 465 U.S. 660, (1984).

116. Cord, *Separation*, at 51–52.

117. Rowland, *Life of Carroll*, at 118.

118. Cord, *Separation*, at 53.

119. Ibid.

120. Ibid.

121. 1 *Statutes at Large* 22 (1791).

122. See, e.g., A. Pfeffer, *Church, State and Freedom* 169 (1973); *Lynch*, 104 S. Ct. at 1381–82 (1984 Brennan, J., dissenting).

123. 1 *Annals* at 685.

124. 1 *Statutes at Large* 50–53 (ch. 8 1789).

125. Ibid. at 51.

126. Ibid. at 52 (Article III).

127. See chapter 5.

128. For example, Richard Henry Lee was president of the Confederation Congress that passed the Northwest Ordinance. Other members of the First Congress who voted for the ordinance in 1787 include James Schureman (New Jersey), William Grayson (Virginia), Daniel Huger (South Carolina), and William Few (Georgia). 32 *Journals of the Continental Congress* 63 (1936) (hereinafter cited as *Journal*). In addition, other members of the First Congress like Madison and Egbert Benson had participated in various land grants for religious purposes, as had Rufus King and William Samuel Johnson.

129. *Journal*, at 63.

130. Copy of Act in Payson Treat, *The National Land System 1785–1820, Appendix II* (1910).

131. Ibid., at 36.

132. *Life of King*, at 47.

133. Madison to Monroe, May 29, 1785, in 1 *Works of Madison* 154 (1865).

134. Chitwood, *Patrick Henry* at 160. See generally Smith, "Freedom of Religion."

135. Treat, *Land System*, at 50–51; *Life of King* at 50.

136. *Life of King* at 50.

137. Ibid.

138. See Sparks, 2 *Writings of George Washington* 181.

139. M. Greene, *The Development of Religious Liberty in Connecticut* 380–82 (1905).

140. See 32 *Journal* at 63; 8 *Letters*, at 621–22.

141. 8 *Letters* at 95.

142. See J. Pratt, *Religion, Politics, and Diversity: The Church-State Theme in New York History* 115 (1967).

143. *Massachusetts Centinel*, January 9, 1790.

144. 34 *Journal* at 540–42.

145. Ibid.

146. Ibid.

147. Cord, *Separation*, at 38.

148. Ibid. at 43–44.

149. See note 130: "And be it further ordained, that the towns of Grandenhutten, Schoenbrunn, and Salem, on the Muskingum, and so much of the lands adjoining to the said towns, with the buildings and improvements thereon, shall be reserved for the sole use of the Christian Indians, who formerly settled there, or the remains of that society, as may, in the judgment of the geographer, be sufficient for them to cultivate."

150. 33 *Journal* at 429–30.

151. 34 *Journal* at 485–87.

152. Cord, *Separation*, at 44.

153. J. Pfohland and A. Fries, *The Moravian Church; Yesterday and Today* 3–4 (1926).

154. Ibid. at 226.

155. Ibid. at 104–6.

156. A 1794 treaty with the Oneida Indians, for instance, obliged the United States to pay $1,000 toward building a "convenient church" in place of one burned by the British in "the late war."

157. Cord, *Separation*, at 38.

158. Ibid.

159. Ibid.

160. Justice Rutledge in *Everson* expressly denied that religious training at public expense could be used to further public purposes. See *Everson* at 52. That view is clearly one not attributable to even Thomas Jefferson, much less to the rest of the founding generation.

161. The specific guarantee was contained in Article I: "No person, demeaning himself in a peaceable and orderly manner, shall ever be molested on account of his mode of worship or religious sentiments, in said teintary." 1 *U.S. Statutes at Large* 51 n.a.

162. Ibid.

163. 2 *U.S. Statutes at Large* 58.

164. Ibid. at 309.

165. Ibid. at 514.

166. Ibid. at 743–47.

167. Ibid. at 238–39.

168. *States of Orleans Territory*, ch. 30, April 19, 1805.

169. Ibid. at ch. 5, May, 2, 1806.

170. Ibid. at ch. 10, March 8, 1809.

171. Ibid. at ch. 31, June 7, 1806.

172. Ibid. at ch. 33, June 7, 1806.

173. Ibid. at ch. 19, March 6, 1810.

174. Ibid. at ch. 6, March 8, 1808.

175. 2 *U.S. Statutes at Large* 743 (1812).

176. *Massachusetts Centinel* July 1, 1789, p. 1.

177. 2 *Collections of the Illinois State Historical Library* 21 (Law Series, T. Pease, ed. 1930).

178. Ibid.

179. Ibid.

180. Ibid.

181. Ibid. at 377–78.

182. 2 *Statutes at Large* 58.

183. Ibid. at 514–15.

184. Ibid. at 367 (1930).

185. Ibid. at 572–73.

186. *Laws of the Indiana Territory*, ch. 35 (1807).

187. Ibid. at ch. 9 (1913), Act of December 7, 1810.

188. Ibid.

189. Ibid.

5

Ratification of the First Amendment: The Whale Satisfied

Congress eventually approved twelve amendments to the Constitution and on September 26, 1789, asked President Washington to forward copies of them to the executives of the states, including the now "foreign" states of Rhode Island and North Carolina. Congress's work was completed, its constitutionally assigned function of "propos[ing]" alterations of the Constitution performed. Yet the amendments had no legal significance until ratified by three-fourths of the states, and the decisive act therefore is not congressional proposal but state assent. Madison saw this clearly. In an 1821 letter to Thomas Ritchie he investigated the "proposal-ratification" dilemma in the cognate context of the 1787 document. His remarks apply with equal force here:

As a guide in expounding and applying the provisions of the Constitution, the debates and incidental decisions of the Convention can have no authoritative character. . . . The legitimate meaning of the Instrument must be derived from the text itself; or if a key is to be sought elsewhere, it must not be in the opinions or intentions of the Body which planned and proposed the Constitution, but in the sense attached to it by the people in their respective State Conventions where it recd. all the Authority which it possesses.[1]

In theory, the understanding of the state legislators should govern historical interpretations of constitutional amendments, including the Establishment Clause.

Unhappily practice has not conformed to theory. Although the Supreme Court has generally affirmed the ascendancy of state ratification—relegating congressional debates to near insignificance—[2] the justices typically find the relevant history to be that of congressional speeches or the views, public or private, of prominent congressional players.[3] Their reasons are simple. The dominant feature of the state legislative record is silence. Comparing, for instance, historical evidence of the 1788 campaign, which included the whale's demand for amendments, to that of the 1790–1791 ratifications is like comparing what we know of the Vietnam War to our knowledge of the Peloponnesian War. The comparison with Congress is no less unequal. Although debates in the Senate were closed during the First Congress, the *Annals* extensively record House discussions, and the recollections of Pennsylvania Senator William Maclay pierce the Senate veil of secrecy. In contrast, state legislative journals of the early national period are as sparse as the generally unilluminating official Senate *Journal*.[4] Not a single state recorded debates, and individual voting behavior was rarely memorialized.

   Most important, not only did state legislators labor in relative obscurity, they were relatively obscure characters. In contrast, all the leading men of the founding generation participated in the great ratification struggle, and many of them served in the First Congress or in the Washington administration. In each instance and especially in the former, they were acutely aware of the magnitude of the historical moment and of the issues they debated and decided. Perhaps the most valuable sources of historical information, then, are the frequently voluminous memoirs and correspondence of these framers and the newspaper coverage of great deeds accomplished by great men. By contrast, ratification of the Bill of Rights was apparently perceived as anticlimactic; newspaper editors paid little attention to it, as did the great men, who went on the other business in the nation's capital. If the state legislators themselves left behind accounts of what they thought when they ratified the amendments, it has escaped the most careful historical detective work. Most judges and scholars have nevertheless too blithely succumbed to the common historiographical temptation to take what is available and make it authoritative. *Everson* is perhaps the extreme example. Jefferson and Madison were, along with Washington and Adams, the most prolific writers of their generation, and each took great care to preserve his personal papers. But there are some who have hesitated to take the path of least resistance, and Leonard Levy is the most celebrated refugee from among those captured by the accessible. His *Legacy of Suppression* gathers much from the evidence of silence. His argument, which assumed an existing, widely accepted definition of liberty of the press, reduces to the proposition that change is louder than continuity, that silence denotes the smooth and steady working of the law of inertia. His application of it was pathbreaking, but the idea was hardly novel. As long ago as 1807, Chief Justice Marshall, presiding over the trial of Aaron Burr, remarked that a "grand departure" from established practice would be clearly demarcated.[5] Raoul Berger made important use of the point in his study *Executive Privilege*,[6] but Levy's expression of it is closer to home and still classic:

If definition were unnecessary [if no one in the state legislatures bothered to explain that norms they were ratifying] because of the existence of a tacit and widespread understanding of "liberty of the press," only the received or traditional understanding could have been possible. To assume the existence of a general, latitudinarian understanding that veered substantially from the common-law definition is incredible, given the total absence of argumentative analysis of the meaning of the clause on speech and press. Any novel definition expanding the scope of free expressions of repudiating, even altering, the concept of seditious libel would have been the subject of public debate or comment.[7]

Nonestablishment, and in the relevant sense free exercise, were certainly subjects of widespread traditional understanding, and they did not occasion significantly more discussion in the states than did liberty of the press. The silent state legislators thus speak in loud, unmistakably clear voices that in ratifying the Establishment Clause, they forbade sect preference by the national government and in no way impaired the government's authority to aid, encourage, and support religion on a nondiscriminatory basis. This provides the operative meaning of the clauses, and it harmonizes with the views actually expressed during 1788 and in the First Congress.

But does this silence speak so resolutely? Professor Anderson, in his recent monograph on freedom of the press, thinks not. "The inference is dubious," Anderson says in express response to Levy. "The premise that lack of debate precludes new meaning is faulty. There is no reason why expansion of an existing concept [like liberty of the press] should require discussion if an adoption of entirely new ones does not."[8] Among the most obvious new norms in the Bill of Rights, Anderson finds the Establishment, Free Exericse, and Due Process clauses.[9] The first two are undoubtedly miscategorized, and the third probably is too.[10] In any event Anderson is on the wrong track in asserting that the Establishment clause, for instance, had "no established common-law meaning."[11] Whether it did or not, it does not follow that it was therefore new or that it had no established meaning. It was, in fact, a norm found in one form or another in every state constitution and found there after exhaustive discussion of its meaning. Also, each state knew what it was like to pass laws under the constraint of nonestablishment. Whatever the validity of Anderson's specific counterpunch to Levy's press freedom interpretation, his general denial of the footprints left by a grand departure is not made out. Indeed its logic is incomplete. The first place to look for settled meanings of Bill of Rights provisions is to the Confederation-era state constitutions, from which most of them were drawn. To look only for common law antecedents is inadequate.

The argument from quiet inertia is, in addition, much stronger here than Levy's application of it to freedom of the press. First, Anderson at least wins the battle because Levy's claim is for an unsullied passage from common law to constitution. Although press liberty appeared in the state constitutions, Levy's definition of it is drawn from common law (frequently British) sources,[12] not from debates in constitutional conventions or from discerning an editorial canopy of statutory scope sufficient to fix the clause's meaning. Moreover, freedom of speech had virtually no constitutional history at all,[13] so that Levy's use of the general point there is less secure than the general point itself. Second, freedom of the press, though mentioned in the 1788 ratification debate as often as freedom of religion, was rarely explained. There is no record of what the antifederalists feared the national government would do to the press comparable to the fears discussed in chapter 3 of this book. Third, nonestablishment was clearly defined, by words and by conduct, in the First Congress, which said almost nothing about liberty of the press and passed no laws evincing an interpretation of it. In combination, the inertial force thus collected in the religion clauses and aimed at the state legislatures far exceeded that of the speech and press clauses. Put metaphorically, if the tub received by the state legislatures was different from the one demanded by the state ratifying conventions (and from the identical one thrown by Congress), would silence have reigned? Fourth, the deviation championed by Anderson and resisted by Levy is minor[14] compared to the gulf between the traditional understanding of the religion clauses and that adopted by the Supreme Court. Put most forcefully, if instead of no sect preference the state legislators thought they were uprooting traditional relationships and ratifying the revolutionary dictate of no aid or encouragement whatsoever, would not there have been as least some noise?

To buttress the point, the silence in the state records is not that of a remarkable or uproarious event unrecorded; it is a fairly complete account of a truly unremarkable occurrence. The legislative journal of each state reveals various details of ratification,[15] and we even know something about the inaction of Massachusetts, Connecticut, and Georgia, states that did not ratify until the sesquicentenial year of 1939.[16] The journals reveal a ratification of the Bill of Rights that was (in composite profile) perfunctory, without significant debate or opposition, which treated all ten amendments as an undifferentiated lump and was accomplished with almost unseemly haste.

Questions informed by the Levy synthesis that need to be asked of these state sources include: Would the New Hampshire House of Representatives have accepted the religion clauses at all if they read it as the Court says it did, much less accept the Bill of Rights as a whole (as it did) at one sitting?[17] Would not that state's senate have spent more than part of one day before accepting the whole (as it did) if the Court is correct?[18] How could the Vermont General Assembly have considered the twelve amendments in grand committee, voted to recommend them to the whole House, passed them in that capacity, and then appointed a committee of three to draft a formal act of ratification, all on the same day, if a grand departure was intended?[19] How to explain the alacrity of the following day when the bill was read a first and a second time, accepted, sent to the governor and council of revision, and returned by them before the day's end?[20] Would Massachusetts have assented to what was to its residents a truly unthinkable no-aid rule, as both its house of representatives and senate did, each in no more than a day?[21] Would Pennsylvania have passed the Bill of Rights without opposition?[22] Would Delaware have done the same in less than a day?[23] Would the New York State Senate have passed them unanimously?[24] Would Rhode Island have ratified all twelve amendments in a single day?[25] Is it conceivable that Maryland departed from the no sect preference reading intended by Congress when the state legislature included Congressmen Joshua Seney,[26] George Gale, and Daniel Carroll,[27] the last of whom participated in the House debate and personally favored aid to religion? Or in the light of the controlling presence (as a member) of Senator Charles Carroll?[28] How to explain North Carolina's gliding through three readings in each house and passage of all twelve amendments in what appears to be less than a full day's work?[29] How can an unprecedented departure from tradition be squared with the nonchalance of states like North Carolina and New York, which not only obviously treated the Bill of Rights as a whole but sandwiched consideration of the amendments between consideration of other spectacularly mundane legislative business?[30]

Even the states refusing to consider the amendments confrim the traditional construction of the clauses. The Georgia legislature considered them long enough—apparently no more than minutes—to decide they were "unnecessary."[31] The upper house in Connecticut took the same position, although the lower chamber was willing to approve.[32] Neither of these states rejected the proffered changes; they were simply considered to be what federalists had called them all along: needless restatements of obvious truths. The record reveals not a single state, except Virginia, that more than respectably paused over the entire Bill of Rights, much less the religion clauses particularly. And the newspaper editors, usually avid, entirely partisan observers of things political, said almost nothing about the journey of the amendments through the states. That the architects of the sacred canopy should swallow the amendments so quietly, so completely, and so effortlessly cannot be squared with the departure urged by the Supreme Court.

Fortunately there is ample independent evidence that in fact the amendments proposed to the states were those asked for by the state ratifying conventions, thus closing the circle around the whale and his tub. The initial newspaper reaction to the congressional proposals was one of relief, portending an anticlimactic ratification by the states.[33] Echoed in the private correspondence of Madison[34] and Washington,[35] the general perception was that Congress had accurately and adequately quieted popular fears insofar as those fears were for personal liberty of the type encompassed by a Bill of Rights.[36]

Among the list of specific satisfied customers was North Carolina. Throughout the summer of 1789, North Carolina federalists stayed in close touch with Madison[37] and advised him of what was necessary, by way of amendments, to reassure the disaffected. William Richardson Davie summarized their needs to Madison as a "guarantee for the free exercise of their religious rights and privileges."[38] Moreover, the record of the 1788 North Carolina convention clearly reveals a paramount fear of domination by a single Protestant sect, coupled with an ardent desire to keep the United States Protestant. Clearly nothing like no aid had ever been part of that state's demands or of its own legistative scheme. When he forwarded the congressional product, Washington speculated that they were sufficient to entice North Carolina into the Union,[39] and within two months,

North Carolina ratified both the Constitution and the amendments.[40] (Washington was not so upbeat about Rhode Island, volunteering that "the majority of that People bid adieu long since to every principle of honor, common sense, and honesty."")[41]

Also contented were Virginia Baptists, whose support Madison assiduously cultivated throughout his career. Baptist disquiet had originally propelled Madison into the pro-amendment camp, and during the congressional debates, he was reminded by correspondents of their "alarm."[42] In November 1789 he was happy to report to Washington that the amendments proposed by Congress had "entirely satisfied the disaffected" of the sect.[43] What had been their fear? Baptist leader Isaac Backus said it was for "rights of conscience,"[44] which was then and thereafter consistent with state aid and support of religion. But the precise cause of alarm more likely appears in a reassuring address by Washington to the Virginia Baptist Associations. What the Baptists sought, the president wholeheartedly endorsed; therefore it is unlikely the Baptists were talking about prohibiting even a general assessment. (Washington supported it.) In fact, the "evil" complained of was the kind of persecution only recently outlawed in Virginia by section 16 of the Declaration of Rights. Washington hastened to state that "no one would be more zealous than myself to establish effectual barriers against the horrors of spiritual tyranny, and every species of religious persecution."[45]

The evidence most devastating to the no-aid thesis surfaces where the silence of the historical record gives way to explicit description of what the Establishment Clause meant. The *Federal Gazette* reflected on Madison's initial nonestablishment proposal: "No self-righteous or powerful church shall set up its impious domination over all the rest."[46] The *Massachusetts Centinel* reprinted this commentary in its Independence day 1789 issue.[47] More important are the surviving debates over the Establishment Clause from the Rhode Island convention convened in March 1790 to consider the original Constitution and twelve proposed amendments[48] and from the Virginia legislative debate of December 1789.[49]

The Rhode Island convention, held in South Kingston, failed to adopt the Constitution, but it recommended to a future conclave adoption of the proposed federal amendments. This initial gathering witnessed a brief exchange over the Establishment Clauses. An antifederalist delegate first opined that the states ought to be prohibited from establishing religion or infringing the rights of conscience.[50] Federalist Henry Marchant thought it was enough to keep it out of the federal government.[51] Then Benjamin Bourne, chief federalist spokesmen and soon to become one of Rhode Island's first senators, responded that there was no such danger in the states in view of "the highest practice and the present General Sentiment of the World on this Subject."[52] Bourne was hardly ignorant of the illiberal practices in neighboring states but instead capitalized on Rhode Island's notorious libertarianism. He remarked that if states should again persecute as they did to "our Ancestors" (mentioning Roger Williams), "it will be a Means of Accession to this State."[53] That a Rhode Islander should define the religion clauses as a common denominator of universal sentiment while drawing attention to New England orthodoxy puts the amendment in the traditional understanding of it and not in Rhode Island's own latitudinarian reading of religious freedom. The Rhode Island legislature supplied further evidence of the clause's meaning in its June 1790 ratification of the Bill of Rights.[54] (A second convention, in May 1790, ratified the Constitution and passed on to the legislature the Kingston meeting's endorsement of the Bill of Rights.)[55] The legislators promptly ratified all but the second proposed amendment (concerning congressional compensation) and in addition recommended further alterations to Congress. That the Rhode Island General Asembly did not understand the First Amendment guarantees to accomplish much at all is clear from their fourth recommendation for further alteration, which was section 16 of the Virginia Declaration of Rights "that no particular religious sect or society ought to be favored or established by law, in preference to others.[56]

The congressional amendments received their initial hearing in Virginia's General Assembly during the first week of November and were discussed off and on throughout that month.[57] Madison no doubt happily witnessed the House of Delegates' adoption of all twelve on November 30, 1789, especially since all of Patrick Henry's tactical maneuvers to prevent consideration finally came to naught.[58] But antifederal resistance was far from stilled. The Virginia Senate, prompted by Henry, Grayson, and Richard Henry Lee, rejected what are now the First, Sixth, Ninth, and Tenth amendments as "too weak."[59] A Madison confidant reported, no doubt correctly, that behind the move was a desire to discredit the new government in Virginia by holding the religion, press, and jury trial guarantees hostage.[60] Also, antifederalists feared that acceptance of the amendments proposed would break the popular fever for change short of the more far-reaching structural changes they had long sought. But whatever the motives, the Virginia Senate accompanied its rejection with a detailed critique of each reject. The senators correctly understood the religion clauses as responsive to the concerns of the Virginia convention expressed in the nineteenth and twentieth proposed articles of amendment.[61] These were, in short, section 16 of the Delcaration of Rights, no sect preference, and exemptions from militia duty for conscientious objectors.[62] Of the Establishment and Free Exercise clauses they wrote:

The 3rd amendment, recommended by Congress, does not prohibit the rights of conscience from being violated or infringed; and although it goes to restrain Congress from passing laws establishing any national religion, they might, notwithstanding, levy taxes to any amount, for the support of religion or its preachers; and any particular denomination of Christians might be so favored and supported by the General Government as to give it a decided advantage over others, and in process of time render it as powerful and dangerous as if it was established as the national religion of the country.[63]

Leonard Levy speaks of the "unbelievable inaccuracy" of the senators' account of free speech and press and seems to pass the same judgment on their view of the religion clauses.[64] The truth is quite the reverse. The report is literally accurate in noting the absence of a conscience guarantee in what was intended by Congress to diminish the protections suggested by "conscience" as opposed to "exercise." The Senate's next interpretation is quite correct: a national religion could not be established, but that did not mean no financial aid to religion. Finally, the senators do not say, as Levy says they did, that Congress may prefer one denomination, though that was surely the impression they intended to convey. But they did so by raising the prospect of a subtle, long-developing insinuation into power that might eventually have the effect of an establishment. The Senate critique was certainly a politically charged, hyperbolic statement but in that regard not nearly the equal of the "Memorial and Remonstrance" eagerly embraced as gospel by the Supreme Court. And however "inaccurate," the senators published their interpretation in the Richmond paper, and it stands as the clearest, most concise, most authoritative definition of the religious clauses in the entire history of ratification by the states.

NOTES

1. Quoted in C. Wolfe, *The Rise of Modern Judicial Review* 34 (1986).

2. *Maxwell v. Dow*, 176 U.S. 581, 601–2 (1900).

3. See, e.g., *Brown v. Board of Education*, 347 U.S. 483 (1954); *Williams v. Florida*, 399 U.S. 78, 92–97 (1970).

4. R. Rutland, *The Birth of the Bill of Rights, 1776–1791* (1955).

5. *United States v. Burr*, F. Case 14693 (1807).

6. R. Berger, *Executive Privilege: A Constitutional Myth* 35 (1976).

7. L. Levy, *Legacy of Suppression* 224–25 (1960). Levy reiterated the point in his revision of *Legacy, The Emergence of a Free Press* 267 (1985).

8. D. Anderson, "The Origins of the Press Clause," 30 *UCLA L. Rev.* 455, 486 n. 192 (1983).

9. Ibid.

10. See G. Gunther, *Constitutional Law: Cases and Materials* 477 (10th ed. 1980).

11. Anderson, "Origins," at 486 n. 192.

12. Levy, *Legacy*. In his preface Levy capsulizes the traditional understanding as Blackstonian.

13. Anderson, "Origins," at 465.

14. Levy maintained that the Blackstonian conception included only freedom from prior restraints. Levy, *Legacy*, at x.

15. See notes 17–30 and accompanying text.

16. J. Nowak, R. Rotunda, and N. Young, *Constitutional Law* 1117 (2d ed. 1983).

17. *A Journal of the Proceedings of the Honorable House of Representatives of the State of New Hampshire*, January 25, 1790.

18. *A Journal of the Proceedings of the Honorable Senate of the State of New Hampshire at a Session of the Great Court*, January 20, 1790.

19. *A Journal of the Proceedings of the General Assembly of Vermont Session at Windsor*, November 2, 1791.

20. Ibid., November 3, 1791.

21. *Massachusetts Centinel*, February 21, 1790.

22. R. Brunhouse, *The Counter Revolution in Pennsylvania 1776–1790* 215 (1942).

23. House of Assembly at a Session Commenced at Dover on Monday the Fourth Day of January 1790 (for January 22, 1790).

24. *Journal of the Senate of the State of New York*, January 26, 1790.

25. General Assembly of Rhode Island and Providence Plantations, begun and held in adjournment at Newport, June 7, 1790.

26. See *Votes and Proceedings of the House of Delegates of the State of Maryland*, November 9, 1789.

27. *Votes and Proceedings of the State of Maryland*, November 25, 1789.

28. Ibid.

29. See *Journal of the House of Commons*, November 23, 25, 26, 30, December 5, 1780; *Journal of the Senate*, November 24, December 8, 1789.

30. North Carolina simultaneously considered bills to extend military authority of the state to the inhabitants south of the French Brood and Holstein Region; for empowering county courts to appoint patrols; to establish boundaries of land granted to one Charles Gerard; to ratify amendments to the Constitution of the United States; and to enable creditors more easily to recover their debts from joint partners and upon joint notes. *Journal of the House of Commons*, November 25, 1789. The New York Assembly forwarded a cache of two bills for consideration by the Senate: one "for the appointment of an Auditor, and the settlement of the public accounts of this state "and another" ratifying in addition to an amendment of the Constitution of the United States of America, proposed by Congress." *Journal of the Senate of the State of New York*, February 22, 1790.

31. J. Bland, *Georgia and the Federal Constitution* 12–15 (1937).

32. T. Curry, *The First Freedoms; Church and State in America to the Passage of the First Amendment* 215 (1986).

33. See, e.g., *Pennsylvania Journal* October 14, December 30, 1789; Massachusetts *Centinal* July 4, 1789.

34. Edward Carrington to Madison, December 20, 1789, in 5 *Documentary History of the Constitution of the United States* 227 (1894, 1965) (hereinafter cited as *Doc. Hist.*); James Madison to George Washington, November 20, 1789, in ibid. at 215.

35. Dr. Stuart to George Washington, September 12, 1789, in 5 *Doc. His.*, at 205; George Washington to Governor Morris, October 13, 1789, in ibid. 212; D. Humphreys to George Washington, October, 29, 1789, in ibid. at 213.

36. Except in Virginia. See notes 56–64 and accompanying text.

37. See, e.g., William Davie to James Madison, in B. Robinson, *William R. Davie* 214 (1957); Benjamin Hawkins to Madison, June 3, 1789, in "Unpublished Letters from North Carolina to James Madison and James Monroe," 14 *N.C. Hist. Rev.* 156, 165 (1937).

38. Robinson, *Davie*, at 214

39. 5 *Doc. Hist.* at 229.

40. See note 29 and accompanying text.

41. 5 *Doc. Hist* at 229.

42. James Manning to Madison, August 29, 1789, in 5 *Doc. Hist.* at 215.

43. Madison to Washington, 5 *Doc Hist.* at 215.

44. Manning to Madison, 5 *Doc. Hist.* at 215.

45. *Columbian Centinel*, November 17, 1790, p. 1.

46. Reprinted in *Massachusetts Centinel*, July 4, 1789.
47. Ibid.
48. *Theodore Foster's Minutes of the Convention* (R. Cotner ed. 1790).
49. H. Beeman, *The Old Dominion and the New Nation, 1788–1801* 62–66 (1972).
50. *Foster's Minutes* at 58.
51. Ibid.
52. Ibid.
53. Ibid.
54. Ibid. at 24–26.
55. Ibid. at 26; P. Conley, *Democracy in Decline* 115 (1977).
56. Refer to chapter 3, note 97, and accompanying text.
57. Beeman, *Old Dominion*, at 62.
58. Ibid.
59. Ibid.
60. Hardin Burnely to Madison, November 5, 1789, in 5 *Doc. History* at 214–215.
61. K. Rowland, *Life of George Mason* 321 (1853).
62. 2 *Doc. History* at 380.
63. Rowland, *Life of Mason*, at 321.
64. Levy, *Legacy*, at 231 n. 1178.

6

The Founders' Worldview: The Sacred Canopy Explained

What the congressional framers and state ratifiers understood by nonestablishment was no sect preference. Joseph Story thus accurately captured the relevant meaning. When the First Amendment was adopted, "the general, if not the universal sentiment in America was, that Christianity ought to receive encouragement from the state, so far as it was not inconsistent with the private rights of conscience and the freedom of religious worship."[1] That the amendment conditioned the manner in which government aided religion, rather than banning all aid, is a distinction that has eluded the Supreme Court. But not Story: "An attempt to level all religions, and to make it a matter of state policy to hold all in utter indifference, would have created universal disapprobation at the time of the adoption of the Constitution."[2]

Story was right. But before elaborately verifying his proposition with historical evidence, it is important to appreciate just what he has gotten hold of. *Everson* grabbed onto the same thing: the Court's "freedom-loving colonials" constitute Story's sentimental universe. Whether such broadly brushed attributions are accurate is one question—and it is clear that Story and the *Everson* Court cannot both be right—the validity of the method displayed is another. And it is questionable, for these are assertions about a critical, relevant portion of the founders' intellectual infrastructure, their mentality or gestalt. The reader may choose any term that correspondingly marks an outer limit on where thought can lead. A good one is horizon, connoting a boundary beyond which vision, whether with one's eyes or one's mind, is impossible. "Separation of church and state," walled or otherwise, is a notion possible only in societies that (1) have clearly differentiated the sacred from the profane, where God's due and Caesar's are distinguished, (2) have a state in the Western sense that is clearly distinguished from society and culture, a concept of state that begins only with the sixteenth century, and (3) that organize religion into some concrete institution properly denoted a church. These factors coalesce only in modern, chiefly Western, societies. That such a separation, where comprehensible, should be thought desirable is quite likely only a product of a twentieth-century Western secularism. In other cultures, such as the theater state described by Clifford Gertz in his *Negara*, separation of church and state is as fathomable as a lecture to a blind person on color. The point is that there are such limits on speculation in every social circumstances, and speculation about the purposive ordering of social norms—that is lawmaking—is similarly bounded. Getting to that boundary line is a matter of unpacking the universal sentiment noted.

Story's observation was rooted in a pair of related premises that wrought an indelible fusion of nondenominational Protestantism and republican government in the early American mind. The first of these notions primarily involved the believer's conception of Protestantism as the consummation of religious development. "In the eighteenth century," says one historian of American religion, "most Americans believed that Protestant Christianity had gathered up within itself the excellences of the Old Testament and, having cleaned itself of the corruptions of Roman Catholicism, now englobed the 'great fundamental principles' of religion."[3] Perhaps the fundamental "fundamental" was individualism in matters of conscience. This was not the fundamental freedom connoted by modern constitutional norms like privacy and autonomy but an ordered liberty that can best be understood in relation to its obverse, Roman Catholicism.

As Elwyn Smith noted, the fundamental Protestant critique of Catholicism was that conscience, "the court of God, was usurped by pope and priests."[4] It was liberated not by unshackling the individual from social obligations, even if they were grounded in orthodox Christianity, but by disciplined recourse to the sacred book. Moral autonomy meant only freedom of access to the commands of God unfiltered by "jesuitical" influences. Even if best understood as simply an antiauthoritarian ecclesiology, this spiritual individualism sufficiently mingled with the premises of republican institutions to generate a single public philosophy. As John Courtney Murray said, religious and political truth were "indisolubly wedded as respectively the religious and the secular aspects of one manner of belief, the one way of life."[5] Appropriately described as an "implicit Protestant establishment" the belief was that "Protestantism in religion . . . produced republicanism in government."[6]

This first notion was filled out by the slightly different contention that the general principles of Christianity both defined and united Americans. Much more than an accurate sociological observation (which it was), John Adams suggested that unity on these general principles made the Revolution possible,[7] an interpretation borne out by the "why" of disestablishment in 1776[8] and evident in the objections to the Article VI ban on religious tests.[9] Benjamin Rush of Pennsylvania, signer of the Declaration of Independence and zealous social reformer, concisely expressed this understanding in a letter to a Universalist theologian. "Republican forms of government are the best repositories of the Gospel," Rush wrote; "I therefore suppose they are intended as prelude to a glorious manifestation of its power and influence upon the hearts of men."[10] One newspaper correspondent wrote in 1789 that Protestantism was the "Bulwark of our Constitution."[11] In short, eighteenth-century Americans viewed the United States as party to a national convenant with God. This cultural hegemony of "republican Protestantism" did not end until the twentieth century, if indeed it ended then.

The second equally powerful engine of social thought has to do with the "missing" Federalist Paper. If liberty presupposed a virtuous citizenry, as Madison maintained in the Federalist Papers,[12] how would the citizenry be kept virtuous? The experimenters in liberty knew that particular habits and traits were essential to self-government. They also knew that, in Walter Berns's formulation of it, they were limited with respect to the means they could adopt to generate the necessary character.[13] As Story put the question: "It yet remains a problem to be solved in human affairs, whether any free government can be permanent where the public worship of God, and the support of religion, constitute no part or of the policy or duty of the State in any assignable shape."[14]

Religion was central to the solution. That Madison's perception was central to the founding generation's thinking is certain. It is expressed in literally countless legislative acts, including the Northwest Ordinance passed by the First Congress. Just as certain is that most of the founders individually could not separate virtue and morality from religion. "Of all the dispositions and habits which lead to political prosperity, Religion and Morality are indispensable supports," Washington said in his Farewell Address.[15] "And let us with caution indulge the supposition, that morality can be maintained without Religion. Whatever may be conceded of the influence of refined education on minds of peculiar structure; reason and experience both forbid us to expect that national morality can prevail in exclusion of religious principle."[16] Reasoning almost precisely the same as Washington's induced Richard Henry Lee to support the 1785 general assessment.[17] John Adams thought that "religion and virtue" were the only foundations not only of republicanism "but of social felicity under all governments and in all the combinations of human society."[18] Jefferson feared for a future America shorn of Christian morality,[19] and even extreme Baptist hostility to New England orthodoxy did not deviate from Washington's caution. Indeed, Reverend Isaac Backus endorsed the animating impulse of Puritan establishments: religion "keeps alive the best sense of moral obligation . . . The fear and reverence of God, and the terrors of eternity are the most powerful restrains upon the minds of men. And hence it is of special importance in a free government, the spirit of which being always friendly to the sacred rights of conscience; it will hold up the Gospel as the great rule of faith and practice."[20]

With this intellectual infrastructure, it is not only easy to see why the founders did not do as the Supreme Court said they did, but it is impossible to see how they could have. Where "Protestant" and "American" were conjoined in the popular mind, the wall of separation—what Paul Freund defined as the "mutual abstention" of the religious and political caretakers[21]—is simply anachronistic. So long as the framers believed that liberty depended on faith, one cannot say that they erected a constitutional barrier to promoting religion. That would, as the framers saw it, make the Constitution a suicide pact.

The framers' horizon is evident in and largely explains two great early American legislative traditions, and it is by these fruits that we shall know of the implicit establishment and the "missing" Federalist Paper. First, given the identification of Protestantism with republican government, it is easy to see why Roman Catholics were the object of discrimination. The Church of Rome was not only a grand spiritual conspiracy against Protestantism, it was politically subversive as well. Roger Sherman's biographer relates his subject's abhorrence of the Catholic church as partly a product of his faith in the new Republic, which was founded on Christianity as he understood it.[22] Indeed for both Sherman and Rufus King, the identity of Christianity—as they understood it—and the United States produced hostility to Anglicanism as well.[23] King wrote to Elbridge Gerry in 1785, upon hearing of Bishop Seabury's appointment to the American episcopacy, in critical terms that each no doubt would have aplied to the Roman church: "I never wished to see the lawn sleeves in America. I never liked the hierarchy of the Church—an equality in the teachers of Religion, and a dependence on the people, are Republican sentiments."[24]

The smothering of conscience by a tyrannical Roman clergy attained the status of popular axiom in the early national period and, like Rhode Island, reigned as a kind of rhetorical extreme wholly negative, and un-American, in its connotation. "Cassius," a federalist pamphleteer, in 1788 accused antifederalists of "presumptuousness in the highest degree" for offering the people "palpable falsehoods" masquerading as cogent arguments. "Their conduct seems to evince, that they harbour sentiments similar to those of the Romish priests, in countries where the common people have scarcely any knowledge . . . and imbibe their principles wholly from what priests think proper to inform them."[25] Cassius boasted that "such artifices" will not succeed upon the inhabitants of America.[26] As late as 1813, John Adams complained to Jefferson that "denunciations of the priesthood" were fulminated against proponents of complete religious freedom.[27] "Jesuitical" was, in popular parlance, what you called a person after running out of epithets like "scoundrel" and "Tory." Even Adams surrendered to the sway of jargon. To prove his point to Jefferson that conscience is always present and that no individual is thus ever completely depraved, he allowed that "Popes, Jesuits, and Sarbonnists, and Inquisitors, have some conscience and some religion."[28]

The fulminations were not baseless. While the nineteenth century, especially the pontificate of Pius IX, is better known for Roman Catholicism's high-profile, unrelenting assault on "liberalism,"[29] that was hardly a retreat from an earlier period of accommodation. An 1832 encyclical letter of Pope Gregory summarized the church's teaching on, or more precisely its disdain for, religious freedom:

"From that polluted fountain of indifference flows that absurd and erroneous doctrine, or rather raving," liberty of conscience.[30] Americans concluded, in the words of Reverend J. F. Berg of Philadelphia, "The pontiff is clearly committed against the first principles of American freedom and regards them as unmitigated abominations."[31]

One solution to the "Catholic" problem—how could Catholics be good Americans?—was to conclude that they could not, and to do everything possible to keep Catholics out of the United States. John Jay favored this solution, and it can be readily seen in Maryland's pre-Revolutionary tax on "papists" and inferred from much of the mourning for Article IV's failure to permit religious tests. A moderate approach was instead adopted by virtually all the states: prevent Catholics from infecting the government by excluding them from public office, or the franchise, or both. The liberal response was to admit Catholics to the body politic in full confidence that they would not long remain Catholic. Embracing Jay's premise while rejecting his conclusion, Catholics could be good citizens so long as they thought and behaved like Protestants. Formal conversion was not important as long as the individual Romanist was sufficiently socialized by Protestant culture and institutions. Reverend Lyman Beecher articulated the "American" response to Catholics in terms that have since dominated this country's historical treatment of immigrant groups, perhaps most especially Catholics:

Let the Catholics mingle with us as Americans and come with their children under the full action of our common schools and republican institutions and the various powers of assimilation and we are prepared cheerfully to abide the consequences . . . If they could read the Bible . . . their darkened intellect would brighten and if they dare to think for themselves, the contrast of Protestant independence with their thraldom, would awaken the desire of equal privileges and put an end to an arbitrary clerical dominion over trembling superstitious minds."[32]

The post-Revolutionary common school indeed was the "indelible fusion" incarnate, society's second broad attempt to perpetuate itself and God's truth by educating its young in Protestant fundamentals. That schools occupied this unique niche can be gleaned from matters already discussed. The Northwest Ordinance, closely inspected, implies that schools would ensure good government by inculcating religion, morality, and knowledge. Federally subsidized sectarian missions among the "heathens" bespoke, in purpose and in rhetoric, an identity between "assimilate" and "Christianize." It can be seen in the five early state constitutions that provided for education and speak just as much of religion as of schools. Broadly, in the period immediately after the War of Independence, the importance of education in fostering religious and republican values was second perhaps only to the family's.[33] According to Pennsylvania's Benjamin Rush and others, the educator was critically significant in shaping and inspiring the new American heart. This was so because the truths of republicanism and

Christianity were so intimately associated that common schools could and should serve as the medium for growing wise and good men.

Plans calling for a publicly supported and systematized education of children were advanced in this early national period. In theory, public education inculcated not only reading, writing, and arithmetic in common (primary level) schools but fostered religious and moral virtue. At their core, this vision comprised beliefs that religion had social utility (the preservation of republican order through brotherly love) and importance for the individual (the salvation of the soul through union with God achieved by reading of Scriptures).[34] Although statewide plans of tax-supported primary-to-college schooling did not mature until the mid-nineteenth century, the notion of a pious, literate population was already well emplaced.[35] But publicly supported colleges also had a religious mission. In establishing a state university in 1785, the Georgia legislature declared that a free government "can only be happy where the public principles and opinions are properly directed, and their manners regulated. This is an influence beyond the Stretch of Laws and punishments and can be claimed only by Religion and Education. It should therefore be among the first objects of those who wish well to the national prosperity to encourage and support principles of religion and morality, and early to place the youth under the forming hand of society, that by instruction they may be molded to the love of virtue and good order."[36] The federal law incorporating Indiana's territorial university in 1807 contained a similar preface.[37]

Newspapers for the years 1789–1790 further reveal a reading (and voting) public interested in the purposes of education, especially in its capacity to make offspring of the "worst" sort of people safe for democracy.[38] A letter to the editor of the *Columbian Centinel* appearing on June 26, 1790, recognized the utilitarian value of instructing Negro children at government expense; schooling in the principles of religion and morality was the "best security for their industry and honesty."[39] The *Pennsylvania Observer* advised in 1790 that public support of schools for "children of poor people" would ensure that "they will never be the instruments of injuring mankind."[40] The printer of a newly published *Independent Catechism* heralded it in a *Boston Gazette* advertisement as an instructional book for both home and schools. The publisher declared that such a catechism was especially desirable under the new republican form of government in that "particular attention ought to be paid to the religious education of youth,— without virtue and piety we never can look for a good administration of government, or for happy and prosperous times."[41] These are but a few examples of the school as a religiously grounded institution of social control.[42]

The actual practice of education conformed to its founders' vision of it. Public schools wholly funded and administered by the state were largely concentrated in New England, were thoroughly religious,[43] and bore the stamp of Congregational hegemony. There, the early national Puritan tradition maintained that children needed literacy to read the Bible and to run commerce. Massachusetts's 1789 act mandated that every town of fifty households provide a schoolmaster to teach children already possessing the rudiments of reading and spelling the following subjects: reading, writing, grammar, arithmetic, orthography, and decent behavior, as well as the principles of piety and love of country. The act authorized all parishes and precincts to vote the raising of taxes to carry out the duty to hire a schoolmaster. Failure to comply resulted in a penalty or fine. School teachers were required to obtain a certificate that he or she was a person of sober life and conversation and well qualified to teach. This certification had to come from both the selectmen of the town and from a learned minister settled in the vicinity.[44]

The town of Boston adopted a proposal for the creation of a system of education in 1789, open to all students who possessed the ability to read and spell. The Bible and other texts were specifically listed for use in the reading classes. The Boston School Committee determined, four weeks after passage of the school plan, that the schoolmasters had the "indispensable duty . . . daily to commence the duties of their office by prayer, and reading a portion of the sacred scriptures, at the hour assigned for opening the School in the Morning; and close the same in the evening with prayer."[45] This committee two weeks later voted a provision that apparently attempted to ensure parents that the particular doctrines of the Congregationalist church would not be foisted on those of other Protestant denominations. On December 28, 1789, the committee voted that

the several School-Masters instruct the Children under their care, or cause them to be instructed in the Assemblies' Catechism, every Saturday, unless the parents request that they be taught any particular Catechism of the religious Society to which they belong; and the Masters are directed to teach such children accordingly.[46]

At stake was not religion in the public schools, for it was inconceivable that it should not be; religion was a raison d'être of the schools in the first place. Sectarianism was the issue, and with Massachusetts as a case study, one can see how the fight to get sect out of the public school was compatible with and even propelled by a desire to keep religion in it. In the process one can see the reflection of disestablishment: sectarian squabbles and preferences had no place in the public square, but state support of nondenominational religion was vital to the country's survival.

This reflection was not easily brought into focus. In 1827 Massachusetts passed a comprehensive school code,[47] section 7 of which addressed the subject of textbook costs and concluded with the following proviso:

Provided, also that said [district school] committee shall never direct any school books to be purchased or used, in any of the schools under their superintendence, which are calculated to favor any particular religious sect or tenet.[48]

During the 1830s sectarian conflict remained the bane of the classroom. Horace Mann, secretary to the state board of education in Massachusetts from 1837 to

1848 and the object of Frankfurter's attention in *McCollum*, led a crusade against denominational proselytizing in the public schools. His annual reports to the board bewailed that problem yet forcefully argued for the continued necessity of moral instruction in the school. Because Mann was sometimes attacked as irreligious by advocates of public school sectarian education, Mann repeatedly asserted his belief in the necessity of promoting moral and religious values, by which he meant pan-Protestant theology.[49]

To back up his claim that the new centralized approach to public schooling embodied in the state board of education had not reduced religious instruction, Mann documented the use of the Bible in school throughout the entire state. His Eighth Annual Report (1845) reported to the state board that of the 308 towns in the state, "the Bible is prescribed by the [local school] committees as one of the reading books to be used in the schools, in 258 . . . In three towns, only, it is found that the Scriptures have not been,—or not been generally,—used in the schools." Indeed, Mann's solution to the problem of sectarian catechietical teaching was to read from the King James version of the Bible,[50] a settlement acceptable to the state's residents until large numbers of Catholics rocked the boat in the latter part of the nineteenth century.

New Hampshire also passed a comprehensive school act in 1789 requiring that schoolmasters be certified by what amounted to the local clergymen.[51] This law for the first time authorized town selectmen to tax residents for school purposes. That this assessment served identifiably religious ends is evident from an early description of the curriculum:

The text-books for many years were few in number and scarcely any two like, except the Testament and the Psalter, which were used for reading and spelling in the more advanced classes. The New England Primer was about the only book used by the younger pupils. They contained . . . the Shorter Catechism, "Prayers for the Young," general rules to incline children to lead pious lives, and religious verses like the "Cradle Hymn" of Dr. Watts . . . The Catechism was the most distinguishing feature of the book. A preface to the reprint . . . says: "Our Puritan Fathers brought the Shorter Catechism with them, across the ocean, and laid it on the same shelf with the family Bible. They taught it diligently to their children every Sabbath."[52]

Connecticut's school were apparently indistinguishable from those of its Puritan neighbors.[53]

What has been described as the New England bibliocracy admitted no exception in libertarian Rhode Island. As late as 1820, Providence public school teachers received the following injunction from the governing school committee:

That they endeavor to impress on the minds of the scholars a sense of the Being & Providence of God & their obligations to love & reverence Him,—their duty to their parents & preceptors, the beauty & excellency of truth, justice & mutual love, tenderness to brute creatures, the happy tendency of self government and obedience to the dictates of reason & religion; the observance of the Sabbath as a sacred institution, the duty which they owe to their country & the necessity of a strict obedience to its Laws, and that they caution them against the prevailing vices.[54]

Of the middle colonies, New York was the most active proponent of public education in the early national period. A 1782 act[55] reserving 400 acres of frontier land for schools (400 were also reserved for "support of the gospel") was supplemented by acts in 1786,[56] 1790,[57] 1801,[58] and 1813[59] establishing a permanent literature fund.

The publicly run common or primary school illustrates the pervasiveness of state-aided and -fostered religion in nonestablishment New York. The history of actual practice as well as the education law of 1812 make clear that common schools were necessary for the dissemination of religion, morality, and learning and that the Bible and Christian moral principles were the instructional vehicle.[60] At the same time, sectarianism had no place in public education. In 1854, an educational theorist contended that the King James Bible was nonsectarian, although the burgeoning Catholic population disagreed.[61] George B. Cheever prefaced this claim by declaring, "While it is essential to forbid sectarianism in the public schools, it is as essential to bring them under the teachings and power of true religion; that religion should not be driven out under cover of repelling sectarianism."[62]

That Cheever believed this so late in New York's history is the only matter of note, for he simply reflected what enlightened New Yorkers had believed since the Revolution: the fostering of Protestantism without sectarian particulars was an inevitable interest and activity of any government, even one that had disestablished religion.[63]

In the remaining middle colonies—Pennsylvania, New Jersey, Delaware— very few public schools existed in 1789. The primary schools extant were usually charity schools run by parishes as part of their duty to care for orphans.[64] The exception was western New Jersey. Quakers there operated common schools supported by local taxation similar to the New England model. Some towns in eastern New Jersey apparently were empowered to operate tax-supported schools if they so chose, but there is no evidence that these townspeople taxed themselves for schools.[65] Pennsylvania, spurred in large part by Benjamin Rush, was nevertheless busy establishing and supporting various sectarian colleges.

Education farther south was largely a haphazard affair, although Maryland had long ago established Protestant common schools.[66] Classrooms in pre-Revolutionary North Carolina were essentially church affairs,[67] and the few academies chartered after disestablishment suggest a continued religious presence in schools.[68] South Carolina did not enact a significant statewide education bill until 1811.[69] The little known of the few schools actually chartered in Georgia accords with the legislature's intention for them. More often than not, they were run by clergymen. The regime at Richmond Academy was perhaps typical; at least students at the state university experienced similar requirements. Scripture reading and prayer opened the day, Sunday worship was required, and pupils were forbidden to swear or say anything of "offense to Religion."[70]

From 1776 to 1786, the established Protestant Episcopal church maintained ownership, control, and responsibility over the charity schools of Virginia. These schools fed, clothed, and educated the poor and orphaned.[71] In 1785–1786, the assembly turned control of charity schools over to nonchurch officials as part of its disestablishment policy. In 1796, the legislature passed an act that enabled counties to establish three-year elementary tuition-free schools. The county courts were charged with administering the first election of aldermen, filling vacancies, and erecting the necessary fund-raising machinery. (County taxpayers bore the schools' expenses.) The preamble to the 1796 act stated that free elementary education impressed youth with respect for government, developed personal happiness, and was conducive to better government. Youngsters should receive capable "knowledge of the true principles of morality and virtue." Governor Tyler's message to the assembly in December 1809, however, revealed that no county had opened a free school under the 1796 enabling legislation.

What occurred instead was a popular movement to charter private schools. The charters allowed funding by lotteries (which were otherwise illegal), subscriptions, and tuition. From 1777 to 1796, the assembly granted at least twenty charters; from 1796 to 1810, thirty more were passed. For example, the Hampton-Sidney Academy (founded by Presbyterians before 1776) sought and received permission from the assembly to hold a lottery to underwrite a building campaign. In some of these charters or in bills during the years following incorporation, the legislature even gave schools escheated lands. In 1784 Hampton-Sidney petitioned for and received from the legislature 412 acres of escheated land; in 1794, it obtained another 1,200 acres. According to one student's recollections, tutors resided with students and enforced strict codes of religious duties by means of fines. These codes and fines remained at the school until 1809. In 1787, the academy's president took a leadership role in a religious revival among the student body; fully half the students found the light and repented of their sins and later became eminent Presbyterian ministers and elders. In addition to Hampton-Sidney, Presbyterians founded and operated two other academies of higher learning and operated at least five secondary-level academies from 1786 to 1790. All these schools were state chartered.

Other denominations participated in the state largesse. The Protestant Episcopal church, in spite of the ongoing controversy over its glebe lands, remained active in education during the 1776–1790 period. It provided instructors and trustees in at least three state-chartered academies. The Methodists maintained three schools, one of which, Ebenezer Academy, was chartered. Apparently all three academies had a highly religious orientation and made provision for excusing students (at parental request) from the "Instruction for Children" sessions. These instruction sessions probably were the doctrinal teaching of the Methodists.

Also of interest is the burgeoning Virginia Sunday school movement, which fully matured only in the 1820s, and thus long after disestablishment occurred (in 1786), Sunday schools taught students "to read and . . . to fear and love God." Prayer and singing were part of this weekend curriculum. These schools, designed to bring up children "in nurture and adminition of the Lord," were run by many denominations. At the same time, the state set up a literary fund intended to promote statewide education, and by 1825 the school commissioners of Richmond, declaring that "the object of the Literary Fund would be promoted by encouraging these institutions," distributed $50 among the Richmond Sunday schools for the purchase of books. The Richmond commissioners increased their aid to Sunday schools to $100 in 1828. Historian Sadie Bell interpreted the lack of notoriety attending these actions:

Apparently there was no recognition, on the part of the advocates of Sunday Schools, of any impropriety in receiving appropriations from the Literary Fund for these schools. This was probably due to the fact that, in many localities, these schools represented combined denominational efforts, and there had arisen a tendency, upon the part of some in Virginia, since the Presbyterian pronouncement of its "Christian" education policy, to regard support for Christian, that is non-sectarian, education, as a perfectly legitimate charge upon the state. It is quite probable that as no objections seem to have been raised by the officers of the Literary Fund, that the precedent set by the school commissioners of Richmond, in appropriating part of their quota to Sunday Schools, was followed in many places without being noted in the Reports of the Second Auditor. There was an evident disposition on the part of many commissioners to favor Sunday Schools.[72]

Here is a true Virginia analogy. After a painfully self-conscious disestablishment, the nonestablishment home state of Jefferson and Madison aided—through tax exemptions, escheated lands, lottery dispensations, and cash grants—sectarian and nondenominational Protestant schools. Given *Everson*'s near obsession with Virginia's experience, is any more necessary to validate (for instance) tuition tax credits for parochial school students? The true, and truly vast, extent of religion's penetration of public education in the early national period should prove that the most basic components of the framers' worldview will not permit the no-aid attribution of the *Everson* Court. Not only did they not erect a wall of separation between religion and government, the givens in their mental world mean that they literally could not.

NOTES

1. J. Story, *Commentaries on the Constitution of the United States* 1868 (1970).
2. Ibid.
3. E. Smith, *Religious Liberty in the United States* 50 (1972).
4. Ibid. at 102–3.
5. J. Murray, *We Hold These Truths* 51 (1960).
6. Smith, *Religious Liberty*, at 104.
7. Adams to Jefferson, June 28, 1813, in C. Adams, ed., 10 *Life and Works of John Adams* 45 (1854).

8. See chapter 2, note 143 and accompanying text.

9. See chapter 3, notes 34–72 and accompanying text.

10. *Letters of Benjamin Rush* 611 (letter of November 12, 1791, to Elhanan Winchester) (L. Butterfield ed. 1951).

11. *Gazette of the United States*, May 6, 1789, at 1.

12. See J. Madison, Federalist 55, in *The Federalist Papers* 456 (1961).

13. Walter Berns, *The First Amendment and the Future of American Democracy* 228 (1976).

14. Quoted in Smith, *Religious Liberty*, at 107.

15. Ibid. at 82.

16. Ibid.

17. See chapter 2, note 193, and accompanying text.

18. 9 *Works of Adams* 635 (letter of August 28, 1811, to Benjamin Rush) (1854).

19. Berns, *First Amendment*, at 31.

20. Smith, *Religious Liberty*, at 20.

21. P. Freund, "Public Aid to Parochial Schools," 82 *Harv. L. Rev.* 1680, 1684 (1969).

22. R. Boardman, *Roger Sherman, Signer and Statesman* 103 (1938). See also J. Pratt, *Religion, Politics and Diversity: The Church-State Theme in New York History* 85 (1967). Paine Wingate recalled a lecture by Professor Wigglesworth while a student at Harvard: "That church is a restless, encroaching, and implacable enemy to Protestants of every denomination. It is indefatigable in its endeavors, compassing land and sea to make proselytes. It utterly denies salvation to any outside of its communion. And its heresies, superstitions, cruelties, idolatries, and other crying wickednesses are such, that you will find it no very easy matter to persuade yourselves that there can be any salvation in it." 2 Wingate *supra* note 125 at 62.

23. See R. Boardman, *Roger Sherman, Signer and Statesman* 319 (1938).

24. Rufus King to Elbridge Gerry, May 9, 1785, in *The Life and Correspondence of Rufus King* 95 (King ed. 1894).

25. *Pamphlets on the Constitution of the United States* (P. Ford ed., 1888) at 41.

26. Ibid.

27. Adams to Jefferson, June 18, 1813, in 10 *Works of Adams* at 43 (1854).

28. Adams to Jefferson of April 19, 1817, in 10 *Works of Adams* at 253.

29. Smith, *Religious Liberty*, at 104.

30. Ibid.

31. J. F. Berg, *Church and State: Or Rome's Influence upon the Civil and Religious Institutions of Our Country* 30 (1851). By 1888, New Hampshire Senator Henry Blair supported his introduction of another Blaine amendment with what Paul Kleppner described as "old logic": "an embattled society needed moral education; morality depended on religious sanctions; only the common school could reach all future citizens; therefore, religious instruction in the public school" (but no assistance to sectarian—especially Catholic—schools). "The preservation of the State demands it," said Blair, "and self-preservation is the first law of nature to the State as to individuals." D. Tyack and E. Hansat, *Managers of Virtue: Public School Leadership in America, 1820–1980* (1982).

32. L. Beecher, *Plea for the West* 63, 128 (1835).

33. Cremin, *American Education*, at 116 examines the republican currents in eighteenth-century American education in chapter 4 and 5 and summarizes this important trend on page 148.

The republican style in American education was compounded of four fundamental beliefs: that education was crucial to the vitality of the Republic, that a proper republican education consisted of the diffusion of knowledge, the nurturance of virtue (including patriotic civility), and the cultivation of learning; that, schools and colleges were the best agencies for providing a proper republican education on the scale required; and that the most effective means of obtaining the requisite number and kind of schools and colleges was through some system tied to the policy.

34. See M. Savelle, *Seeds of Liberty: The Genesis of the American Mind* 267–73 (1965), for a description of plans for public education by the pietiest John Woolman and by the rationalist Benjamin Franklin. For a brief treatment of statewide public systems of primary through university education, see Benjamin Rush's plan for Pennsylvania and Thomas Jefferson's series of plans for Virginia in Cremin, *American Education*, at 116–21 and 107–14, respectively.

35. In addressing the legislature in 1784, Governor George Clinton remarked: "Neglect of Education of Youth is among the Evils consequent on War—Perhaps there is scarce anything more worthy your Attention, than the Revival and Encouragement of Seminaries of learning; and nothing by which we can more satisfactorily express our Gratitude to the Supreme Being for his past Favours; since Piety and Virtue are generally the offspring of an enlightened Understanding." J. Pratt, *Religion, Politics and Diversity* 115 (1967).

36. R. Strickland, *Religion and the State in Georgia in the 18th Century* 178 (1939).

37. *Illinois Historical Collections* at 532.

38. Then, as now, a kind of undereducated, permanent lower class loomed as a potential menace to social stability.

39. *Columbian Centinel*, June 26, 1790.

40. *Pennsylvania Observer*, January 27, 1790.

41. *Boston Gazette*, February 24, 1789.

42. See R. Mohl, "Education as Social Control in New York City, 1784–1825," 51 *N.Y. Hist.* 127 (1970).

43. See Richard J. Purcell, *Connecticut in Transition, 1775–1818* (1918), at 914–95.

44. S. Schultz, *The Culture Factory: Boston Public Schools, 1789–1860* (1973), at 13–15.

45. *Massachusetts Centinel*, January 9, 1790 at 1.

46. Ibid.

47. *Laws of Massachusetts*, ch. 143.

48. Ibid.

49. W. Dunn, *What Happened to Religious Education?* 141–50 (1958). The text of Mann's reports may be found in H. Kleibard, ed., *Religion and Education in America: A Documentary History* 67–75 (1969).

50. Kleibard, *Religion*, at 67–75.

51. C. Kinney, *Church and State: The Struggle for Separation in New Hampshire, 1630–1900* (1955), at 152–53.

52. Ibid.

53. Purcell, *Connecticut*, at 94–95; Dunn, *What Happened*, at 71.

54. Dunn, *What Happened*, at 71.

55. *Session Acts*, 1782, ch. 22, Art. 7. The legislative citations are taken from G. Miller, *The Academy System of the State of New York* (1922), at 27–28.

56. *Session Acts*, 1786, ch. 67.

57. Ibid., 1790, ch. 38.

58. Ibid., 1801, ch. 126.

59. Ibid., 1813, ch. 187.

60. George B. Cheever, *Right of the Bible in Our Public Schools* 201–13 (1854). Griffin notes that the Bible-in-the-schools movement was part of the anti-Catholic movement in the mid-nineteenth century. C. Griffin, *Their Brothers' Keepers: Moral Stewardship in the United States, 1800–1865* 140–43.

61. Griffin, at 140–43.

62. Cheever, *Right of the Bible*, 37–38.

63. Smith, *Religious Liberty*, at 108.

64. N. Burr, *Education in New Jersey 1630–1871* 240–45 (1942).

65. D. Sloan, *Education in New Jersey in the Revolutionary Era* 7 (1975).

66. See chapter 2, notes 310–12, and accompanying text.

67. See chapter 2, notes 271–76, and accompanying text.

68. P. Conklin, "The Church Establishment in North Carolina," 42 *N.C. Hist. Rev.* 11, 20 (1955).

69. Ibid. at 20–21. See chapter 2, notes 230–33, and accompanying text.

70. R. Strickland, *Religion and the State in Georgia in the Eighteenth Century* 178–79 (1939).

71. The material on Virginia's schools is drawn from S. Bell, *The Church, the State, and Education in Virginia* (1930), unless otherwise indicated.

72. Ibid. at 249.

7

The Meaning of the Words:
Yesterday and Today

A rigorous historical inquiry into the adoption of the Establishment Clause has shown that it prohibits sect preferences in the government's dealings with religion—including state efforts to promote, encourage, and assist faith—but does not forbid those efforts altogether. The Court has therefore been fundamentally in error since 1947, and condemnably so. The right answer—sect equality—was strenuously pressed upon the *Everson* Court and also by Edward Corwin in an important article published almost before the ink on that opinion was dry.[1] Since then various commentators[2] and an occasional jurist[3] have reminded the Court of this fundamental alternative, but the Court has never looked back. It also has never articulated a convincing justification for either its brusque dismissal of these entreaties or for its no-aid regime, beginning with the preemptorial *Everson* opinions. Still, the justices should confess their sin and embark at the earliest opportunity on the path first forsaken in 1947.

A major objection to this departure—stare decisis, or respect for precedent— is insufficient to stay the change of course. The chief virtue of stare decisis is its assurance that individuals who organize their affairs in the light of the law will be protected in their understandable and reasonable reliance on it.[4] But that purpose is hardly served by fortifying the *Everson* regime. First, the precedents are so erratic and so often inscrutable that few responsible actors rely heavily on them, a factor that belies the other main reason for stare decisis: avoiding the appearance given by conflicting results that mere judicial will, and not constitutional principle, is at work. Second, many of the rulings have been so contrary to American culture and popular sentiment that repudiating the cases will harmonize rather than disturb expectations. Third, and unlike most other provisions of the Bill of Rights (including the Free Exercise Clause), government institutions and corporate bodies of believers, and not individuals as such, are the ordinary subjects of the Court's haphazard nonestablishment rulings. Finally, the practical effects of switching to a sect-neutral constitutional order are, most emphatically, not to be confused with turning the clock back to 1790. The intellectual reorientation attending the switch is certainly much greater than the everyday consequences.

The conclusion is sect equality, and it is recommended as an immediate replacement for prevailing law. But due largely to the harmful tendency of both judicial and academic writers to lump all historically grounded accounts of constitutional law together as explications of original intent the precise statement of the result here is important. It is not offered as the original intent of the Establishment Clause's framers, for two built-in distortive tendencies disqualify that term from further use in serious discussion of constitutional meaning. Empirically, the original intent of the framers may be, as in *Everson*, a reference to the undisclosed views of one or two leading personalities on the some part of the issues addressed by the Constitution but not on the constitutional language itself. It may be, as the Bill of Rights synthesis suggests, a more inclusive reference, perhaps to all relevant players, but again not to the Constitutional language. It may also regard exchanges like those among members on the House floor about the constitutional language but that were unknown to the state legislators who ratified the amendment. More problematic are private exchanges among the same persons about the same thing, as well as confidential correspondence between Madison and Jefferson, for example, concerning the amendments. It is sometimes even supposed that original intent represents our best guess at what Madison would say about some contemporary problem. Such an undifferentiated vocabulary inpoverishes critical appraisal of historically aided interpretation and is productive of a judgment on the entire historical enterprise due to one grievously flawed use or (abuse) of the past. *Everson*'s is a hopelessly flawed historical approach to constitutional meaning, and it has nothing to do with the methodology here save for a gaze backward in time that is common to most constitutional exegesis.

Logically, original intent of the framers suggests a distinction between the meaning of the words used and the users' understanding of them and implies the interpretive superiority of the latter. Some writers locate this distinction— and a consequent need to arbitrate among the distinguished meanings—elsewhere in constitutional law,[5] but it certainly is not present in the Establishment Clause. The evidence instead reveals both a standard definition and the framers' subscription to it. Most important, these connotations constitute a theoretically improper constitutional analysis. First, ratification is the key event. Congress merely proposes amendments; the state legislatures enact them.[6] Second, John Hart Ely is right in saying that only the language is ratified, not the undisclosed opinions of even the most prominent proponents of the alteration.[7] Consequently, the search for constitutional meaning is for the meaning apprehended by the ratifiers, and all the evidence adduced in this book contributes to that objective. The conclusion specifically stated is that the ratifiers understood their ratification of the Establishment Clause to interdict sect preferences by the national government. It is not that they intended it, connoting the presence in their minds of something not evident in the words they ratified. It is the meaning of the words.

Much more than mere preference among available labels is at stake here. The value of the contribution of original intent to constitutional interpretation is dubious. Whose intentions, and about what (precisely), count? Does Madison's intent matter more than the contrary intent of Patrick Henry or Fisher Ames? But even scholars unimpressed with the search for something called original intent share[8] the Supreme Court's unwavering view that the plain meaning of a constitutional provision is conclusive.[9] Not only does the clear import of a term overcome contrary intimations derived from accompanying intentions, there is no need to investigate those intentions. They do not matter, whatever they are. Even the *Everson* Court confirmed the unassailability of plain meaning. However misinformed, the justices there said that they had hold of an unambiguous textual command, and there was no deflecting it.

More oblique confirmation of this ascendancy is provided, ironically, by a major obstacle to its more widespread influence in constitutional law. What I call the burden of proof objection is typified by Leonard Levy in his recent recasting of the seminal work on freedom of the press, *Legacy of Suppression*. In *Emergence of a Free Press*, he warns, "No one can say for certain what the Framers had in mind because enough evidence does not exist to justify cocksure conclusions, even though all the evidence points in one direction."[10]

The first criticism is that Levy probably searches for an irrelevancy; "what the Framers had in mind" is not the issue so much as the meaning of the words is. Still, assuming that he would offer the same observation on the latter endeavor, requiring "cocksure conclusions" is guaranteed to paralyze historical analysis, as well as any other form of human speculation. Certainty does not come easily in human affairs; even the physical sciences understand themselves as dealing with statistical probabilities and regular occurrences, not laws or necessities. It is most ironic that Supreme Court justices should demand "cocksure conclusions"; they engage in the frail practice of human judging based on the exceedingly limited record presented to them. Further, their handiwork is generally marked by less rigorous standards of scholarship than one might wish and fueled by highly speculative social theory. Indeed, if such a rigorous burden were placed on other sources of constitutional law—inference from structure, tradition, community sentiment, governmental practice, empirical propositions about human behavior and motivation—their opinions would be blank pieces of paper. Blanker still would they be if the chief sources of law in this area—the justices' personal philosophies and views on religion and society—were required to be certain.

That this crippling burden of proof is selectively applied to historical retrieval

138   CHURCH-STATE RELATIONSHIPS

reveals it as a transparent effort to avoid unpalatable results and therefore to free
the justices to introduce other, usually more speculative, criteria into the cases.
Put differently and with more impact, it is an ad hoc device to escape, effectively
but indirectly, the regnancy of plain meaning by denying that it can be reliably
captured. Since the Court is understandably wary of defying a concededly obvious
meaning of a particular constitutional phrase, requiring "cocksure conclusions"
allows the justices to honor plain meaning but as a theoretical or imaginary
construct only. The transparency is theoretically deficient, for it fails to address
the subsequent question: what should be the governing criteria or sources of law
(if any) when historical aids falter? That a particular constitutional provision is
historically indeterminate—shrouded in the mists of history—may mean that the
party relying on the Constitution in a lawsuit loses; since constitutional meaning
cannot be reliably ascertained, the constitutional challenge fails. That historical
ambiguity by itself justifies resort to other sources—most usually to judicial
value preferences—is as common in practice as it is unsupported and unexplained
in theory.

A different problem superficially resembling this one is to what level of
generality historical recovery should aspire. Formulating the issue in this manner
allows us to see that despite the fragmentation of church-state analysis, all
analyses of this area, if not of all constitutional law, are historically grounded.
The only necessary illustration is that what are usually taken as polar extremes
in the discussion—popularly rendered, they are Attorney General Edwin Meese's
original intent theory[11] and Justice William Brennan's living Constitution
method[12]—differ only in the level of generality with which they approach the
past. To emphasize, each admittedly and emphatically says he looks to the
framers for the solution to present problems. Ironically neither looks at the
Constitution.

The Meese approach corresponds to one currently fashionable on the Court,
a method favored more by some (for instance, Justice Rehnquist's views appear
to tightly mimic the attorney general's) than by others (Justice Brennan is an
unenthusiastic, desultory practitioner) but employed by all the justices at one
time or another. One need appreciate that until recently, historical inquiry dominated just the search for stable Establishment Clause doctrine and therefore
resolved cases through the meditation of principles traceable to the framers. In
Everson, for instance, the extended discourse on the colonial experience produced
a no aid to religion doctrine that was itself the basis of decision. The famous
three-part Lemon test was derived largely from historical questioning, but again
it, and not the historical data, purported to decide cases. Some recent opinions
have abandoned this sensible priority of doctrine in which historical inquiry
produces autonomous, general principles. The derailment is attributable to a
pithy Holmesianism, one quoted approvingly by Justice O'Connor in Wallace
v. Jaffree, moment of silence case: "If a thing has been practiced for two
hundered years by common consent it will need a strong case for the Constitution
to affect it."[13] The justices have refashioned a widely accepted, circumscribed

deference to unbroken governmental practice[14] into what I label the "roll-call of ancient analogues." In this rendition, a virtually impossible burden is imposed on those challenging a practice (not a principle) accepted when the Constitution was adopted. For example, in *Marsh v. Chambers*[15] (the legislative chaplains case) and in *Lynch v. Donnelly*[16] (the Nativity scene case), a majority of the Court asked whether the challenged practice had an eighteenth-century counterpart. If so, the modern equivalent was consistent with the First Amendment. But asking whether the framers actually countenanced an analogous practice, without more, is best understood as a total abandonment of the search for principled norms, and thus an abdication of responsible judicial review. More than that, it is unintelligent and, in effect, evil.

Lynch v. Donnelly best illustrates the stakes of reducing constitutional adjudication to an antiquarian matching game. The majority in *Lynch* found President Washington's Thanksgiving day proclamation the most persuasive counterpart.[17] The dissent (including Justice Brennan) inquired more directly after the intent of the framers respecting Nativity scenes.[18] In fact, the dissent had the better of it, since the then-dominant pietistic sects regarded Christmas celebration, as they did all other merriment, as suspect, thus confirming Mencken's caustic observation on Puritans and their hostility to good times. While such head counting may slightly inform a search for the principles contained in the Establishment Clause, it can do no more than that. Otherwise one wonders if the next case will witness the Court's asking the framers whether they intended Nativity scenes with wise men and the Angel Gabriel in them or if they preferred just the shepherds and a few donkeys.

Nevertheless Justice Rehnquist in particular continues to be impressed by Washington's Thanksgiving prayers. He recounted the episode in great detail in *Wallace*. There, Washington's "endorsement of prayer" was a warrant to sustain Alabama's endorsement of it in *Wallace*.[19] Justice Rehnquist closed his analysis with this ominous historical challenge: "History must judge whether it was the father of his country in 1789, or a majority of the Court today, which has strayed from the meaning of the Establishment Clause."[20]

Actually there were analogues on all fours; Maryland's public schools are an example. But one element of Court history, as distinguished from historical fact, is that (as Justice O'Connor remarked in *Wallace*) "free public education was virtually non-existent in the late 19th century,"[21] a proposition for which she cited two footnotes from Justice Brennan's *Abington* opinion.[22] Therefore, O'Connor reported, Justice Rehnquist could not suggest that the framers actually approved school prayer. In fact, every one of the original states had drawn up plans for public schooling, and all but South Carolina and Georgia had implemented them. Not surprisingly, these public (or common) schools were thoroughly and unabashedly Protestant. But perhaps sufficient proof of this overly specific method's inadequacy resides in the other great early American legislative tradition (besides Protestant common schooling). One who is following this method must be prepared to validate civil disabilities for Catholics and for all non-Christians. That the anti-Catholic prejudices and legal enactments of the framers, however steadfast, should not affect contemporary doctrine—even doctrine historically retrieved—is to say that principles are retrieved, not specific (mis)applications of them. Chief Justice Burger in *Waltz* supplied the necessary normative criticism: the purpose of the Establishment Clause was more to state an objective than to write a statute.[23] In other words, constitutional meaning is more general than the narrow specifics found in ordinary statutes.

The quest for ancient analogues and questers like Meese and Rehnquist ignore what the framers actually wrote into the Constitution: a ban on sectarian privilege. Justice Brennan instead criticizes this technique as thinly veiled political conservatism, rooted in the expectation that ancient analogues generally correspond to the Republican agenda[24]—and understandably, for Justice Brennan looks at the Constitution neither more often nor more closely than his conservative colleague. Whatever the accuracy of Brennan's political effects critique, the analogues method is certainly defective, but it is hardly the exclusive property of conservatives. Leonard Levy is no political conservative, yet he employs precisely the same methodology in his second look at the Free Press Clause, with the effect (and likely the intention) of justifying more liberal effects than his earlier work wrought.[25] In *Legacy*, Levy concluded the law was narrow; the legal term *freedom of the press* had a restrictive definition built up over the years, one authoritatively restated by Blackstone. The Blackstonian definition of press freedom was unchanged at the time of the First Amendment and, by inference owing to the silence of inertia, entered into the Constitution. Now, after examining what newspaper editors actually got away with during the early national period, Levy concludes that a practice of press freedom existed despite the restrictive legal definition of it: "The American experience with a free press was as broad as the theoretical inheritance was narrow."[26] One need not doubt this as a matter of observation to wonder at the next step in Levy's new rendition:

The obvious conclusion from this—which I failed to draw in *Legacy* . . . is that the framers of the press clause of . . . the first amendment could only have meant to protect the press as they knew it. In other words they constitutionally guaranteed the *practice* of freedom of the press.[27]

This breathtaking elevation of practice over the accepted legal definition of terms used in what was, after all, a legal document (the Constitution) is not further defended, just presented. Why the framers used a phrase whose antiquated meaning was well known to them to constitutionalize a radically different practice, also supposed to be known to them, is left for speculation. We need not pause to pursue it; for now, two observations will suffice. First, Levy still relies on his "sounds of silence" argument—that is, the absence of discussion signals continuity but simply substitutes practice for law as the subject of that predicate. Here he implicitly succumbs to the Bill of Rights synthesis, presuming that the First Amendment stood at the cutting edge of political experience. Second, this is the roll call of ancient analogues in pristine form. He does not retrieve a principle from the past; he takes a snapshot of it. Levy freezes in time a set of specific eighteenth-century practices that may well be outmoded, even reactionary, by now. Instant gratification is provided by the absence of prior restraints on publication in practice then, so they are unconstitutional now. Levy must now overcome the theoretical respectability his method bestows on complete suppression of nonpolitical (narrowly defined as anything not pertaining to governmental affairs) literature offensive to Puritan sensibilities. Consider only the blasphemy prosecutions that occurred well into the nineteenth century. One can be sure that the net tally here will hardly warm liberal hearts.

If this account of original intent—the conceptual cheapskate—is flawed, so is its opposite, the conceptual glutton. Overgeneralization of historical meaning to suit a new age is just as common and is much more a liberal than a conservative temptation. Still, one popular, politically oriented overgeneralization of history may be traced to so-called conservatives. "We are a Christian nation" was an accurate sociological observation in 1790, and is still largely so. From this some, and not just Jerry Falwell, would conclude that governmental Christian observances are necessarily constitutional. The defect here is obvious: it simply substitutes the mentality that produced the Constitution for the Constitution itself. However appealing, the Constitution does not so read, and indeed there is abundant evidence that the framers fully appreciated the difference. While they hoped and expected that the United States would remain Christian, they knew that the Constitution was not a guarantor of that homogeneity, as their extensive discussion of the ban on test oaths reveals. The founders anticipated that social processes and nongovernemtal institutions, and perhaps the sheer fortuity of favorable immigration, would work that result. Legal efforts to that end were permissible so long as they did not include test oaths, abridge free exercise, or violate sect neutrality. Thus the Constitution was a restrictive condition, and intentionally so, on the maintenance of a Christian United States.

Nevertheless, exceedingly abstract renditions of original intent are characteristic of liberal jurists and writers. For instance and despite widespread contrary impressions, Justice Brennan expressly grounded his own constitutional theorizing in the eighteenth century and unequivocally eschewed personal philosophy and value preferences as a basis for constitutional law: "Justices are not platonic guardians appointed to wield authority according to their personal moral predictions."[28] Rather, the proper judicial role is to implement substantive value choices made by the framers as evidenced in (especially) the Bill of Rights they produced. Brennan rejected the particularism of Meese (though without apology for using it himself at times) chiefly because the methodology is unworkable. We cannot retrieve the desired historical information. Indeed Brennan too subscribes to the paramountcy of plain meaning derived from historical inquiry and seems to say that the most reliable account of it is necessarily quite general. Brennan's more realistic—the only attainable—historical fidelity would extract great principles form the document and reject its anachronistic contours, implement majestic generalities, and apply them to our time, not as the framers did to theirs.[29]

This is fine so far, and if Justice Brennan found sect equality majestic or general enough, there would be an end to it. At first blush, he goes way beyond that: "The Constitution embodies the aspiration to social justice; brotherhood, and human dignity that brought this nation into being."[30] Sect equality is comparatively pedestrian, but then Brennan renders it unspeakably trivial beside the substantive value choice he would implement without donning the garb of Platonic Guardian: now the Constitution is a "sublime oration on the dignity of man," the judical commission no less than ordering the relationship of the individual to the state.[31] Evidently, no more specific direction from the framers (or the text) is either necessary or welcome.

Brennan so collapses any distinction between the rejected Platonic Guardian and fideistic originalism that further comment is dispensable. Less grandiose attempts at the same exercise, however, abound and warrant comment. Neutrality,[32] separation,[33] and voluntarism[34] are assertedly prominent values put in the Constitution by the framers and extracted by modern courts charged with providing their contemporary meaning. Perhaps the short answer to this historical approach is, to the extent that the values recovered lead analysis to no aid, that the approach is flawed. Put most plainly, any sequence of historical questions or value extractions that results in attributing no aid to the framers had no more validity than *Everson*. If the generation of Americans who debated, drafted, and ratified the First Amendment can be made to say that, then any constitutional theory that prizes original intent is truly useless because that category will have been emptied of all objective content.

But that is just the first line of response to value extractors. The next question is, Why bother? If the words mean no sect preference, what is the purpose of generalizing further unless one is trying to legitimize the substitution of one's own values for those of the framers? This is not an instance of applying underlying or inchoate values to situations unforeseen by the drafters as the only way to keep the Constitution relevant. School prayer, Bible reading in the classroom, religious school funding, tax exemptions, and other aids to churches were all eighteenth-century issues, and no sect preference is as much a solution now as it was then. The second question is, Is it worth it? How much have neutrality, separation, and voluntarism actually told us about how to decide cases? Is it not likely that the morass that is Establishment Clause jurisprudence is largely the residue of trying to figure out what those values mean in actual situations? Since they are so indeterminate, their political attraction is (or should be) nil. In the hands of courts bent on implementing a political agenda, they will serve liberal and conservative masters equally well. Third, and related, is Henry Monaghan's point: "excessive generalization as to 'intent' seems at war with any belief that a constitutional amendment is a *conscious* alteration of the frame of government whose major import should be reasonably apparent to the ones who gave it life."[35] (Emphasis in original.) For instance, if the wall of separation metaphor was first used in 1802 (as the Court admits it was),[36] how could its meaning be apparent to the 1788 conventioneers who demanded nonestablishment or to the state legislators who ratified that stricture in 1790? More important, if the founding generation wished to institute requirements of voluntarism or separation, why didn't they say that instead of no sect preference?

Monaghan's point also cuts deeply into perhaps the last resort of politically motivated historical retrievers: that the founders not only prohibited a national church or an official establishment but anything like an establishment of religion. Probably first used (incorrectly) by Madison in 1811,[37] this paraphrase of *Everson* "means at least this" pronouncement was most recently reiterated by the dissenters in *Lynch v. Donnelly*.[38] The *Lemon* opinion stated it most precisely. The language "respecting an establishment of religion" obliges courts to invalidate a law that "might not establish a state religion but nevertheless be one respecting that end in the sense of being a step that could lead to such establishment and hence offend the First Amendment."[39] This attribution is historically unsustainable and is applied unfaithfully since the Court is hardly talking about steps on the road to sect inequality. Further, since this imposing prophylaxis is unparalleled in constitutional law, it can only be viewed as an ad hoc justification for constitutionalizing the world of church and state where the Constitution did not. In any event, how is a notion such as "anything like an Establishment" a "conscious alteration" with a reasonably apparent plain meaning? Finally, it is deceitful simultaneously to profess devotion to another's intentions (for example, the framers') and to capture those intentions so abstractly that no objective constraint on discretion is also captured. Indeed, if the justices long ago ceased executing anybody's intentions but their own, they ought to admit it so that its propriety can be candidly evaluated.

Fidelity to the framers is also not accomplished by focusing on the evils they sought to protect against. Sometimes the problem here is just shoddy history. *Everson* is one example. *Lemon*—where the Court similarly identified ends like "sponsorship, financial support and active involvement of the sovereign in religious activity"[40]—is another. Divisiveness is nevertheless the consummate examplar, and while its precise meaning is elusive, its theoretical place in constitutional law is not: it authroizes judicial carte blanche in church and state. Properly, a focus on evils is of help in accurately interpreting the words containing the founders' prescription for the evil, but it is not constitutional interpretation at all to ignore that prescription. The founders' remedy for whatever demons haunted them was sect equality, and the Court has not seen fit to implement that solution. More, the Court even contradicts itself. The justices have frequently remarked that we are, at this point in the twentieth century, quite far removed from the dangers that prompted nonestablishment. True or not, if the justices believe it, one would expect that when the other shoe drops, it would land next to the Third Amendment[41] and the Marque and Reprisal Clause,[42] provisions that addressed and solved problems—quartering soldiers in private homes and outfitting private navies, respectively—that no longer exist. But rather than allow the Establishment Clause thereby to drift into well-deserved oblivion, the justices have, in Byron White's formulation, "carved out what they deemed to be the most desirable national policy governing various aspects of church-state relationships."[43] White's candor is uncharacteristic of the judicial conscience.

Did the framers intend nondiscriminatory aid? Michael Malbin is one careful scholar who rejects the Court's no-aid rule on the strength of his analysis of the primary sources but hesitates to conclude that the same sources reveal an intention to aid religion.[44] Does it matter? Probably not. None of the Bill of Rights provisions is an empowering declaration, so that one cannot ask of their drafters what affirmative powers, or particular uses of them, they intended. In other words, one cannot reason from the Bill of Rights story to the affirmative reach of federal power.

The historical answer is also practically irrelevant because separate constitutional developments since 1790 render the founders' situation incomparable to ours. Most important is the incorporation of the Establishment Clause by the Fourteenth Amendment and its application to the states. (*Everson* accomplished this too.) Now the states and not just the federal government must observe nonestablishment constraints. Since most of the controversial church-state rulings concern state practices—tax exemptions, school prayer, and Nativity scenes, for instance—affirmative state power and intentions matter most. These have nothing whatsoever to do with the Constitution or its creators. Second, two centuries of constitutional decision making have expanded the reach of federal taxing, spending, and commerce powers so far beyond the framers' conception of them (for reasons theoretically unrelated to the development of Establishment Clause doctrine) that their intentions or conceptions of those powers are antiquated. For instance, two recent Establishment Clause cases arose not from an asserted Congressional "power over religion" but from spending enactments. Federal financial aid to underprivileged and handicapped students prompted church-state rulings in the *Aguilar*[45] and *Witters*[46] cases. And this is precisely why Leonard Levy's reading of nonestablishment as "no power over religion" is no help.

But for those who persist, the answer is a qualified yes. To be sure, there is no enumerated power over or concerning religion, so that intentions to aid religion are shadowy. But like the Fourth Amendment's prohibition of general warrants, which makes no sense if the government is powerless to issue warrants at all (and there is no such enumerated power), the no-sect preference command of the First Amendment logically implies power to legislate affecting religion. And like the power to issue warrants, the power to legislate on religion is found in the necessary and proper execution of other enumerated powers—which is precisely what the framers intended or expected, an intention manifested in the behavior of the First Congress and in the universal practice of the states. Where the federal government was empowered to act directly upon individuals without state buffers—that is, in the territories and in the military, in relations with the Indians, and within Congress itself—the First Congress did in fact aid religion. If one replaces *intent* with *contemplate* (a better sense of the state of mind at issue), Story's observation rightly ends the inquiry. One must then add, even if as a footnote, the Huntington-Madison exchange on the House floor. The framers there expressly put aid to religion alongside the First Amendment and make their verdict of consistent quite clear. So yes, if you like, the framers intended non-discriminatory aid to religion.

The historical command is indeed as the Court would have it: unambiguous. And while no sect preference is firmly rooted in the past, it is not necessarily antiquated. It may not please some modern ears, but it is not the less modern for it. Nor is it the dead hand of those long buried. It undoubtedly corresponds more closely with modern American sentiment than no aid, and it cannot be more difficult of application to twentieth-century problems than that discredited formula has proved to be. Indeed, one commentator has cataloged the "legendary inconsistencies" of church-state jurisprudence and attributed them largely to the inherent unworkability of concepts like separation and no aid or support to a religiously grounded culture and polity.[47]

Sect equality is not particularly conservative or liberal, and so overthrowing *Everson* may be a wash when upset expectations are counted. Just as it cuts a middle way between Meese and Brennan, it neatly bisects the views of (for instance) the religious New Right of Jerry Falwell and the separationist People for the American Way, founded by "All in the Family" creator Norman Lear. It would validate legislative schemes aiding private schools so long as all religious sects operating schools were eligible. Tax exemptions for all religious institutions would continue to pass muster, but it would be unnecessary to invent an entanglements prong, as the *Waltz* court did, to save them. Equal access laws similarly present little difficulty so long as school facilities were available to all. But this historically verified principle would not, for example, overturn the school prayer and Bible reading cases. As we have seen, even if it were possible in 1790 to derive a sect-neutral prayer, it is no longer. (Of course, Catholics and others could be as sectarian as they wish in their own publicly aided parochial schools.) More generally, contemporary conditions militate strongly against any kind of governmental observance intended to capture a spiritual common denominator. A truly voluntary moment of silence in a public schoolroom might survive constitutional challenge in a sect-neutral regime but only if conceived and executed without bias, especially in the form of subtle (and not-so-subtle) indications from teachers and administrators that specifically religious reflection—much less sect-specific prayer—is favored.

Lynch v. Donnelly would not necessarily come out the way that it did, although it might. The creche, of course, could be recognized as the Christian sign that it is and not as some neutered, universal folk symbol. The question need no longer be whether government sponsored religion but whether it did so on an evenhanded basis. The issue is perhaps best cast in terms of equal access: is government willing to aid other groups endeavoring to clothe the public square in sacred garb?

Whether the Court will decide that no sect preference is a better idea than no aid is pure conjecture, for only Justice Rehnquist has evinced any attraction to the idea. One may at least hope that in the future, the other justices give the plain meaning of the words a fairer hearing than they did in *Everson*. Before they further leave behind sect equality for some other preferred norm—that is, before they embark on another journey from someplace to what will likely be no place—they might well consider the counsel of Jefferson, who stressed that the meaning of the Constitution is "to be found in the explanations of those who advocated it, upon which the people relied in adopting the Constitution."[48] Or perhaps Madison should have the last word after all. If the "sense in which the Constitution was accepted and ratified by the Nation . . . be not the guide in expounding it, there can be no security for a consistent and stable government, more than for a faithful exercise of its powers."[49]

NOTES

1. E. Corwin, "The Supreme Court as National Board," 14 *L. & Contemp. Prob.* 3 (1949).

2. See, e.g., R. Cord, *Separation of Church and State* 5 (1982).

3. See, e.g., *Wallace v. Jaffree*, ———. U.S. ———. 105 S. Ct. 2479, 2520 (1985) (Rehnquist, J., dissenting).

4. On stare decisis, see generally, H. Monaghan, "Taking Supreme Court Opinions Seriously," 39 *Md. L. Rev* 1 (1979). See also the exchange between Justices Stevens and White in *Thornburgh v. American College of Obstetricians and Gynecologists*, 54 U.S.L.W. 4618 (1986).

5. D. Anderson, "The Origins of the Press Clause," 30 *UCLA L. REV.* 455, 462 (1983); M. Nimmer, "Introduction: Is Freedom of the Press a Redundancy: What Does It Add to Freedom of Speech?" 26 *Hastings L.J.* 639, 640 (1975).

6. *Maxwell v. Dow*, 176 U.S. 581, 601–2 (1900).

7. J. Ely, *Democracy and Distrust* 27 (1980).

8. See, e.g., P. Brest, "The Misconceived Quest for the Original Understanding," 60 *B.U.L. Rev.* 204, 237 (1980).

9. *Sturges v. Crowninshield*, 17 U.S. (4 Wheat.) 122, 202–3 (1819).

10. L. Levy, *Emergence of a Free Press* 268 (1985).

11. See *New York Times*, October 16, 1985, July 25, 1986, Pp. 23.

12. W. Brennan, "The Constitution of the United States: Contemporary Ratification," speech delivered October 12, 1985 at Georgetown University.

13. *Wallace* at 2502 (1985) (O'Connor, J., concurring).

14. *Ex parte Quirin*, 317 U.S. 1, 41–42 (1942).

15. *Marsh v. Chambers*, 463 U.S. 783 (1983).

16. *Lynch v. Donnelly*, 465 U.S. 660 (1984).

17. Ibid. at 1360.

18. Ibid. at 1382–86 (Brennan, J. dissenting).

19. *Wallace* at 2514.

20. Ibid. at 2520.

21. 105 S. Ct. at 2503 (O'Connor, J. concurring).

22. Ibid.

23. *Waltz v. Tax Commission*, 397 U.S. 664, 668 (1970).

24. Brennan, "Constitution," at 45.

25. See generally his *Emergence of a Free Press*. See also L. Levy, "The Legacy Reexamined," 37 *Stan. L. Rev.* 767 (1986).

26. Levy, "Legacy," at 769.

27. Ibid.

28. Brennan, "Constitution," at 3.

29. Ibid. at 7.

30. Ibid. at 1.

31. Ibid. at 8.

32. See P. Freund, "Public Aid to Parochial Schools," 82 *Harv. L. Rev.* 1680, 1684 (1969); Van Alstyne, "Comment: Trends in the Supreme Court: Mr. Jefferson's Crumbling Wall—A Comment on Lynch v. Donnelly," 1984 *Duke L.J.* 770, 774–76 (1984); Comment, "Beyond Seeger/Welsh: Redefining Religion under the Constitution," 31 *Emory L.J.* 973, 975 n. 12 (1982).

33. See *Everson*, 330 U.S. 1 16–18 (1947). See also *Lynch v. Donnelly*, 465 U.S. 698 (1984) (Brennan, J., dissenting); Comment, *"Mueller v. Allen*; Do Tuition Tax Deductions Violate the Establishment Clause?" 68 *Iowa L. Rev.* 539 (1982).

34. *Everson* at 18; *Lynch*, 465 U.S. at 698 (1984) (Brennan J., dissenting); *Roemer v. Maryland Pub. Works Bd.*, 426 U.S. 736 (1976); *Abington School Dist. v. Schempp*, 374 U.S. 203, 222 (1963).

35. H. Monaghan, "The Constitution Goes to Harvard," 13 *Harv. C.R.-C.L. L. Rev.* 117, 127 (1978). See also J. Ely, *Democracy and Distrust* 67 (1980); T. Sandalow, "Constitutional Interpretation," 79 *Mich. L. Rev.* 1033, 1046 (1981).

36. *Lynch*, 104 S. Ct. at 1359 n. 1.

37. "The Constitution of the U.S. forbids everything like an establishment of religion," quoted in Van Alstyne, "Comment," at 776.

38. *Lynch*, 104 S. Ct. at 1572.

39. *Lemon v. Kurtzman*, 403 U.S. 602, 612 (1971).

40. Ibid.

41. "No Soldier shall, in time of peace be quartered in any house, without the consent of the owner, nor in time of war, but in a manner to be prescribed by law." U.S. Const. amend. 3.

42. Congress shall have power to "grant Letters of Marque and Reprisal." U.S. Const. art. I, § 8, cl. 11.

43. *Committee for Public Education v. Nyquist, 413 U.S. 756, 821 (1973) (White, J., dissenting).*

44. M. Malbin, *Religion and Politics: The Intentions of the Authors of the First Amendment* 9 (1978).

45. *Aguilar v. Felton*, 105 S. Ct. 3232 (1985).

46. *Witters v. Washington*, 106 S. Ct. 748 (1986).

47. W. Marshall, "We Know It When We See It": The Supreme Court and Establishment," 59 *S. Cal. L. Rev.* 495 (1986).

48. 4 *J. Elliot, Debates in the Several State Conventions on the Adoption of the Federal Constitution* 446 (2d ed. 1836); see also R. Berger, *Executive Privilege* 138 (1974).

49. 4 *Writings of Madison* 191 (1865).

Appendix 1 ———————————————

Jefferson's Bill for Religious Liberty, 1785

Well aware that the opinions and belief of men depend not on their own will, but follow involuntarily the evidence proposed the their minds; that Almighty God had created the mind free, and manifested his supreme will that free it shall remain by making it altogether insusceptible of restraint; that all attempts to influence it by temporal punishments, or burdens, or by civil incapacitations, tend only to beget habits of hypocrisy and meanness, and are a departure from the plan of the holy author of our religion, who being lord of body and mind, yet chose not to propagate it by coercions on either, as was in his Almighty power to do, but to extend it by its influence on reason alone; that the impious presumption of legislators and rulers, civil as well as ecclesiastical, who, being themselves but fallible and uninspired men, have assumed dominion over the faith of others, setting up their own opinions and modes of thinking as the only true and infallible, and as such endeavoring to impose them on others, hath established and maintained false religions over the greatest part of the world and through all time: That to compel a man to furnish contributions of money for the propagation of opinions which he disbelieves and abhors, is sinful and tyrannical; that even the forcing him to support this or that teacher of his own religious persuasion, is depriving him of the comfortable liberty of giving his contribution to the particular pastor whose morals he feels most persuasive to righteousness; and is withdrawing from the ministry those temporary rewards, which proceeding from an approbation of their personal conduct, are an additional incitement to earnest and unremitting labours for the instruction of mankind; that our civil rights have no dependence on our religious opinions, any more than our opinions in physics or geometry; that therefore the prescribing any citizen as unworthy of the public confidence by laying upon him any incapacity of being called to offices of trust and emolument, unless he profess or renounce this or that religious opinion, is depriving him injuriously of those privileges and advan-

Source: Thomas E. Buckley, *Church and State in Revolutionary Virginia* 190–91 (1977).

tages to which, in common with his fellow citizens, he had a natural right; that it tends only to corrupt the principles of that very religion it is meant to encourage, by bribing, with a monopoly of worldly honours and emoluments, those who will externally profess and conform to it; that though indeed these are criminal who do not withstand such temptation, yet neither are those innocent who lay the bait in their way; that the opinions of men are not the object of civil government, nor under its jurisdiction; that to suffer the civil magistrate to intrude his powers into the field of opinion and to restrain the profession or propagation of principles on supposition of their ill tendency is a dangerous fallacy, which at once destroys all religious liberty, because he being of course judge of that tendency will make his opinions the rule of judgment, and approve or condemn the sentiments of others only as they shall square with or differ from his own; that it is time enough for the rightful purposes of civil government for it offers to interfere when principles break out into overt acts against peace and good order; and finally, that truth is great and will prevail if left to herself that she is the proper and sufficient antagonist to error, and has nothing to fear from the conflict unless by human interposition disarmed other natural weapons, free argument and debate; errors ceasing to be dangerous when it is permitted freely to contradict them.

, We the General Assembly of Virginia do enact that no man shall be compelled to frequent or support any religious worship, place, or ministry whatsoever, nor shall be enforced, restrained, molested, or burthened in his body or goods, nor shall otherwise suffer on account of his religious opinions or belief; but that all men shall be free to profess, and by argument to maintain, their opinion in matters of religion, and that the same shall in no wise diminish, enlarge, or effect their civil capacities.

And though we well know that this Assembly, elected by the people for the ordinary purposes of legislation only, have no power to restrain the acts of succeeding Assemblies, constituted with powers equal to our own, and that therefore to delcare this act irrevocable would be of no effect in law; yet we are free to declare, and do declare, that the rights hereby asserted are of the natural rights of mankind, and that if any act shall be hereafter passed to repeal the present, or to narrow its operation, such act will be infringement of natural right.

Appendix 2 —————————————————

A Bill Establishing a Provision for Teachers of the Christian Religion, Virginia, 1784

WHEREAS the general diffusion of Christian knowledge hath a natural tendency to correct the morals of men, restrain their vices, and preserve the peace of society, which cannot be effected without a competent provision for learned teachers, who may be thereby enabled to devote their time and attention to the duty of instructing such citizens, as from their circumstances and want of education, cannot otherwise attain such knowledge; and it is judged that such provision may be made by the Legislature, without counteracting the liberal principle heretofore adopted and intended to be preserved by abolishing all distinctions of preeminence amongst the different societies or communities of Christians;

Be it therefore enacted by the General Assembly, That for the support of Christian teachers, ————per centum on the amount or ————in the pound on the sum payable for tax on the property within this Commonwealth, is hereby assesed, and shall be paid by every person chargeable with the said tax at the time the same shall become due; and the Sheriffs of the several Counties shall have power to levy and collect the same in the same manner and under the like restrictions and limitations, as are or may be prescribed by the laws for raising the revenues of this State.

And be it enacted, That for every sum so paid, the Sheriff or Collector shall give a receipt, expressing therein to what society of Christians the person from whom he may receive the same shall direct the money to be paid, keeping a distinct account thereof in his books. The Sheriff of every County, shall, on or before the ————day of ———— in every year, return to the Court upon oath, two alphabetical lists of the payments to him made, distinguishing in columns opposite to the names of the persons who shall have paid the same, the society to which the money so paid was by them appropriated; and one column for the names where no appropriation shall be made. One of which lists, after being recorded in a book to be kept for that purpose, shall be filed by the Clerk in

Source: Everson v. United States, 330 U.S. 1, 72–74 (1947).

his office; and the other shall by the Sheriff be fixed up in the courthouse, there to remain for the inspection of all concerned. And the Sheriff, after deducting a five per centum for the collection, shall forthwith pay to such person or persons as shall be appointed to receive the same by the Vestry, Elders, or Directors, however dominated of each such society, the sum so stated to be due to that society; or in default thereof, upon the motion of such person or persons to the next or any succeeding Court, execution shall be awarded for the same against the Sheriff and his security, his and their executors or administrators; provided that ten days previous notice be given of such motion. And upon every such execution, the Officer serving the same shall proceed to immediate sale of the estate taken, and shall not accept of security for payment at the end of three months, nor to have the goods forthcoming at the day of sale, for his better direction wherein, the Clerk shall endorse upon every such execution that no security of any kind shall be taken.

And be it further enacted, That the money to be raised by virtue of this act, shall be by the Vestries, Elders, or Directors of each religious society, appropriated to a provision for a Minister or Teacher of the Gospel of their denomination, or the providing places of divine worship, and to none other use whatsoever; except in the denominations of Quakers and Menonists, who may receive what is collected from their members, and place it in their general fund, to be disposed of in a manner which they shall think best calculated to promote their particuar mode of worship.

And be it enacted, That all sums which at the time of payment to the Sheriff or Collector may not be appropriated by the person paying the same, shall be accounted for with the Court in manner as by this Act is directed; and after deducting for his collection, the Sheriff shall pay the amount thereof (upon account certified by the Court to the Auditors of Public Accounts, and by them to the Treasurer) into the Public Treasury, to be disposed of under the direction of the General Assembly, for the encouragement of seminaries of learning within the Counties whence such sums shall arise, and to no other use or purpose whatsoever.

Appendix 3 ──────────────────

Memorial and Remonstrance Against Religious Assessments to the Honorable the General Assembly of the Commonwealth of Virginia, 1785

We, the subscribers, citizens of the said Commonwealth, having taken into serious consideration, A bill printed by order of the last Session of Generally Assembly, entitled "A Bill establishing a provision for Teachers of the Christian Religion," and conceiving that the same, if finally armed with the sanctions of a law, will be a dangerous abuse of power, are bound as faithful members of a free State, to remonstrate against it, and to declare the reasons by which we are determined. We remonstrate against the said Bill,

1. Because we hold it for a fundamental and undeniable truth, "that Religion or the duty which we owe to our Creator and the Manner of discharging it, can be directed only by reason and conviction, not by force or violence." The Religion then of every man must be left to the conviction and conscience of every man; and it is the right of every man to exercise it as these may dictate. This right is in its nature an unalienable right. It is unalienable; because the opinions of men, depending only on the evidence contemplated by their own minds, cannot follow the dictate of other men: It is unalienable also; because what is here a right towards men, is a duty towards the Creator. It is the duty of every man to render to the Creator such homage, and such only as he believes to be acceptable to him. This duty is precedent both in order of time and degree of obligation, to the claims of Civil Society. Before any man can be considered as a member of Civil Society, he must be considered as a subject of the governor of the Universe: And if a member of Civil Society, who enters into any subordinate Association, must always do it with a reservation of his duty to the general authority; much more must every man who becomes a member of any particular Civil Society, do it with a saving of his allegiance to the Universal Sovereign. We maintain therefore that in matters of Religion, no man's right is abridged by the institution of Civil Society, and that Religion is wholly exempt from its cognizance. True it is, that no other rule exists, by which any question which

Source: Everson v. United States, 330 U.S. 2, 63–72 (1947).

may divide a Society, can be ultimately determined, but the will of the majority; but it is also true, that the majority may trespass on the rights of the minority.

2. Because if religion be exempt from the authority of the Society at large, still less can it be subject to that of the Legislative Body. The latter are but the creatures and vicegerents of the former. Their jurisdiction is both derivative and limited: it is limited with regard to the coordinate departments, more necessarily is it limited with regard to the constituents. The preservation of a free government requires not merely, that the metes and bounds which separate each department of power may be invariably maintained; but more especially, that neither of them be suffered to overleap the great Barrier which defends the rights of the people. The Rulers who are guilty of such an encroachment, exceed the commission from which they derive their authority, and are Tyrants. The People who submit to it are governed by laws made neither by themselves, nor by an authority derived from them, and are slaves.

3. Because, it is proper to take alarm at the first experiment on our liberties. We hold this prudent jealously to be the first duty of citizens, and one of [the] noblest characteristics of the late Revolution. The freemen of America did not wait till usurped power has strengthened itself by exercise, and entangled the question in precedents. They say all the consequences in the principle, and they avoided the consequences by denying the principle. We revere this lesson too much, soon to forget it. Who does not see that the same authority which can establish Christianity, in exclusion of all other Religions, may establish with the same ease any particular sect of Christians, in exclusion of all other Sects? That the same authority which can force a citizen to contribute three pence only of his property for the support of any one establishment, may force him to conform to any other establishment in all cases whatsoever?

4. Because, the bill violates that equality which ought to be the basis of every law, and which is more indispensable, in proportion as the validity or expediency of any law is more liable to be impeached. If "all men are by nature equally free and independent," all men are to be considered as entering into Society on equal conditions; as relinquishing no more, and therefore retaining no less, one than another, of their natural rights. Above all are they to be considered as retaining an "equal title to the free exercise of Religion according to the dictates of conscience". Whilst we assert for ourselves a freedom to embrace, to profess and to observe the Religion which we believe to be of divine origin, we cannot deny an equal freedom to those whose minds have not yet yielded to the evidence which has convinced us. If this freedom be abused, it is an offense against God, not against man: To God, therefore, not to men, must an account of it be rendered. As the Bill violates equality by subjecting some to peculiar burdens; so it violates the same principle by granting to others peculiar exemptions. Are the Quakers and Menonists the only sects who think a compulsive support of their religions unnecessary and unwarrantable? Can their piety alone be intrusted with the care of public worship? Ought their Religions to be endowed above all others, with extraordinary privileges, by which proselytes may be enticed from all others? We think too favorably of the justice and good sense of these denominations, to believe that they either covet preeminencies over their fellow citizens, or that they will be seduced by them, from the common opposition to the measure.

5. Because the bill implies either that the Civil Magistrate is a competent Judge of Religious truth; or that he may employ Religion as an engine of Civil policy. The first is an arrogant pretension falsified by the contradictory opinions of Rulers in all ages, and throughout the world: The second an unhallowed perversion of the means of salvation.

6. Because the establishment proposed by the Bill is not requisite for the support of the Christian Religion. To say that it is, is a contradiction to the Christian Religion itself; for every page of it disavows a dependence on the powers of this world: it is a contradiction to fact; for it is known that this Religion both existed and flourished, not only without the support of human laws, but in spite of every opposition from them; and not only during the period of miraculous aid, but long after it had been left to its own evidence, and the ordinary care of Providence: Nay, it is a contradiction in terms; for a Religion not invented by human policy, must have preexisted and been supported, before it was established by human policy. It is moreover to weaken in those who profess this Religion a pious confidence in its innate excellence, and the patronage of its Author; and to foster in those who still reject it, a suspicion that its friends are too conscious of its fallacies, to trust it to its own merits.

7. Because experience witnesseth that ecclesiastical establishments, instead of maintaining the purity and efficacy of Religion, have had a contrary operation. During almost fifteen centuries has the legal establishment of Christianity been on trial. What have been its fruits? More or less in all places, pride and indolence in the Clergy; ignorance and servility in the laity; in both, superstition, bigotry and persecution. Enquire of the Teachers of Christianity for the ages in which it appeared in its greatest lustre; those of every sect, point to the ages prior to its incorporation with Civil policy. Propose a restoration of this primitive state in which its Teachers depended on the voluntary rewards of their flocks; many of them predict its downfall. On which side ought their testimony to have greatest weight, when for or when against their interest?

8. Because the establishment in question is not necessary for the support of Civil Government. If if be urged as necessary for the support of Civil Government only as it is a means of supporting Religion, and it be not necessary for the latter purpose, it cannot be necessary for the former. If Religion be not within [the] cognizance of Civil Government, how can its legal establishment be said to be necessary to civil Government? What influence in fact have ecclesiastical establishments had on Civil Society? In some instances they have been seen to erect a spiritual tyranny on the ruins of Civil authority; in many instances they have been seen upholding the thrones of political tyranny; in no instance have they been seen the guardians of the liberties of the people. Rulers who wished to subvert the public liberty, may have found in established clergy convenient auxiliaries. A just government, instituted to secure and perpetuate it, needs them not. Such a government will be best supported by protecting every citizen in the enjoyment of his Religion with the same equal hand which protects his person and his property; by neither invading the equal rights of any Sect, nor suffering any Sect in invading those of another.

9. Because the proposed establishment is a departure from that generous policy, which, offering an asylum to the persecuted and oppressed of every Nation and Religion, promised a lustre to our country, and an accession to the number of its citizens. What a melancholy mark is the Bill of sudden degeneracy? Instead of holding forth an asylum to the persecuted, it is itself a signal of persecution. It degrades from the equal rank of Citizens all those whose opinions in Religion do not bend to those of the Legislative authority. Distant as it may be, in its present form, from the Inquisition it differs from it only in degree. The one is the first step, the other the last in the career of intolerance. The magnanimous sufferer under this cruel scourge in foreign Regions, must view the Bill as a Beacon in our Coast, warning him to seek some other haven, where liberty and philanthrophy [sic] in their due extent may offer a more certain repose from his troubles.

10. Because, it will have a like tendency to banish our Citizens. The allurements

presented by other situations are every day thinning their number. To superadd a fresh motive to emigration, by revoking the liberty which they now enjoy, would be the same species of folly which has dishonoured and depopulated flourishing kingdoms.

11. Because, it will destroy that moderation and harmony which the forbearance of our laws to intermeddle with Religion, has produced amongst its several sects. Torrents of blood have been spilt in the old world, by vain attempts of the secular arm to extinguish Religious discord, by proscribing all difference in Religious opinions. Time has at length revealed the true remedy. Every relaxation of narrow and rigorous policy, wherever it has been found to assuage the disease. The American Theatre has exhibited proofs, that equal and compleat liberty, if it does not wholly eradicate it, sufficiently destroys its malignant influence on the health and prosperity of the State. If with the salutary effects of this system under our own eyes, we begin to contract the bonds of Religious freedom, we know no name that will too severely reproach our folly. At least let warning be taken at the first fruits of the threatened innovation. The very appearance of the Bill has transformed that ''Christian forbearance, love and charity,'' which of late mutually prevailed, into animosities and jealousies, which may not soon be appeased. What mischiefs may not be dreaded should this enemy to the public quiet be armed with the force of law?

12. Because, the policy of the bill is adverse to the diffusion of the light of Christianity. The first wish of those who enjoy this precious gift, ought to be that it may be imparted to the whole race of mankind. Compare the number of those who have as yet received it with the number still remaining under the dominion of false Religions; and how small is the former! Does the policy of the Bill tend to lessen the disproportion? No; it at once discourages those who are strangers to the light of [revelation] from coming into the Region of it; and countenances by example the nations who continue in darkness, in shutting out those who might convey it to them. Instead of levelling as far as possible, every obstacle to the victorious progress of truth, the Bill with an ignoble and unchristian timidity would circumscribe it, with a wall of defense, against the encroachments of error.

13. Because attempts to enforce by legal sanctions, acts obnoxious to so great a proportion of Citizens, tend to enervate the laws in general, and to slacken the bands of Society. If it be difficult to execute any law which is not generally deemed necessary or salutary, what must be the case where it is deemed invalid and dangerous? and what may be the effect of so striking an example of impotency in the Government, on its general authority[?]

14. Because a measure of such singular magnitude and delicacy ought not to be imposed, without the clearest evidence that it is called for by a majority of citizens: and no satisfactory method is yet proposed by which the voice of the majority in this case may be determined, or its influence secured. ''The people of the respective counties are indeed requested to signify their opinion respecting the adoption of the Bill to the next Session of Assembly.'' But the representation must be made equal, before the voice either of the Representatives or of the Counties, will be that of the people. Our hope is that neither of the former will, after due consideration, espouse the dangerous principle of the Bill. Should the event disappoint us, it will still leave us in full confidence, that a fair appeal to the latter will reverse the sentence against our liberties.

15. Because, finally, ''the equal right of every citizen to the free exercise of his Religion according to the dictates of conscience'' is held by the same tenure with all our other rights. If we recur to its origin, it is equally the gift of nature; if we weigh its importance,

it cannot be less dear to us; if we consult the Declaration of those rights which pertain to the good people of Virginia, as the "basis and foundation of Government," it is enumerated with equal solemnity, or rather studied emphasis. Either then, we must say, that the will of the Legislature is the only measure of their authority; and that in the plenitude of this authority, they may sweep away all our fundamental rights; or, that they are bound to leave this particular right untouched and sacred: Either we must say, that they may control [sic] the freedom of the press, may abolish the trial by jury, may swallow up the Executive and Judiciary Powers of the State; nay that they may despoil us of our very right of suffrage, and erect themselves into an independent and hereditary assembly: or we must say, that they have no authority to enact into law the Bill under consideration. We the subscribers say, that the General Assembly of this commonwealth have no such authority: And that no effort may be omitted on our part against so dangerous an usurpation, we oppose to it, this remonstrance; earnestly praying, as we are in duty bound, that the Supreme Lawgiver of the Universe, by illuminating those to whom it is addressed, may on the one hand, turn their councils from every act which would affront his holy prerogative, or violate the trust committed to them: and on the other, guide them into every measure which may be worthy of his [blessing, may re]dound to their own praise, and may establish more firmly the liberties, the prosperity, and the Happiness of the Commonwealth.

Bibliographical Essay

The bibliographical innovation of this book is not the exhumation and careful inspection of hitherto forgotten or ignored sources, dusty tomes that unexpectedly shed bright light on a familiar subject. Rather, it is the organization of more or less familiar sources into a discussion firmly grounded in a (hopefully) coherent theory of constitutional lawmaking. Because the chapter notes exhaustively identify the sources reviewed and relied on, reiteration here would be wholly gratuitous. Two examples of the innovation, however, deserve note. Ben Perley Poore's *Federal and State Constitution of the United States* (two volumes, 1972) is a well-known, reliable compilation. Better-kept secrets are the laws of the thirteen original states, which are now more accessible to researchers due to the ongoing editing project of John D. Cushing. Cushing has so far provided edited versions of the legal corpus of all the important states save Pennsylvania and North Carolina. Used in conjunction, these sources should reveal the standard definition of many terms used in the U.S. Constitution since that document, and more so the Bill of Rights, relied most heavily on the post-Revolutionary state constitutions for its lexicon, idiom, and grammar.

Besides descriptions of the state legal regimes, another underused source of federal constitutional meaning resides in the Articles of Confederation era, where (unlike the product of the Poore-Cushing partnership) the gems are not so much the laws passed but the lawmakers passing them. The records of the Confederation Congress reveal the public position of a majority of the Constitution's framers on a host of important national political issues, church-state prominently among them. The *Journals of the Contintental Congress* should be read with Jack N. Rakove's masterly political history, *The Beginnings of National Politics* (1979).

A roadmap to further exploration of the constitutional law of church-state, and its ever-burgeoning scholarly commentary, is perhaps the most useful aspect of a critical guide to further reading. The starting point is the case law since 1947 and (unless one is prepared to read each opinion in the official *United States Reports*) the best summary account is J. Nowak, R. Rotunda, and N. Young, *Constitutional Law* 1028–1081 (2d ed. 1983). Legal academic commentary is legion. Among the best recent attempts to synthesize and explain the cases is W. Marshall, "We Know It When We See It: The Supreme Court and Establishment," 59 *Southern California Law Review* 495 (1986), which argues that the norm unifying the cases is an aversion to the symbolic union of church and state. J. Garvey's "Another Way of Looking at School Aid," 1985 *Supreme Court Review* 61, focuses on parochial school financial assistance cases and draws an important parallel to the state action doctrine of the Fourteenth Amendment. See also my own "Dogmatomachy—A 'Privatization' Theory of the Religion Clause Cases," 30 *Saint Louis University Law Journal* 275 (1986) and "The 'No Religious Test' Clause and the Constitution of Religious Liberty: A Machine That Has Gone of Itself," 37 *Case Western Reserve Law Review*.

There is undoubtedly no more currently debated issue in constitutional law than the role of original intent. Chapter 7 represents one attempt to shed light on that debate by suggesting that the more fruitful inquiry is whether there is persuasive (but not "cocksure") evidence of the "plain meaning" of a constitutional provision, with secondary effort directed at identifying the various connotations of original intent and their (often abundant) inadequacies. Still, unless or until my suggestion takes, the debate will rage in familiar categories. The best brief introduction to the controversy is John Hart Ely, *Democracy and Distrust: A Theory of Judicial Review* 1–41 (1980). A briefer, more polemical view by an appellate judge frequently touted as a future Supreme Court nominee is R. Bork, "Styles in Constitutional Theory," 26 *South Texas Law Journal* 383 (1985). The most inveterate academic defender of originalism in constitutional theory is Raoul Berger, whose caustic articles seem to annoy more people than they persuade. Still, his work is an anchor in shifting currents. For a recent sample, see his "Original Intention in Historical Perspective," 54 *George Washington Law Review* 101 (1986) and "New Theories of 'Interpretation': The Activist Flight from the Constitution," 47 *Ohio State Law Journal 1* (1986). The best-known explicit rejection of originalism is Michael Perry, *The Constitution, the Courts and Human Rights* (1982). Statesmanlike reviews of the debate include Henry Monaghan, "Our Perfect Constitution," 56 *New York University Law Review* 353 (1981), and W. Van Alstyne, "Interpreting *This* Constitution: The Unhelpful Contributions of Special Theories of Judicial Review," 35 *University of Florida Law Review* 209 (1983). Illustrative of the discouraging state of affairs is H. Powell, "The Original Understanding of Original Intent," 98 *Harvard Law Review* 885 (1985), which wonders whether the framers intended future interpreters to seek constitutional meaning in their (the framers') intent. These citations are to some of the best and most prominent work in the field by legal academics; they are not remotely exhaustive.

The 1980s have engendered an outburst of writings on religion in U.S. history and on the constitutional law of church and state by nonlawyers or at least scholars outside the legal academy. Among the former is Reichley's *Religion in American Public Life* (1985). See, in addition, W. Miller, *The First Liberty: Religion and the America Republic* (1985), and especially the excellent work, primarily a view of the nineteenth century, by R. Laurence Moore, *Religious Outsiders and the Making of Americans* (1986). Thomas Curry's *The First Freedoms* (1985) is the best recent contribution by a nonlawyer to our understanding of church-state relations in colonial America, although it is vulnerable to criticism when viewed (as occasionally it seems to invite) as a work of constitutional law. Robert Cord's *Separation of Church and State* masterfully reviews the historical materials as well as developments since, but it is (from the perspective of the lawyers' debate about constitutional meaning just surveyed) susceptible to charges of naiveté. Useful historical information on both the Constitution's proscription of religious tests and about the Jewish struggle for civil rights in the United States is in Morton Bordon, *Jews, Turks, and Infidels* (1984). The most recent contribution of Curry's mentor falls far short of the scholarly standards he previously set and which he obviously required of Curry. See Leonard Levy, *The Establishment Clause: Religion and the First Amendment* (1986). Christopher Wolfe's *The Rise of Modern Judicial Review* (1986) is an excellent interpretive account of how the Supreme Court's understanding of their constitutionally assigned task has changed since the Founding era.

Index

About the Author

GERARD V. BRADLEY, Assistant Professor of Law, University of Illinois at Urbana-Champaign, co-authored *Labor Racketeering* and has written numerous articles published in law journals.

DATE D'